PERKINS ON U.S. FINANCIAL HISTORY AND RELATED TOPICS

Edwin J. Perkins

University Press of America,® Inc.
Lanham · Boulder · New York · Toronto · Plymouth, UK

4501 Forbes Boulevard
Suite 200
Lanham, Maryland 20706
UPA Acquisitions Department (301) 459-3366

Estover Road
Plymouth PL6 7PY
United Kingdom

Printed in the United States of America
British Library Cataloging in Publication Information Available

Library of Congress Control Number: 2008937439
ISBN-13: 978-0-7618-4420-4 (paperback : alk. paper)
ISBN-10: 0-7618-4420-1 (paperback : alk. paper)
eISBN-13: 978-0-7618-4421-1
eISBN-10: 0-7618-4421-X

™ The paper used in this publication meets the minimum requirements of American National Standard for Information Sciences—Permanence of Paper for Printed Library Materials, ANSI Z39.48—1984

Contents

Contents

Preface

The motivations for this edited volume were threefold. First, there was the powerful influence of the "ego" factor. The chance, once again, to get my treasured manuscripts into print. Most of these selections are reprints of previously published material, but three of the entries are originals. I tried half-heartedly to publish the three manuscripts in scholarly journals, but I failed for a variety of reasons.

The second motivation was to offer easy access to a broad sample of my publications to a wider range of scholars in various fields. What I discovered over the years (make that decades) was that scholars who had discovered one of my publications useful in their research were often unaware that some of my other publications in different outlets or formats might be equally pertinent. Some readers of my books were not aware of my journal articles, and, likewise, journal readers were not always aware of my books. This volume will help to alleviate that problem among currently active researchers--and hopefully future generations of scholars.

The third motivation was to produce a condensed volume of my works that might attract modest textbook sales in university courses taught by financial historians.

Chapter One

The Entrepreneurial Spirit in Colonial America: The Foundations of Modern Business History

Among the fields of scholarly inquiry within the American spectrum, colonial history and business history have undergone remarkable rejuvenations and expansions over the last three decades. At first glance, the two fields might appear to have few overlapping interests, and thus this observation about their recent flowering might be quickly dismissed as mere coincidence--two separate events portending no mutual consequences. However, closer inspection suggests a different conclusion. Indeed, when recent developments within the fields of colonial and business history are viewed in tandem, numerous opportunities for cross-disciplinary reinforcement are illuminated. This conjuncture of interests and concerns is the focus of this essay; my goals are, first, to survey much of the pertinent literature and, second, to redirect the conceptualization of issues and themes currently floating about within these scholarly areas. The emphasis is on the pervasiveness of entrepreneurial attitudes and aspirations associated with a range of occupational groupings in the seventeenth and eighteenth centuries.

After moving forward steadily, but unspectacularly, as a field of scholarly endeavor during the first half of the twentieth century, colonial history has undergone a remarkable resurgence during the last quarter century. This revival and expansion were recently explored in Jack P. Greene and J. R. Pole's wide-ranging 1984 essay, which served as an introduction to a collection of historiographical papers drafted by noted scholars and covering the status of research in a variety of subfields. The authors observed that, after decades of relatively modest gains, colonial history had become, as a result of a conjunction of forces still not fully understood, "one of the most exciting and attractive areas of American historical study" over the course of the last quarter century. (1) The number of graduate students entering the colonial field climbed rapidly in the 1960s and 1970s.

Soon thereafter the publication of books and articles multiplied dramatically. Coincident with this colonial rejuvenation, the *William & Mary Quarterly* attained a leading place among the ranks of the nation's most stimulating and esteemed forums for lively intellectual exchange; the range of articles accepted expanded to include social and economic topics and fresh research on the everyday lives of common people.

One subfield within the colonial realm that prospered during this upsurge of general interest was economic history. Prior to mid-century, economic history as a field of research within the larger scheme of U.S. history was relatively undeveloped. Historical knowledge about the economic forces at play in the colonial era was extremely sparse, and the slight amount of information in print was often superficial or was inaccurate. Bernard Bailyn's The *New England Merchants in the Seventeenth Century* (1955), a monograph combining aspects of economic and political history, opened the path to new directions in scholarship. (2) Still, as late as 1965, when Stuart Bruchey wrote *The Roots of American Economic Growth, 1607-1861*, a synthesis of the existing literature devoted to the first 250 years after the arrival of European settlers, the chapters on the colonial origins of the nation's economy were rather spotty. The fault lay not with the author's failure to recognize the vital importance of the colonial background, but rather with the absence of a solid body of published literature to draw on for analysis.

Beginning in the late 1960s, and growing at an accelerated pace in the next decade, a new group of historical investigators converged on the colonial scene. Many were scholars trained formally as economists, demographers, or geographers--social scientists who brought to their research activities the specialized tools of quantification. Their focus varied from macroeconomic topics, such as the analysis of data related to overseas trade and payment balances or aggregate growth rates, to detailed studies of narrower markets, such as indentured servants and slaves. Meantime, scholars trained in more traditional history curricula stepped up their involvement in research on topics either clearly economic in origin or with strong economic dimensions. Some historians familiarized themselves with the more advanced tools of quantification and computerization, whereas others diligently collected data and followed the institutional and narrative tradition of historical analysis. The contributions of many of these participants were recently surveyed and assessed in a remarkably comprehensive book with an exhaustive bibliography published in 1985 by John McCusker and Russell Menard. (3)

My interest lies with the intersection of these two burgeoning fields-- namely, scholarly definitions and interpretations of the nascent business sector in the seventeenth and eighteenth centuries. Most accounts, whether written by colonialists or by business historians, have usually pointed primarily, or exclusively to urban merchants as the forerunners of the business entrepreneurs who responded, in the decades after independence, to new economic opportunities fostered by an improved transportation network, new forms of industrial machinery, and new sources of inanimate energy. Colonial merchants clearly should be counted among the precursors of subsequent generations of business owners and managers, but the singular concentration on this new occupational group is, in my view, too restrictive.

As an alternative interpretative approach, I offer a more sweeping proposition: that most occupational categories in colonial society quality as legitimate antecedents of the nineteenth-century entrepreneur. The only groups excluded are Native Americans, sailors (but not all mariners), enslaved blacks in rural areas (but not all slaves in urban settings), and the small number of genuinely subsistence farmers on the frontier and in other remote regions. It follows as a corollary to this general hypothesis that my conception of colonial society reflects a culture permeated with market values and capitalist principles.

OTHER VIEWS OF COLONIAL ENTREPRENEURSHIP

This all-inclusive approach is not wholly original. Thomas Cochran has explored similar themes about the importance of business values throughout American history in numerous publications over a long and vigorous academic career. In *Business in American Life: A History*, published in 1972, Cochran cited the ownership of land, in combination with the European settlers' efforts to develop its productive capacity and gain access to transportation facilities, as an essentially business proposition. Over the decades the price of land in areas near the coast and east of the frontier typically climbed steadily in value, and property owners realized financial returns not only from greater agricultural output but also from capital gains associated with the rising value of farmland. Concomitant with that analysis, Cochran stressed the great importance of "the legacy of commercialized agriculture passed on by planters and farmers." (4)

In two subsequent books on the interrelationship between business and culture, Cochran skipped quickly over the colonial era, beginning his coverage of events after 1776. In *200 Years of American Business,* which appeared in 1977, he argued that the half-century following the War for Independence was "the period of the Business Revolution." The context of his general discussion suggests that Cochran was thinking mainly of new institutional arrangements, such as the corporate form of organization, but the impression left with most readers was that the business orientation of American society prior to independence was relatively immature and unadvanced. In his *Frontiers of Change: Early Industrialism in America,* Cochran identified immigrants to the colonies as "a segment of European populations with an unusual willingness to take risks," but again his focus was almost exclusively on the first half of the nineteenth century. (5)

In this article I seek to rekindle and reinforce the views Cochran originally espoused in the 1972 volume and to carry forward even further that general line of argument. Rather than pinpointing the years from 1780 to 1830 as a particularly revolutionary period in terms of business practices and principles, I would push back the starting point for these developments to the initial years of English settlement on the North American continent. The emergence of one of the first early modern societies with pervasive entrepreneurial values was itself a revolutionary development and the impact was as pronounced during the seventeenth century as in any subsequent period of American history. These early patterns of thought and action created the broad institutional framework for all subsequent economic activity. And a particularly revolutionary aspect of the society was the existence of the emerging entrepreneurial orientation among a broad swath of occupation groups.

Within the last decade several historians have recognized and assessed more positively the role of entrepreneurial forces in shaping colonial society. In an economic history textbook published in 1979, James Soltow, who wrote the chapters on the colonial period, unambiguously identified southern planters and artisans as the owner-managers of their business enterprises. Soltow cited Robert Carter as "the prototype of the Chesapeake planter-tycoon," and he characterized artisans as "independent entrepreneurs." (6) Soltow's choice of the word "tycoon" to describe the operations of great planters in the eighteenth century may be overblown, but the thrust of his argument was that commercial attitudes were prevalent in southern society.

In *America's Business* (1985), a broad synthesis covering the entire sweep of American history in a brief 250 pages, James Oliver Robertson was even more emphatic about the business aspects of colonial society. Robertson stressed active markets in land and humans--indentured servants and slaves--plus the multifaceted activities of several prominent northern merchants and southern planters, among them William Pynchon, Daniel Dulany, and William Fitzhugh, as clear evidence of the existence of a strong business outlook. (7)

The entrepreneurial bent of colonial Americans has been noted by other scholars whose expertise lies beyond the fields of economic and business history. Carl Degler's famous quip about capitalism arriving in the first boats crossing the Atlantic merits repetition here. In a careful study of the conceptualization of economic life in the eighteenth century, J. E. Crowley focused on two factors: frugality and industry (meaning in the latter instance the attribute of steady work habits). According to Crowley, a positive attitude toward the fruits and benefits of trade and commerce was the norm: "Americans demonstrated the trait which is essential to the success of a market economy, a personal motivation to raise one's standard of living." In pinpointing the motivations of thousands of British emigrants who paid their own passage to the colonies on the eve of independence, Bailyn likewise observed: "Almost all, searching rationally for personal betterment or greater security, were, or hoped to be, family-scale entrepreneurs." (8)

In a recent book on two smaller Massachusetts ports that competed fairly successfully with Boston in the first half of the eighteenth century, Christine Heyrman noted that, although the towns' residents placed an increased emphasis on commercial values as the decades passed, the profit motive failed to undermine the bonds of communal cohesion. In a review of her book, John McCusker criticized the author for assuming that the attitudes of earlier generations had been somehow less oriented toward business affairs: "Even the most religious of the early Puritan settlers of Massachusetts Bay were alert to the need to create and maintain a viable economy." He added, "As I see it, the set of values that informed the economic behavior of the inhabitants in the eighteenth century was already present and operating in the seventeenth century." McCusker was particularly critical of Heyrman's failure to examine more closely the precedents established over the previous half-century: "To imply that the earliest settlers of the towns were somehow aloof from commercial concerns and the pressures of business is simply to ignore (or, perhaps, misread) considerable evidence to the contrary." According to McCusker, the seventeenth-century residents of these maritime towns already "were, in the jargon of the economist, utility maximizers." (9)

Some of the best evidence of entrepreneurial activity in New England during the seventeenth century relates to the establishment and development of new towns. Fred Martin studied over one hundred persons who were involved in establishing over 60 towns, of which 39 were located in Massachusetts and 10 in Connecticut. These profit-oriented entrepreneurs, to use Martin's explicit terminology, obtained private corporate charters from provincial legislatures to finance and manage speculative settlements. Some developers were involved in several town projects over a lifetime. Cornelius Waldo, for example, was associated with the founding of Chelmsford, Massachusetts, in the 1650s and other towns as late as the 1670s. These seventeenth-century towns had dual identities; they were both private, commercial organizations and public, communal institutions. The shareholders in town projects controlled the local government, and residents who were not investors were typically denied participation in civic affairs.

Entrepreneurial land developers were involved in myriad activities. They built roads, constructed meetinghouses, recruited settlers, hired ministers for local churches, negotiated with Native Americans, and served, in emergencies, as military commanders. These investors risked their organizing talents and their own monies in one or more settlement projects, and they profited only if a town was successfully launched. Martin concluded that these land developers were as critical to the settlement of New England in the seventeenth century as they were in the eighteenth century. (10)

THE CURRENT DEBATE: COMMUNALIST OR CAPITALIST?

Over the last quarter-century, a vigorous debate has erupted among scholars about whether colonial society was essentially capitalist or decidedly pre-capitalist in character. Opinions are so divided at present that no resolution of this ongoing controversy appears likely within the foreseeable future. It should be noted, however, that my perception of a colonial society imbued with business values differs greatly from positions advocated by other scholars such as James Henretta, Christopher Clark, Michael Merrill, Robert Mutch, Rona Weiss, and Allan Kulikoff. In general they have tended to emphasize the communal, cooperative aspects of colonial economic behavior and to downplay the role of the marketplace and capitalist forces in influencing the decisions of individuals and households in early America.

In a seminal article published in 1978, Henretta sparked the whole debate by asserting that farmers in New England possessed a communal mentalite. He argued that communal, family-oriented values held sway over individualistic, profit-maximization impulses, and that, as a consequence, agricultural entrepreneurship was stifled In these northern colonies, the maintenance of strong kinship ties between generations had a higher priority than the personal accumulation of property. Two years later in a published intellectual exchange, Henretta reiterated the basic proposition: "The economic behavior of northern farm families was not fundamentally determined by market forces and values." (11)

Other historians echoed the communal, cooperative theme. In discussing the behavior of many New England farm households, Clark concluded that they were not profit-oriented as late as the early nineteenth century. Most trading activity did not require the use of cash, and debts and credits were settled mainly by swaps of goods and services--in other words, a mostly barter economy existed. The main objective of farm households was not a high degree of self-sufficiency, according to Clark, but rather local independence from the destabilizing aspects of outside market forces. Merrill emphasized the prevalence of reciprocal exchange agreements among households. In the same vein, Mutch claimed that farmers operated in essentially "pre-market societies." Weiss perceived most colonial workers, farmers and artisans, as "petty producers" living in what was fundamentally still a feudal world. In a sweeping article published in 1989, Kulikoff initiated a discussion aimed at identifying more precisely when the rural transition to new forms of capitalism might have occurred in the United States. Although not yet prepared to cite a specific date in the nineteenth century, Kulikoff was nonetheless certain that the alleged transition had occurred well after the close of the colonial era. (12)

The contrary position in this scholarly debate, argued most forcefully by James Lemon, Winifred Rothenberg, and Carole Shammas, offered convincing evidence that market forces outweighed communal values. These three scholars leaned toward the argument that most colonists were caught up in a market-oriented society that was already capitalistic in terms of its functions and attitudes. Inadequate transportation facilities in remote areas precluded the participation of every colonist in the market economy on any given date, but most settlers aspired to gain access to the market mechanism, both for the sale of surplus production and for the acquisition of affordable goods in short supply within their households. As population density rose in formerly frontier areas and roads were widened to accommodate carts and wagons, the number of individuals involved in market activity steadily expanded.

Vigorously disputing Henretta's communal hypothesis, Lemon conceded that countervailing influences such as church, community, and kinship groups might have mitigated the power of impersonal market forces. But he was adamant about the driving mechanism. "The basic dynamic was toward economic growth, toward success defined by wealth. . . , and toward accumulation as a goal in its own right," he wrote in a rebuttal letter published in 1980. Shammas calculated that up to one-quarter of household income was spent on items that moved across provincial borders. She argued that most colonial farmers were unavoidably involved in a host of market transactions because the high cost of equipment to spin thread, weave cloth, mill grain, and perform many other household tasks normally prohibited self-sufficiency. Rothenberg defined capitalism as an economic system featuring private ownership, the use of markets to allocate goods and investments, and a legal tradition to enforce contracts. By those criteria, she concluded that the colony of Massachusetts, on which most of her research had focused, was clearly a functioning capitalist society by the mid-eighteenth century. (13)

The consensus arising from a survey of the contributions of Cochran, Soltow, Robertson, McCusker, Martin, Lemon, Shammas, and Rothenberg points to the emergence of a new interpretative framework for historical discussions of the major themes recurrent in the culture of colonial America. The new format places greater emphasis on the economic and business aspects of colonial society, and it includes a wider array of occupational groups within the business sector. I concur with Rothenberg's definition of utility maximization within households--as distinguished from the narrower concept of mere profit maximization, and I believe it can be fully and usefully applied to colonial society. She defined utility maximizers as follows: 1) households that recognize tradeoffs, for example between more leisure and more income; 2) households that know their income or budget constraints; and 3) households that rank-order their preferences and then choose the alternatives that would leave them better off over the choices that would leave them worse off. Rothenberg rejected the terminology of Henretta's earlier depiction of colonial farmers in New England as possessing a pre-capitalist, communal mentalite, and endorsed the idea that Americans possessed instead a "commercial mentalite." (14)

COMPONENTS OF THE ENTREPRENEURIAL GROUP

Before proceeding, we must pause to define more precisely some additional terminology relating to the degree of involvement by various individuals and groups in business and entrepreneurial activities. Two categories have been created for this purpose. The first grouping includes persons strongly oriented toward entrepreneurship as evidenced by both their actions and attitudes; they were individuals willing to risk the expenditure of capital and labor in an effort to increase their income levels over the long run and to accumulate greater property and wealth. The second category comprises persons who were involved in similar types of economic activities, but to a much more limited extent. They were prepared to work diligently to bring their income and property holdings up to a reasonably sufficient level of comfort, but thereafter they were content to maintain the status quo; their motivation for further advancement faded. I call such people "maintainers." These individuals can be described as petty traders, if shopkeepers and smaller merchants with limited inventories, or petty producers, if mainly artisans or family farmers. (15) The primary aim of these individuals, and their households, were to maintain the status quo in their living standards rather than to enhance them. (In Europe these groups would probably be lumped together and labeled "petit bourgeois," but for some reason that term still sounds inappropriate in the American context.)

Members of the mercantile community were among the most active full-fledged entrepreneurs in colonial society. Merchants accounted for 2 to 5 per-cent of aggregate employment, with greater concentrations in port cities and towns. In addition to facilitating the exchange of goods in internal and foreign markets, they were the conduits for the extension of credit from areas with surplus working capital down through the chain of mercantile firms to the final consumers. (16) The source for much of the credit that supported the carrying of inventories and the sale of imported goods in the colonial market can be traced to British traders and manufacturers, as Jacob Price has demonstrated in a series of scholarly publications. (17) Given the undeniable importance of merchants as mainstays of the business establishment in colonial society, this occupational group can be passed over with little discussion, since virtually all historians have agreed that these wholesalers ranked high among the legitimate precursors of nineteenth-century entrepreneurs.

Not every merchant conformed to the bold entrepreneurial model, however. Like some farmers and artisans, a few shopkeepers were content merely to reach a comfortable living standard, with no aspirations for acquiring greater wealth. These merchants were content to operate small to medium-scale businesses, avoiding the risks of an expanded inventory. Meanwhile, at the top of the mercantile pyramid, some merchants who had accumulated great wealth through their involvement in risky ventures subsequently became exceedingly conservative and focused their energies mainly on preserving existing capital. Thomas Doerflinger has explained how many formerly successful merchant households in Philadelphia withdrew from trading activities and invested their funds in urban rental properties. (18) Thus, though the mercantile sector included a higher percentage of active entrepreneurs within its ranks than other occupational groups, some merchants were not consistently bold risk-takers, and some tried to protect previously accumulated assets from the threat of possible losses.

In addition to merchants, many artisans, if not most, deserve inclusion in any discussion of the pre-industrial roots of American entrepreneurship. Many historical accounts place craft workers squarely in the labor sector of the economy, whereas others depict them straddling the line between business and labor. These workers can be viewed as laborers, since they produced various goods using hand tools; at the same time, master artisans may be classified with equal validity as the owners and managers of small business firms. Most operated proprietorships, or they occasionally worked in partnerships with one or two other men. Youthful apprentices and journeymen were subordinate employees, but usually their dependent status was merely a temporary stage along the route to independence. By their early thirties, most craft workers were married and self-employed, although exceptions to this generalization might be found in a large urban area such as Philadelphia, where a substantial number of craft workers remained journeymen employees throughout their working lives. Master artisans owned their own tools, maintained inventories of raw materials and goods-in-process, accepted orders from customers, managed their daily schedules, handled their own monies and accounts, and generally performed all the functions typically associated with the operation of small business enterprises, past and present. Of course, some artisans had no grander ambition than to remain independent, small-scale producers--that is, "maintainers"--but most artisans were prevented from expanding their scale of operations, irrespective of their attitude about possible opportunities beyond the local market, by limited access to distant markets resulting from inadequate transportation services.

Mounting evidence from analyses of estates suggests that moderately successful artisans frequently owned a few acres near their homes for limited cultivation, and that many maintained a sufficient number of livestock—cows, cattle, hogs, and chickens--to provide a steady source of meat, milk, and eggs for their households. (19) In Philadelphia, the largest port city over the last quarter century of the colonial era, master artisans frequently occupied homes whose values, or rents, were comparable to the residences of the small and medium-sized merchants who composed the majority of the mercantile community. (20) We also know that many of the new manufacturing establishments created after independence to serve wider markets were organized and managed by persons who had initially operated small artisan shops and later made the transition to employer status. (21) Thus, the entrepreneurial tradition that emerged on a grander scale in the nineteenth century can be traced as validly to the activities of colonial artisans as to any other occupational category.

A substantial share of farm households also legitimately belongs in the entrepreneurial camp. Farm workers made up from 60 to 85 percent of the tree colonial work force--with the exact percentage depending on geographical location and how we categorize persons also engaged on a part-time basis in related pursuits, such as crafts and occasional day labor. The criterion for the assignment of farm households to the business and entrepreneurial sector hinges on whether they aimed at the steady accumulation of property in land, livestock, bonded labor, fences, barns, and other productive assets. The distinction lies between farmers seeking further capital formation and farmers content to maintain to existing levels of productivity. How many would quality by this standard is admittedly difficult to determine, since ascertaining the motivations of thousands of farmers who left no written records is hazardous at best. After the labors of earlier generations had created a certain level of wealth, some families were content simply to maintain the resources and skills necessary to ensure a modestly comfortable life by the standards of the time. Thus, historians who have argued the persistence of communal and family values in the lives of farm households may be correct in asserting that those attitudes were foremost in the minds of certain groups--especially of some New Englanders in areas long-settled and relatively heavily populated, as well as of those in some of the older counties of Virginia and Maryland. These farmers were the equivalent of the petty traders and small-scale producers in the mercantile and artisanal sectors. But considering the thirteen colonies as a whole, the vast majority of farm households in the middle and southern colonies, plus a fair share of those in New England, were seeking the means to further material advancement for themselves and their children. Perhaps one-half of all farm households met the basic qualifications outlined above for inclusion in the entrepreneurial category. Few of them may have actually achieved great wealth, but they nonetheless aimed at steadily accumulating productive assets. (22)

Entrepreneurially-oriented farm households had several important characteristics in common. First, they tended to defer immediate consumption and to save a healthy share of their annual income; those savings were invested in making capital improvements to their properties. This investment behavior was exhibited mainly through non-pecuniary activities such as clearing forests, constructing barns, building fences, and otherwise augmenting the productive capacity of their farms. These farmers tried to expand the total agricultural output of their lands by hiring extra labor to plant and harvest more cropland than was required for a comfortable subsistence. Households then faced several options in the disposition of surpluses. On the one hand, they could sell excess output in the marketplace and use the sale proceeds to purchase other goods or services designed to satisfy their desires fur immediate consumption, or, alternatively, they could follow investment strategies leading to the improvement of their productive capacity. (23)

Among the prime vehicles for agricultural investment were livestock herds. Two strategies, pursued either separately or in combination, led to capital accumulation. Surplus foodstuffs could be withheld from sale in the marketplace and fed to livestock--mainly cattle and hogs, thus increasing meat and dairy supplies available to members of the household in later periods. Another investment strategy, and one that the first second generations of landowners often chose, was to concentrate on building livestock herds by deferring the slaughter of females and adding more animals to breeding stock. By postponing immediate gratification from a tastier and more varied diet, the household could enjoy enhanced income in subsequent years either from increased meat consumption or from the sale of surplus livestock in the marketplace. (24)

These strategies of saving and investment were employed not only by independent yeomen who held title to their own farms, but also by numerous colonial tenant households as well. The whole issue of tenancy has been poorly understood, and only recently have the studies of Sung Bok Kim, Stephen Innes, Gloria Main, Paul Clemens, Lucy Simler, and Mary Schweitzer begun to throw clearer light on the overall picture. (25) Many tenant farmers were, of course, genuinely trapped in situations of nearly hopeless dependency. (26) But others were on an entirely different track.

For younger households, headed by single or married males under the age of thirty-five, tenancy was often strictly a voluntary, temporary career stage that aided in the accumulation of wealth and subsequently led to land ownership and independence. Even some persons with sufficient financial resources to purchase unimproved land close to the frontier opted instead for tenancy status on improved farms that already possessed the potential for higher yields and better access to waiting markets. Rental terms were frequently attractive to potential tenants for several reasons. First, many wealthy individuals had investments in numerous properties, both developed and undeveloped, and they wanted some immediate financial return on their vast holdings. Second, landlords holding undevelope4 tracts wanted to attract settlers who would invest the time and labor required to convert the raw land into productive farms. Third, these same landlords wanted a readily available source of occasional day labor for their own fields during the spring and full seasons. In short, the supply of rental properties was large relative to the supply of potential tenants, which translated into a reasonable level of rents, whether paid in cash or in kind.

Colonial tenants with an entrepreneurial orientation frequently used their initial capital stock plus the sums saved from yearly profits to invest in a series of productive assets. In the southern and middle colonies, many tenants decided to invest surplus funds in human capital--servants or slaves--before moving on to acquire their own cropland. Some devoted their surpluses to building livestock herds. Others used their own labor and surplus funds to make leasehold improvements on rented properties. When their leases expired, some tenants, notably in Maryland, were allowed to remove the easily portable assets. Moreover, the laws in some colonies sometimes prescribed financial compensation by landlords for improvements impossible to transport--such as erecting barns, building fences, or clearing forestland and converting it into fertile cropland. In New York, where some contractual agreements ran on for several decades, tenants had the right to negotiate the reassignment of their leases to third parties under terms that permitted tenants to recapture the cost of leasehold improvements; in other words, tenants could profit from the sale or reassignment of farms in their possession even in the absence of clear title to the property.

In villages and towns, artisans frequently leased small farms, a few fields, or even more commonly pasturage for their livestock. Most craft workers maintained at least one cow for dairy products, plus several cattle, sheep, or hogs. The income generated from collateral agricultural activities, in the form of either food consumption in the home or sale in the marketplace, supplemented the earnings from regular craft labor. In addition to helping to care for the livestock, the wives and children of male artisans were often engaged part-time in agricultural pursuits and thus made substantial contributions to household income. (27)

Although some Marxist historians may vehemently disagree, I believe that southern planters and other farmers with investments in indentured servants or slaves quality for inclusion in the entrepreneurially oriented classification because they sent bonded workers out into the fields with the aim of producing surpluses for sale in the marketplace. (28) The prime markets for many of these products--especially tobacco, rice, and indigo--were located overseas. Farmers with investments in other human beings normally sought to expand the scope of future operations; the profits expropriated from their bonded workers were frequently reinvested in additional land and labor. In the South, moderately successful planters tried to emulate their more prosperous neighbors, hoping one day that they or one of their progeny might eventually reach the elevated status of "great planter." (29) Large planters hired overseers for their huge work forces. This practice of employing full-time supervisors who did not hold an ownership stake in a business enterprise was the forerunner of developments relating to the emergence of an independent managerial class in manufacturing firms and railroads in the nineteenth century.

Although historians have previously noted that perhaps no more than one-third of all southern farmers in most regions in any given year in the eighteenth century actually possessed slaves, Allan Kulikoff has recently shown that this statistic, although accurate, may nonetheless be misleading if improperly interpreted. Many non-slaveholding farms were cultivated by younger households with limited assets. During the early years of marriage, many white families who coveted slaves could not yet afford to purchase them; in other cases, there was a lag of a decade or so before these younger households began to inherit bonded workers from their aging or deceased parents and relatives. In the Chesapeake region that he studied, for example, Kulikoff revealed that, over an entire life cycle, a majority of white males who survived to middle age could anticipate the ownership of one or more slaves. (30) If this pattern prevailed throughout the southern colonies, then we can argue that perhaps one-half or more of all southern families headed by males aged thirty-five and above became slaveholders and that members of these households at some point in their life cycle were active participants in the commercial aspect of staple agriculture.

Another group that, on balance, deserves inclusion in the ranks of the entrepreneurially oriented are indentured servants. This statement may surprise many readers, but the new evidence uncovered within the last decade--primarily by David Galenson, Farley Grubb, and Bernard Bailyn--has cast an entirely new light on the whole operation of markets for indentures and redemptioners. (31) Most existing accounts of indentured servants not only place them exclusively within the working-class sector, but also depict them as persons grossly exploited by their owners, in a manner similar to slaves. But the similarities between servitude and slavery have been overemphasized to the neglect of the vast differences in their origins and outcomes. Except for that 10 percent or so of the total who were transported to North America from England's crowded jails in the eighteenth century, most servants voluntarily agreed to business contracts covering a period ranging from four to seven years. Slaves, in contrast, were involuntary captives, and the term of their service was indefinite--usually not only for their own lifetimes, but also for the lifetimes of all future generations unless manumitted.

Servants are best viewed as ambitious persons who elected to make an investment in their personal welfare based on an exchange of labor services over a fixed term of years for the benefit of regaining complete freedom in a new society where opportunities were vastly greater than in Europe. They risked an uncertain fate in a distant land because of a desire to increase appreciably the chance of eventually acquiring ownership of their own farm or artisan shop. By a ratio of three or four to one, more males than females ventured forth across the ocean to the Western Hemisphere in search of a better life, but the motivations for emigration were essentially the same for both sexes. Most were youths between the ages of fifteen and twenty-five. In their European environment, the vast majority of these adventurers faced the prospect of eking out a meager existence as husband or wife in a tenant household on croplands permanently controlled by landlords. The probability of escape from this degrading status was very slight. The greatest danger of migrating to the Western Hemisphere was the possibility of an early death. Mortality rates during the ocean voyage and for the first year after arrival were very high--but not appreciably higher for servants than for free persons making similar crossings of the Atlantic Ocean. Migration across thousands of miles of ocean was a risky enterprise, and those who ventured forth anticipated difficult living conditions in the months ahead.

In all, over a quarter-million Europeans chose to trade a temporary claim on their future economic output for the immediate financing required to transport them to a new environment where land was inexpensive and thus accessible to persons with limited assets. The vast majority traveled to the Chesapeake region or to the middle colonies, with few arriving in New England or the Lower South. Servants swapped one service for another: their own future labor units were traded for long-distance transportation, plus regular meals and some clothing. Prospective migrants negotiated the terms of their individual indenture contracts before their departure from European ports. A few people were kidnapped and shipped overseas involuntarily, but most transactions took place in generally competitive markets involving numerous merchant contractors.

Prospective migrants bargained over the final geographical destination, length of contract, and the size of freedom dues at the expiration of their term. The inclusion of freedom dues was crucial, because these sums provided the financial resources to start a new life on a higher economic plane; in many cases the money was a good start toward making the down payment on a small farm, the purchase of a few head of livestock, or the acquisition of the tools required to stock an artisan's shop. (32) Persons with craft skills or the ability to read and write were usually in a position to bargain for the most favorable contractual terms. Females, who generally entered domestic service, were in significantly shorter supply 'than males, and they generally obtained more favorable contracts requiring fewer months of labor.

The material lives of servants were rarely below the standards to which they had been accustomed in Europe. Servants became members of their employers' households; they shared meals, heat from the fireplace, and even bedding. Since most households with the financial resources to acquire servants lived above the colonial average, the accommodations were normally quite adequate. Many servant contracts stipulated weekly rations of meat and generous allotments of beer and spirits. Males normally labored in the fields or in the shop, often performing the same tasks as their employers; females were usually engaged in domestic service --cooking, washing, childcare, feeding all the livestock, and other related household duties. The status of servants was clearly subordinate, and they were routinely called on to perform the least desirable work assignments. Once freed, however, their previous condition of servitude was no handicap on the road to upward social and economic mobility.

In sum, markets in servant contracts functioned fairly efficiently from an economic standpoint, since all parties involved in these transactions, including those persons agreeing to the indentures, usually received the services agreed on in advance. If English merchants or colonial owners tailed to live up to the terms of the written agreement, servants had the legal right to take the offending parties to court for breach of contract--although it should be noted that the court system was controlled by local property holders, who were rarely sympathetic to the complaints of bonded workers. An owner judged to be acting in violation of a servant's contract could be penalized, however, through a reduction in the term of required service or, in extreme cases, the granting of immediate freedom. The most frequent offense was the failure to pay freedom dues on the expiration of a contract, and suits alleging nonpayment were common in local courts. According to the research of Mary Schweitzer, the actual conditions of servitude in Pennsylvania in the eighteenth century were in reasonable conformity with the terms of written contracts and the laws of the province.

More evidence on the entrepreneurial aspects of indentured servants arises from new knowledge about the frequency with which colonists born in North America were drawn into service contracts. Orphans and the young children of indigent parents were prime candidates for indenture by judicial order, but older youths and some adults also signed contracts for varying terms. In Pennsylvania, Schweitzer discovered, poor youths seeking a specific sum of money payable at a fixed date in the future occasionally decided that the indenture system provided the safest and surest method of accumulating forced savings. A young person with no tangible resources was thereby able to sell a temporary claim on labor services to gain a small amount of future capital for investment in productive assets. (33) In addition to most indentured servants, a majority of those persons performing what was usually termed "common" or "day" labor also had a budding entrepreneurial orientation. In discussions of the colonial economy, historians have invariably assigned participants in these markets to the lower classes, since analyses of estates reveal that such workers tended to have few material possessions. Such persons also accounted for a large share of the population, comprising one-third or more of all adults in most regions. How, then, can one argue for the inclusion of so many visibly poor individuals within the entrepreneurial classification? The answer is revealed by an examination of the age distribution of common laborers. The vast majority were teenagers and young adults--persons ranging from fifteen to thirty years in age, generally unmarried. They were, in fact, mainly the children of economically independent parents; these youths were only beginning to participate in labor markets, and they started out near the bottom of the wage scale.

Prior to marriage in their early to mid-twenties, male youths routinely worked in the fields of nearby farms, and occasionally in an artisan shop, and young females assisted older women in neighboring households with domestic chores. These activities brought in a modest income and, perhaps equally important, the exposure to other family economic units served as a learning experience, since it acquainted these young people with the traditional roles of husbands and wives within an independent household. This pattern of youth employment was a mutual exchange arrangement among a majority of colonial households, extending over virtually all income levels, including some very wealthy families who naturally sent their offspring to labor only within the confines of other wealthy homes and estates. Youths therefore passed though a predictable stage in their life cycle: a period when their incomes were relatively low and their accumulated assets small. Males employed throughout the year could earn up to £30 per year (roughly $3,000 in 1990 dollars), whereas females received less than half that figure. These youthful laborers lived in the nearby homes of their parents or in the households of their employers. Their work as common laborers was a temporary arrangement--merely the beginning step along the path to more successful careers after marriage. (34)

Youths of both sexes usually saved a substantial share of their modest earnings and used those sums, along with inheritances, to assist in financing the formation of their own new households. Despite the relatively high percentage of workers performing common labor for low wages, this generally youthful group did not form the core of a permanently deprived class of workers. Most youths that engaged in common labor in the colonial period anticipated marriage and immediate promotion to landowner sometime before age thirty. The fundamental position of this stratum of society can be assessed, therefore, not by observing how its members fared economically as youths, but rather by considering the general level of wealth they had achieved on reaching middle age. By that criterion, most colonial youths clearly belong within the mainstream of an economic system imbued with enterprising attitudes.

THE EXCLUDED GROUPS

Enslaved blacks constitute the largest group of workers excluded from the entrepreneurial ranks. By the 1770s they made up just over 20 percent of the total population of the thirteen colonies. Unlike indentured servants, most slaves had no hope fur a more prosperous future either for themselves or for their children. This hopelessness was especially prevalent in rural areas, where the overwhelming number of slaves resided. In a few towns and cities, however, some urban slaves were granted permission to hire out their labor to third parties, sharing their earnings with owners on the basis of some prearranged formula. The system of self-hire was most common in Charleston, where blacks were a majority, and many slaves in that South Carolina port were engaged full-time in a variety of artisan activities. These slave artisans frequently maintained their own shops, and some were able to accumulate sufficient earnings to purchase freedom from accommodating owners. In his recent study of black employment patterns in Charleston, Philip Morgan has labeled some of these workers slave entrepreneurs. (35) His categorization appears justified, because these bonded workers had the means of steadily accumulating property, with the goal of enhancing permanently their general welfare. Enterprising slaves nevertheless constituted only a minuscule fraction of the total slave population in the colonies.

The vast majority of sailors employed on vessels in ports all along the coastline constitute another small but recognizable occupational group that should be excluded from any entrepreneurial classification. Colonial ships carried a substantial share of British and American cargoes in the North Atlantic trade, and they completely dominated the coastal trade, a rapidly growing market in the last quarter of the colonial era. These vessels provided employment in jobs requiring little advance training for thousands of sailors at relatively low wages and, more important, in positions with few opportunities fur advancement. Even in this instance, however, a few enterprising sailors who managed to survive the hazards of multiple voyages did move up to higher paying positions--first as mariners and perhaps later even to ship captain, a responsible job generating a fairly steady income. (36)

In rural areas there existed a very small category of adult workers, over the age of thirty and usually never married who continued to seek employment as day laborers throughout their working lives. Probably no more than 2 or 3 percent of the entire free rural population fit within this lowly occupational group. In urban areas, which accounted for a mere 7 percent of colonial population in 1775, the number of poor day laborers was probably relatively greater-perhaps as high as 10 percent of the overall work force.

What about women? Did they possess an entrepreneurial orientation? This question is difficult to answer satisfactorily because we need to distinguish, first, between married women and widows and, second, between women as individuals and as members of household units. Since by law and custom, males --mostly fathers or husbands (but sometimes brothers or other close relatives)-- usually exerted control over the property of daughters and wives, the vast majority of women, when considered as individuals, cannot have functioned as entrepreneurs. For example, a married woman could not sign a legal contract without the permission of her husband.

If, however, we view colonial society from the perspective of the household unit, then the issue becomes clouded. Most wives identified with the acquisitive traits of their spouses and contributed through their labor activities to the shared goal of accumulating property and enhancing economic opportunities for the benefit of their immediate families and the later welfare of their children. Seen in this light, wives may be considered as full participants in households with an entrepreneurial outlook. They contributed by providing essential domestic services and by working in the fields at critical periods such as the annual harvest; in addition, the output from supplementary housewifery activities, such as churning butter and spinning thread, generated extra income for consumption or investment in productive assets. (37)

Widows were more diverse in terms of wealth and income, and that diversity is revealed in this group's linkage to the entrepreneurial spirit. Most widows were far removed from that concept, especially women beyond their prime childbearing years, roughly age forty. Under English law, widows normally received a dower--a one-third lifetime interest in the property of their deceased spouses. (38) Although settlement terms differed depending on the number, age, and sex of surviving children and grandchildren, most widows aimed at conserving their remaining assets and eking out a modest living. Younger widows with several children, older widows without male teenagers still residing at home, and the few single women who had never married together constituted a group that consistently ranked among the households with the lowest incomes and wealth. (39)

On the other hand, a small minority of widows and unmarried daughters who gained control over substantial property through inheritance were able to exercise a quasi-entrepreneurial role in society. These propertied women had free rein to manage their enterprises, including the hiring and firing of employees and the legal right to negotiate contracts of all varieties. They could sue and be sued. Moreover, women who had inherited ownership of farms, artisan shops, or mercantile firms were generally accepted by the commercial community and encouraged to behave in a businesslike manner. Law and custom were generally conducive to the accumulation of further wealth, although some colonies had restrictions on the ability of women to purchase additional land. Of course a woman owner could not exercise complete discretion in decision making, since, like her male counterparts, she was limited by custom to hiring only males as assistants for any position with supervisory authority and responsibility. Males as a gender group possessed the opportunity to start their work careers in entry-level positions (overseers, supercargoes, clerks) and to accumulate sufficient experience and savings to move gradually toward independent status. Women, in contrast, either began their business careers as full-fledged owner-managers, or they did not participate in the business world at all. (40)

If women owners exercised all the power and authority of males in identical positions, then why use the prefix "quasi" to describe their seemingly entrepreneurial activities? The explanation relates not to their daily activities, but rather to their motivation and goals. Women were not expected to oversee the operations of farms and commercial enterprises because of a personal desire to succeed in the business world; in addition, they were generally not allowed to pass on the bulk of accumulated wealth to daughters or to other female relatives. Rather, they were viewed as persons who had assumed power in the marketplace on a strictly temporary basis as a result of extraordinary circumstances, conserving and expanding assets fur male progeny or male relatives until some future date. So long as it was clearly understood that ownership and control were eventually destined for transfer to a male somewhere within the family structure, it was perfectly acceptable for a woman to assume the burden of business responsibilities following the death of a husband or father. (41)

Therefore, such women are best viewed as persons functioning primarily as trustees for future generations of males. The situation is reasonably analogous to the power occasionally assumed by a queen mother in Europe when acting as a regent for an underage son who was heir to the throne. Because of limitations imposed by custom and low on their right to dispose of their property and the business enterprises periodically coming under their managerial control, colonial women even in the most favorable circumstances remained strictly on the periphery of the entrepreneurial class. (42)

CONCLUSION

If the general hypothesis of this essay about the broad occupational swath of the business sector in the seventeenth and eighteenth centuries is valid, it must lead eventually to a profound reorientation of teaching and scholarship within the fields of colonial and business history. Based on the accumulated wisdom of numerous recent investigations of the patterns of economic behavior exhibited in colonial society, that reorientation is fully merited. Entrepreneurial attitudes and strategies for upward economic mobility pervaded the tree population of the British North American colonies throughout the first two centuries of European settlement. These attributes were shared by the vast majority of colonial households: not only by merchants but by artisans, most farmers (including many tenants), indentured servants, unmarried and still youthful day laborers, and even a few exceptional slaves operating in the urban self-hire market. In retrospect, the business and social historian Thomas Cochran was on the mark when he first stressed the revolutionary character of the American economic system and the depth of business values within the society.

In the larger perspective of U.S. history, historians should henceforth stress that the majority of the free population from colonial times forward were active participants in an economic, social, and political system heavily imbued with entrepreneurial values--a system characterized by high savings rates, a market orientation, and positive attitudes toward the accumulation of wealth. How wide a swath did the business sector cut in the U.S. colonial past? It encompassed most occupational groups even in that earlier pre-industrial era. This theme remains one vital part of an abiding continuity in American history from 1607 to the present.

Notes

1. Jack P. Greene and J, R. Pole, "Reconstructing British-American Colonial History: An Introduction," the lead essay in their co-edited anthology, *Colonial British America: Essays in the New History of the Early Modern Era* (Baltimore, Md., 1984), quotation from p. 4.
2 Bernard Bailyn, *The New England Merchants in the Seventeenth Century* (Cambridge, Mass., 1955).
3. John McCusker and Russell Menard, *The Economy of British America, 1607-1789* (Chapel Hill, N.C., 1985). Other surveys of recent literature include Gary M. Walton and James F. Shephard, *The Economic Rise of Early America* (New York, 1979), and Edwin J. Perkins, *The Economy of Colonial America*, 2d ed. (New York, 1988).
4. Thomas Cochran, *Business in American Life: A History* (New York, 1972), 57. Verification of the rising price of land in settled areas can be found in Jackson Turner Main, *Society and Economy in Colonial Connecticut* (Princeton, N.J., 1985), 31-33, and Richard Beeman, *The Evolution of the Southern Backcountry: A Case Study of Lunenburg County, Virginia, 1746-1832* (Philadelphia, Pa., 1984), 33, 64. For an even earlier advocacy of themes related to the pervasiveness of capitalist attitudes in early American society, see Louis Hartz, *The Liberal Tradition in America: An Interpretation of American Political Thought since the Revolution* (New York, 1955).
5. Cochran, *200 Years of American Business* (New York, 1977), 4, and *Frontiers of Change: Early Industrialism in America* (New York, 1981), 11.
6. Sidney Ratner, James H. Soltow, and Richard Sylla, *The Evolution of the American Economy* (New York, 1979), 48, 69.
7. James Oliver Robertson, *America's Business* (New York, 1985), 11-46.
8. The Carl Degler quotation is a chapter subtitle from *Out of Our Past: The Forces That Shaped Modern America* (New York, 1959), 1. See also J. E. Crowley, *This Sheba, Self: The Concepualization of Economic Life in Eighteenth-Century America* (Baltimore, Md., 1974), 77; Bernard Bailyn, *Voyagers to the West: A Passage in the Peopling of America on the Eve of the Revolution* (New York, 1986), 200.
9. Christine L. Heyrman, *Commerce and Culture: The Maritime Communities of Colonial Massachusetts, 1690-1750* (New York, 1984); McCusker's review appeared in the *Business History Review* 60 (Summer 1986): 296-97.
10. John Frederick Martin, "Entrepreneurship and the Founding of New England Towns: The Seventeenth Century" (Ph.D. diss., Harvard University, 1985). His book is forthcoming from the University of North Carolina Press.
11. James Henretta, "Families and Farms: Mentalite in Pre-Industrial America," *William & Mary Quarterly* 35 (1978): 3-32; the quotation comes from Henretta's printed reply to a rebuttal letter from James Lemon "Comment on James A. Henretta's 'Families and Farms: Mentalite in Pre-Industrial America'" *ibid.* 37 (1980): 699. The broad parameters of this debate are reviewed in much greater depth in the second revised edition of my *Economy of Colonial America*, 67-71; the accompanying bibliographical essay lists much of the pertinent literature published through the mid-1980s. Because so many participants espouse such divergent views, the question about whether colonial society was capitalist or pre-capitalist appears unresolvable--at least for years to come. Some historians have tried to take an intermediate position between the two extremes--among them Michael Bellesiles, T. H. Breen, and Bettye Hobbs Pruitt; see Bellesiles, "Community Strategies for Dealing with Poverty: The New England Frontier, 1760-1820," unpublished paper distributed at the University of California's economic history conference, Laguna Beach, May 1986; Breen, "Back to Sweat and Toil: Suggestions for the Study of Agricultural

Work in Early America," *Pennsylvania History* 49 (1982): 241-58; and Pruitt, "Self-Sufficiency and the Agricultural Economy of Eighteenth -Century Massachusetts," *William & Mary Quarterly* 41 (1984): 333-64. For a broader theoretical discussion of related issues in a wider perspective, see Albert O. Hirschman, *Rival Views of Market Society and Other Recent Essays* (New York, 1986).

12. Christopher Clark, "Household Economy, Market Exchange, and the Rise of Capitalism in the Connecticut Valley, 1800-1860," *Journal of Social History* 13 (1979): 169-89; Michael Merrill, "Cash Is Good to Eat: Self-Sufficiency and Exchange in the Rural Economy of the United States," *Radical History Review* 3 (1977): 42-71; and Robert Mutch, "Yeoman and Merchant in Pre-Industrial America: Eighteenth-Century Massachusetts as a Case Study," *Societas* 7 (1977): 279-302. Allan Kulikoff focuses on the evolution of the agricultural economy in "The Transition to Capitalism in Rural America," *William & Mary Quarterly* 46 (1989): 120-44; I disagree with Kulikoff's thesis because I believe that little transition was required.

13. Lemon, "Comment," 688-700; Carol Shammas, "How Self-sufficient Was Early America?" *Journal of Interdisciplinary History* 13 (1982): 247-72, and "Consumer Behavior in Colonial America," *Social Science History* 6 (1982): 67-86; Winifred Rothenberg, "The Market and Massachusetts Farmers, 1750-1855," *Journal of Economic History* 41 (1981): 283-314; and "Markets, Values, and Capitalism: A Discourse on Method," *ibid.* 44 (1984): 174-78.

14. Her definition of utility maximization is round in Rothenberg's book review of Steven Hahn and Jonathan Prude, eds., *The Countryside in the Age of Capitalist Transformation: Essays in the Social History of Rural America* published in *Reviews in American History* 15 (1987): 633. She endorsed the term "commercial mentalite" in "The Market and Massachusetts Farmers, 1750-1855."

15. Harold Livesay was the inspiration for the term "maintainers"; he proposed it while serving as discussant on a panel at the Economic and Business Historical Society's annual convention, Toronto, Canada, 1988. If the focus here were on the post-revolutionary era, it would be tempting to label artisans and others who aimed mainly at achieving independence from employers--or landlords--and who feared excessive concentrations of wealth in society as persons exhibiting "republican virtues." I do not believe that terminology or that conceptual context is appropriate for the colonial period, however. Forrest McDonald, in discussing the intellectual origins of the Constitution, observed that, although historians have devoted much energy to analyzing the tensions between republican virtues and aristocratic vices, they had unfortunately inadequately addressed the counterpart tensions between communitarian consensus and possessive individualism; see his *Novus Ordo Seclorum: The Intellectual Origins of the Constitution* (Lawrence, Kans., 1985), viii.

16. An excellent source on the role and functions of merchants is Stuart Bruchey, ed., *The Colonial Merchant: Sources and Readings* (New York, 1966).

17. To cite one prominent example, see Jacob Price, *Capital and Credit in British Overseas Trade: The View from the Chesapeake, 1700-1776* (Cambridge, Mass., 1980).

18. Thomas Doerflinger, *A Vigorous Spirit of Enterprise: Merchants and Economic Development in Revolutionary Philadelphia* (Chapel Hill, N.C., 19816).

19. See, for example, Main, Colonial Connecticut, and Paul Clemens and Lucy Simler, "Rural Labor and the Farm Household in Chester County, Pennsylvania, 1750-1820," in *Work and Labor in Early America*, ed. Stephen Innes (Chapel Hill, N.C., 1988).

20. Doerflinger, *Vigorous Spirit of Enterprise.*

21. The artisanal origins of many early manufacturers are documented in Steven J. Ross

Workers on the Edge: Work, Leisure, and Politics industrializing Cincinnati, 1788-1890 (New York, 1985).
22. Lemon makes a similar argument in his "Comment," 688-696.
23. Shammas, "How Self-Sufficient Was Early America?"
24. According to Bruce Daniels, the typical farmer in Connecticut by the 1770s owned 10 cattle, 16 sheep, 6 pigs, 2 horses, a team of oxen, and some poultry; see his "Economic Development in Colonial and Revolutionary Connecticut: An Overview," *William & Mary Quarterly* 37 (1980): 427-50. Alice Hanson Jones estimated for the same period that middling farmers throughout the colonies (estates of £100 to £400) held about 15 percent of their total wealth in livestock, with smaller farmers (estates under £99) holding just over 25 percent in livestock; the data are from tables 7.21 and 7.22 in *Wealth of a Nation To Be: The American Colonies on the Eve of the Revolution* (New York, 1980). The colonists' expansion of livestock herds presaged the business strategies of many rural households in the modem U.S. economy. In the late twentieth century, the bulk of all harvested grain ends up as fodder for gigantic herds of hogs and cattle since high income levels permit Americans to exercise their preference for obtaining a disproportionate share of their nourishment from meat and dairy products. Although colonial farms were a far cry from the modem mechanized farm, the increased size of crop surpluses and their allocation to boost the output of meat and dairy products was a trend already under way by the eighteenth century.
25. Sung Bok Kim, *Landlord and Tenant in Colonial New York: Manorial Society, 1664-1775* (Chapel Hill, N.C., 1978); Stephen Innes, "Land Tenancy and Social Order in Springfield, Massachusetts, 1652 to 1702," *William & Mary Quarterly* 35 (1978), 33-56, and *Labor in a New Land: Economy and Society in Seventeenth-Century Springfield* (Princeton, N. J. , 1983) Gloria Main, *Tobacco Colony: Life in Early Maryland* (Princeton, N.J., 1982); Clemens and Simler, "Rural Labor"; and Mary Schweitzer, *Custom and Contract: Household, Government, and the Economy in Colonial Pennsylvania* (New York, 1987).
26. Downwardly mobile tenants are the focus of Gregory Stiverson, *Poverty in a Land of Plenty: Tenancy in Eighteenth-Century Maryland* (Baltimore, Md., 1977).
27. In "Rural Labor," Clemens and Simler identified a significant number of tenant farmers in eastern Pennsylvania who earned a living from a combination of activities: producing crops on rented land, periodic day labor in the landlord's fields, and occasional craft work for the landlord. Indeed, landlords often charged very low rents for contiguous farms because they wanted to hold nearby a "captive" source of supplementary day labor during certain critical weeks in the cycle of planting and harvesting, and they anticipated that tenants would bring new land under the plow. When wheat began to ripen, farmers with sizable commitments to commercial agriculture were always willing to pay occasional day laborers substantial wages--up to 4 shillings per day (about $23 in 1990 prices)--if extra hands were available in the surrounding countryside.
28. The inclusion of southern planters in the entrepreneurial category is incompatible with the Marxian analysis of southern slave society advanced by Elizabeth Fox-Genovese and Eugene Genovese. They are unwilling to grant the U.S. slave society the status of full-fledged capitalism. Instead, they view the slave South as a region that "emerged as a bastard child of merchant capital and developed as a non-capitalist society." Their depiction of the slave south is outlined in *Fruits of Merchant Capital: Slavery and Bourgeois Property in the Rise and Expansion of Capitalism* (New York, 1983); quotation from p. 5.
29. T. H. Breen recently estimated the share of households qualifying for great planter

status to be in the range of 3 to 10 percent; see his *Tobacco Culture: The Mentality of the Great Tidewater Planters on the Eve of Revolution* (Princeton, N.].., 1985), 32-38.
30. Allan Kulikoff, *Tobacco and Slaves: The Development of Southern Culture in the Chesapeake, 1680-1800* (Chapel Hill, N.C., 1986), 118-61.
31. The contributions of these scholars include Galenson, *White Servitude in Colonial America: An Economic Analysis* (New York, 1981); Grubb, "Immigration and Servitude in the Colony and Commonwealth of Pennsylvania: A Quantitative Economic Analysis" (Ph.D. diss., University of Chicago, 1984), plus numerous derivative articles, including "Immigrant Servant Labor: Their Occupation and Geographic Distribution in the Late Eighteenth-Century Mid-Atlantic Economy," *Social Science History* 9 (1985): 249-75; "The Market for Indentured Immigrants: Evidence on the Efficiency of Forward-Labor Contracting in Philadelphia, 1745-1773," *Journal of Economic History* 45 (1985): 855-68; "Colonial Labor Markets and the Length of Indenture: Further Evidence," *Explorations in Economic History* 24 (1987): 101-6; and Bailyn, *Voyagers to the West*. Two very useful essays are James Horn, "Servant Emigration in the Chesapeake in the Seventeenth Century," 51-95, and Lois Green Carr and Russell Menard, "Immigration and Opportunity: The Freedman in Early Colonial Maryland," 206-42, in The *Chesapeake in the Seventeenth Century: Essays on Anglo-American Society*, ed. Thad Tate and David Ammerman (Chapel Hill, N.C., 1979). An excellent survey of the literature on both forms of bonded labor is Richard Dunn, "Servants and Slaves: The Recruitment and Employment of Labor," in Greene and Pole, *Colonial British America*, 157-94. For a useful bibliography, see Perkins, Economy of Colonial America, 110-14.
32. In *Tobacco Colony*, Gloria Main estimated freedom dues in Maryland at around £3.5 in the seventeenth century--or about $350 in 1990 prices.
33. Details of the indenture contracts of the native born, are found in Schweitzer, *Custom and Contract*.
34. The best data on work patterns during a male's life cycle are found in Jackson Turner Main, *Colonial Connecticut*. Information on females is sketchier, but Schweitzer, *Custom and Contract*, and Shammas, "The Female Social Structure of Philadelphia in 1775," *Pennsylvania Magazine of History and Biography* 107 (1983): 69-83, are useful sources.
35. Philip Morgan, "Black Life in Eighteenth-Century Charleston," *Perspectives in American History*, n.s., I (1984), 187-232.
36. Marcus Rediker, *Between the Devil and the Deep Blue Sea: Merchant Seamen, Pirates, and the Anglo-American Maritime World, 1700-1750* (New York, 1987). On the economic status of seamen, mariners, and captains, see Main, *Colonial Connecticut*, 280-95. Eighty percent of all ship captains in the colony listed land in their estates.
37. Joan Jensen, *Loosening the Bonds: Mid-Atlantic Farm Women, 1750-1850* (New Haven, Conn., 1986).
38. Marylynn Salmon, *Women and the Law of Property in Early America* (Chapel Hill, N.C., 1986). A strictly lifetime interest meant that, on the widow's death, the property was turned over to whoever was named in the husband's will or, alternatively, it was divided according to the customs and laws of the colony. In neither case did the widow have the right to alter or dictate the disposition of the property on which she had relied for economic support during her widowhood.
39. Shammas, "Female Social Structure," 69-83.
40. A good source on the special status of women as managers of farms and commercial enterprises is Julie A. Matthaci, *An Economic History of Women in America: Women's Work, the Sexual Division of Labor, and the Development of Capitalism* (New York, 1982). With the explicit consent of their husbands, women in some colonies were granted

the privilege of opening business enterprises, usually small mercantile firms; they received all managerial powers, including the right to negotiate contracts, under the legal device called "feme sole."

41. For more information on differing provincial laws, see Carole Shammas, Marylynn Salmon, and Michel Dahlin, *Inheritance in America: From Colonial Times to the Present* (New Brunswick, N.J., 1987).

42. Eliza Lucas, who later married a Pinckney, is perhaps the best example of a colonial businesswoman. She managed successfully several rice and indigo plantations for extended periods of time on two separate occasions--the first at the bidding of her father and once again following the death of her husband. Predictably, after her sons had matured, they eventually assumed ownership and managerial control over the plantation properties.

Chapter Two

"Introduction" to *American Public Finance and Financial Services, 1700 - 1815*

This book focuses on the evolution of financial services from the colonial period through the early national era, emphasizing their importance in laying the foundation for the future development of the American economic and political systems. During the seventeenth and eighteenth centuries, the British colonies in North America made substantial progress in shaping a financial environment that generally provided a fair degree of stability and, secondly, fostered steady economic advancement. Partially as a result of improved financial services, the rate of economic growth in the British colonies, on both an aggregate and per capita basis, was among the highest in the world from 1650 to 1775.

After the achievement of political independence, the expansion of financial services continued unabated. Experimentation was evident in virtually every financial market, and improvements became more pronounced as the decades passed. A diverse and responsive financial sector was one of the great strengths of the American economy in the pre-industrial era--and thereafter as well. By 1815 the most institutionally advanced sector of the U.S. economy was the broad-based financial infrastructure. A quarter century after the formation of the new federal government, incorporated commercial banks and insurance companies were numerous and typically well managed; in combination, they attracted millions of dollars in private investment in their common stock. By comparison, most contemporary transportation and manufacturing firms were relatively small enterprises, with the majority in manufacturing still operating as partnerships or proprietorships.

From the mid-eighteenth century forward, a more sophisticated capital market was in the process of emerging, and was progressing at accelerating rates. By the early nineteenth century, the market accommodated the placement and the subsequent trading of the common stock of many financial services firms and,

*Excerpt from Perkins, *American Public Finance and Financial Services, 1700-1815.*

equally importantly, the long-term bonds of the federal government. Meanwhile, the monetary system, based on the circulation of specie wins and bank notes continuously convertible into specie, was generally sound and secure--the only exception being the temporary suspension of conversion privileges caused by the economic dislocations surrounding the War of 1812. The solid base established in the financial sector laid the groundwork for growth and development in other complementary sectors of the economy after 1815.

This study concentrates largely on the institutional development of the American financial services sector from the last decade of the seventeenth century through the first fifteen years of the nineteenth century. New technologies made no significant impact during that time; the innovations were exclusively institutional arrangements. Most of the services discussed here originated in European financial markets and migrated to Great Britain; thereafter, they crossed the ocean to the North American colonies. The study identifies the continuities that persisted throughout the colonial, confederation, and early national eras, and, when appropriate, it highlights a series of innovative departures from financial traditions.

One of the book's main claims to originality rests on its broad chronological sweep. Most previous examinations of American financial history have concentrated strictly on the colonial period or, alternatively, started with Alexander Hamilton's bold initiatives in the early 1790s and moved forward in time. E. James Ferguson's *Power of the Purse* remains one of the few accounts of financial activities during the intervening confederation years. Within the fields of political, social, and intellectual history over the last quarter century, overlapping studies of the colonial and early national periods have become much more common in scholarly circles, and this book adds more fuel to that historiographical trend.

To convey the scope, I chose the term "financial services sector" to describe the breadth of the analysis. That descriptive phrase entered the language of business journalists in the late twentieth century and was completely unfamiliar to contemporaries two hundred years ago. Nonetheless, I was attracted by its comprehensive context. Financial services sector is an umbrella term designed to unite under its shadow a host of related but varying functions. In this book that umbrella encompasses all of the following: the money stock, governmental loan facilities (land hanks), commercial banking, and capital markets plus, in a secondary role, the occupations of investment banker, stock and bond broker, foreign exchange dealer, lottery organizer, and insurance underwriter.

Three overriding themes dominate these pages: continuity, innovation, and maturation. Governments in North America consistently sought to establish financial systems responsive to the needs of the population. Most legislatures enacted laws designed to permit the wide-scale participation by diverse groups of citizens--both as the providers and the consumers of financial services. That legacy eventually became a pillar of the Jeffersonian-Jacksonian political tradition. When economic and political conditions changed, American society possessed the flexibility to alter institutional arrangements within the financial sector. Almost immediately after independence, the general movement was from public to private control of money and banking. In the colonial era, provincial legislatures were directly involved in the provision of financial services: but in the 1790s state governments retreated, in part because of constitutional restrictions. Private enterprises were granted greater leeway, and entrepreneurs took advantage of the opportunities to create new institutions.

The revolution in financial services moved ahead at a faster pace than corresponding revolutions in transport, energy, and manufacturing. Even before independence, colonial legislatures were innovators in the use of fiat currency, a form of governmel1lissue paper money unconvertible into coin at fixed exchange rates. A healthy share of those monies entered the economy through government-owned mortgage loan offices, which made long-term loans in moderate amounts (the maximum sum was restricted by law) to private citizens secured by real estate. Most borrowers used the funds to increase productive assets, including more land, new barns, fences, tools, livestock, and the contracts of bonded workers--both indentured servants and slaves.

The use of fiat currency was a departure from monetary traditions in the mother country. Fiat paper had an unsavory reputation Europe and was not a component of the money stock in Great Britain. Its issuance in the colonies was regularly challenged by imperial officials, who nevertheless reluctantly approved most emissions after warning of the dangers of depreciation and the potential for financial catastrophe. In several colonies, primarily in New England, fiat monies did in fact lose most of their purchasing power; they were steadily withdrawn from circulation under parliamentary directive after 1751. But in the middle colonies and every southern colony except North and South Carolina, fiat currency never succumbed to spiraling depreciation. Instead, it continued to play a positive role in facilitating everyday trade and served as a fairly reliable store of liquid wealth.

Fiat currency also provided the mechanism to finance approximately two-thirds of the cost of the War for Independence. The solid reputation fiat currency had established during the third quarter of the century allowed it to provide sufficient purchasing power to carry the American military forces through the first five years of the war--a notable achievement critical to the final victory. Although fiat currency, both the congressional and state varieties, depreciated irreversibly from 1778 to 1780 and finally fell to less than one percent of face value in relation to hard monies, in the postwar decade seven state legislatures voted for its reissuance. Only the constitutional prohibition on direct state emissions of currency after 1789 eliminated fiat paper as a component of the nation's money stock.

Other innovative features of the colonial economy were the birth of a market for short-term government debt and expanded marine and fire insurance. After the parliamentary ban on their fiat currency issues, the New England colonies financed periodic budget deficits through the direct sale of treasury bills, with maturities ranging from one to five years, to private investors. Prior to 1750 investors seeking a safe harbor for their capital had little choice but to invest their savings in real estate, make well-secured mortgage loans to neighbors, or hoard specie-a sterile, unremunerative asset. Treasury bills, which typically paid interest at the legal limit, were a new investment vehicle. They provided the seedbed for the broader capital market that emerged in the last decade of the century.

The insurance market also witnessed substantial development during the eighteenth century. Initially, American shippers arranged marine coverage through their London agents. Syndicates of underwriters operating from waterfront coffeehouses, of which Lloyd's was the most famous, accepted the risks associated with overseas trade. Beginning in the second quarter of the eighteenth century, independent American underwriters began to cover the risks on shipments to the Caribbean and southern Europe, plus intercoastal routes. A decade or so later, Benjamin Franklin spearheaded the movement to establish the first successful American fire insurance company in Philadelphia. That firm was organized as a nonprofit, mutual enterprise--another American first.

As a result of advances and refinements dating back centuries, but more pronounced after 1650, the fundamental techniques of insuring ships and buildings, plus their contents, against various hazards were generally well understood by the last quarter of the eighteenth century. In the colonies the indigenous institutional framework was woefully deficient, although a few American underwriters entered the market beginning in the 1720s. This arrested financial sector was transformed after independence; the U.S. insurance market literally exploded. Numerous state-chartered companies, with millions of dollars in equity capital, began operations between 1790 and 1815, and they had the blessings of political leaders of every stripe. Generally speaking, those firms engaged in marine and fire insurance (but not life insurance) had already traveled far down the road to maturation on the eve of the War of 1812.

The adaptive and innovative character of the American financial system was likewise evident in the movement toward the privatization of currency issuance in the postwar era. Firms issuing monies convertible into coin at the holder's option were commonplace in Great Britain by the mid-eighteenth century, but similar enterprises had never been sustained in the colonies. In the 1780s state-chartered commercial banks with transferable shares opened their doors in three states--Pennsylvania, New York, and Massachusetts. These chartered banks endured some controversy during their first decade of operations, especially in Philadelphia, but all carried out faithfully their responsibility to provide a sound currency, and they operated profitably. Based partially on the success of that experiment, chartered financial institutions assumed total responsibility for providing the American public with paper monies in the 1790s.

Although state legislatures were required to abstain from the issuance of fiat currency after ratification of the Constitution, they often joined private citizens in acquiring shares in the commercial banks operating within their borders. The federal government made the greatest public investment in commercial banking when it took 20 percent of the equity in the Bank of the United States. Mixed enterprises, partially private and partially public, were commonplace in the early national era. Continuing their bias in favor of wide-scale citizen participation and access to financial services, a legacy from colonial times, Americans opted for a decentralized, atomistic system of commercial banks linked closely to their communities. Many of the initial objections to the creation of a well-capitalized, centrally administered, and federally chartered national bank dissipated in the first year after the board of directors voted to spread the benefits geographically throughout the nation by opening a chain of branch offices. The branches received capital allocations from the Philadelphia office; branch capital grew over lime and eventually exceeded the amount retained at headquarters. Meanwhile, the branches functioned largely independently of central control. Each branch's local board of directors made loans strictly to local customers.

In the state systems, in contrast branch banking sprang up in some areas, but even the most ambitious institutions rarely operated more than three or four satellite offices. The most common organizational form was the single-unit banking enterprise. Federalists and Republicans alike agreed on this bask concept: namely, the importance of local control over commercial banking services. The scattered institutional pattern persisted in the United States well into the twentieth century. Interestingly, no other nation around the world chose to imitate the fragmentation of the U.S. banking system--another fact lending support to historians who argue the uniqueness of the American experience. .

The American capital market that sprang forth in the 1790s was composed of government bonds and the equities of private banks and insurance companies. The bonds, which totaled approximately $70 million face value, were remnants of the leftover debts incurred in fighting the War for Independence. The long delay in repaying the principal ran counter to the policies implemented by most colonial legislatures following the largest previous military confrontation in North America--the Seven Years' War. In the 1760s the thirteen colonies had increased taxes, and aided by reimbursements from Parliament, the majority set out to retire the bulk of their outstanding debts within a decade or so. Most colonies actually accomplished their goals or at least made substantial progress in reducing their outstanding obligations. In the 1780s most states hoped to duplicate the success of their efforts a generation earlier. Legislative factions that felt a heightened sense of urgency passed joint taxation and debt retirement acts designed to put a huge dent in their respective indebtedness by the end of the decade. Many states tentatively adopted optimistic plans to eliminate their entire public debt by the mid-1790s at the very latest. Generally ignoring the pleas of the Continental Congress for financial contributions to help service the federal debt, the several states decided instead to draw on local resources to make inroads on local obligations.

The urgency factions in state capitals justified programs of high taxes, huge budget surpluses, and systematic debt retirement on several grounds. They maintained that accelerated principal repayment would save taxpayers money in the long run by reducing the aggregate revenues spent on interest. Other anticipated societal benefits included fewer opportunities for speculation in the public debt. By retiring the public debt promptly, citizens would also discourage the emergence of a permanent monied class--a group of allegedly unproductive parasites who owned a disproportionate share of the public debt and lived off the interest income, generation after generation. Those classes were prominent in allegedly corrupt European states but were unwelcome in the new United States. At the national level, Jeffersonian Republicans adopted most of the principles of the urgency factions in debates about how to service the nation's wartime debts.

Urgency factions took the lead in most states, but after the mid-1780s they backed off and gave way to the gradualist position almost everywhere, with the notable exception of Massachusetts. The size of the public debt after the War for Independence was many times greater than what had accumulated during the Seven Years' War, and the taxes necessary to extinguish it were burdensome. Even raising enough revenues to maintain interest payments was difficult; retiring the principal with dispatch required too much sacrifice over too long a time. Some states, like Virginia, made progress for one or two years but then decided to maintain the status quo.

Gradualists like Alexander Hamilton in New York, argued that the emphasis should be placed on generating only sufficient tax revenues to meet recurring interest obligations. The retirement of principal should proceed slowly, extending over a quarter century or more. Federalists rejected Jefferson's axiom that each generation should assume the entire financial burden for the military expenditures it had incurred. Correspondingly, Hamilton hoped a perpetual national debt would provide the core for an American capital market that might eventually rival London. The financial strain on citizens in the late 1780s allowed Hamiltonian strategies to come to the fore at both the federal and state levels in the 1790s.

Massachusetts was the exception in that context. The urgency faction adopted a plan to retire the state's public debt over a five-year period starting in 1785. When citizens protested the accelerating taxes and threatened revolt, the state government refused to budge. Shays' Rebellion was the result. The outcome was a consequence of political miscalculation and gross fiscal mismanagement, pure and simple. Given the unprecedented magnitude of the public debt, patience and good common sense were seriously lacking within the legislative leadership. The irony remains that if Massachusetts had waited until the congressional committee charged with settling wartime debts among 'the thirteen states had finished its work, which finally occurred in 1793, the legislature would have learned that its creditor position was sufficiently large to cover all the state's wartime obligations. In truth, heavy local taxation was not required--not in Massachusetts, a state that had done more than its share on a per capita basis to aid the cause. The intervening federal assumption of the states' outstanding debts was not a necessary condition for that result. Federal assumption represented a preemptive advance payment, so to speak; Massachusetts would have received overwhelming financial relief from the national government three to five years later in any event. The preceding nutshell analysis provides only a preview. How the complex events, with all the elements of a comic-tragic opera, transpired in Massachusetts during the 1780s consumes an entire chapter of this volume.

Once the state and federal debts were consolidated in the early 1790s, the American capital market blossomed. The prices of the new federal bonds rose as the confidence of investors in the government's ability to sustain interest payments strengthened. Shares in the Bank of the United States came on the market soon thereafter and were gobbled up by eager investors. State-chartered commercial banks and insurance companies floated stock issues as well; the new firms were generally profitable and paid regular dividends, which supported the value of their securities. Once Jefferson assumed the presidency and actually began to retire the federal debt in earnest, the reputation of American securities received an added boost.

What emerged in the first decade of the nineteenth century was essentially a Jeffersonian-Hamiltonian hybrid. The nation possessed a maturing capital market, fulfilling Hamilton's dream, but its core steadily shifted away from public bond issues, which drew on tax revenues, toward the securities of a multitude of private firms, most of which were concentrated in the financial services sector. They operated under charters issued by state governments that periodically expired and thus became subject to renegotiation, thereby making the enterprises accountable to the general public. No highly visible monied class --no easily identifiable group of rentiers living in perpetual luxury off the proceeds of government interest payments--arose in American society.

Meanwhile, the maturation of the financial services sector was a mutually supportive and reinforcing phenomenon. The successes of the U.S. Treasury's debt retirement program as well as the operations of a host of private financial enterprises--not generally manufacturing and transportation firms--invigorated the institutional structure of financial markets, broadly speaking, and lubricated the wheels of commerce. Financial firms and corresponding financial markets--in the latter case, securities trading and foreign exchange transactions, for example--progressed in parallel during the nation's first quarter century. Improved and expanded financial services became the first pillar in the underlying infrastructure of the American economy.

Although this volume was not written with the intention of testing the applicability of broader theories about the links between republican and capitalist ideology in the early national era, especially the hypotheses advanced by Joyce Appleby about the market orientation of Jeffersonian Republicans. The compatibility of many of those revisionist concepts and the conclusions of this study are undeniable. Regarding the shape and character of the emerging financial services sector, many leaders of the two major political factions shared similar values and attitudes. They agreed by and large on the following: 1) the importance of establishing a sound monetary system (convertible bank notes were not controversial after 1790); 2) the importance of local control over local financial institutions; 3) the importance of widespread access to financial services; and 4) the importance of meeting the government's legitimate debt obligations, with only the timing of principal repayments a matter of debate.

After 1795, Republicans were as entrepreneurial as the Federalists in seeking state charters for commercial banks and insurance companies. Once they realized that commercial banking would evolve as a decentralized system, most Jeffersonians modified their complaints about the dangers of financial privatization. Once they could see that the national debt was not destined to climb to new heights and attract thereby a swarm of speculators and stockjobbers, most Jeffersonians welcomed the emergence of a functioning capital market that financed new enterprises and provided liquidity for persons seeking to adjust their investment portfolios. Admittedly, reservations about the constitutionality of the First Bank of the United States lingered, but the congressional refusal to renew the federal charter in 1811 should not be interpreted as anything more than a Republican repudiation of Hamilton's centralizing principles. The financial services sector that developed in the early national era was compatible with the ideological outlook of the vast majority of Americans. After the turn of the century, its development reflected the expressed goals of Jeffersonians and Hamiltonians alike.

Chapter Three

Conflicting Views on Fiat Currency: Britain and its North American Colonies in the Eighteenth Century

Political and business attitudes concerning the inclusion of fiat currency in the money stock differed tremendously between England and Great Britain's North American colonies in the eighteenth century. All 13 American colonies, at one time or another, embraced the emission of fiat paper as a supplement to the circulating coinage, whereas Parliament vehemently disavowed any possibility of its issuance in England and generally discouraged its usage anywhere within the British Empire. As the years passed, frequent disagreements over the management of monetary affairs within the Empire soured relations between colonies and crown. From Parliament's passage of the Current Act of 1764 until its modification in 1773, the controversy over the emission of fiat currency was, after taxation, the second most divisive issue in imperial relations, and it ranks high among the underlying causes for the American rebellion in the mid-1770s. This article examines how these transatlantic differences in theory and practice arose, and why they persisted for so long. (1)

England

By the eighteenth century, most political and business leaders in England held diametrically opposed opinions regarding the legitimacy of the two main forms of paper money. As a rule, they voiced few objections to emissions of paper monies by chartered banks and most private firms whenever these issuers stood ready to convert currency into coin or bullion upon demand by drawing upon their accumulated reserves. Convertible paper money was recognized both as a convenient medium of exchange and also, since it rarely depreciated, as a relatively safe means of holding wealth. At the same time, British leaders generally opposed emissions of fiat currencies by governmental bodies, including Parliament itself, because history had shown, or at least the European

*Reprinted article with permission of *Business History* (1991), pp. 8-30.

history with which they were generally familiar had revealed very clearly, that fiat monies invariably depreciated and caused havoc within a national economy. Members of parliamentary committees with responsibility for colonial affairs drew upon their wisdom and experience to steer political sub-units away from the potential dangers of fiat currencies. In North America, however, they met persistent opposition from local leaders who cited consistently favourable results with unconvertible governmental issues.

To round out the argument before proceeding to more controversial matters, we should discuss briefly the form of paper money to which few critics in Britain raised substantial objections, namely currencies and banknotes issued by chartered banks and private firms. The origins of circulating private monies can be traced mainly to the functions of goldsmiths. They issued warehouse receipts to depositors of specie, and these receipts evolved into negotiable instruments which circulated as money, starting in the seventeenth century. At first goldsmiths held one hundred per cent reserves, but over the years they discovered that holding only fractional reserves against their note issue was reasonably prudent. Later several mercantile houses also entered the financial services market, providing banking and other more sophisticated financial services for their regular customers. Firms engaged in banking made loans both through deposit creation and the issuance of non-legal tender promissory notes convertible into coin at their premises.

In 1694, as is well known, Parliament granted a limited-liability charter to the Bank of England. During the next six decades, three public banks in Scotland likewise received limited-liability charters. (2) These chartered institutions issued currencies supported by specie reserves. The Bank of England emitted currency only in large denominations so that few of its bills circulated among the general population, but the Scottish banks printed currency in small denominations--£1 and even lower--and paper money eventually replaced much of the circulating coinage in Scotland. In both England and Scotland, the paper monies of the chartered banks were convertible into specie upon demand, and despite the limited liability clauses in their charters, the public had faith in their solvency and viability. (3)

Non-chartered private bankers in England and Scotland operated without the protection of limited liability. If specie reserves proved inadequate or loans went sour, currency holders were free to proceed through the courts against the business and personal assets of issuers. The unlimited liability of currency issuers gave the appearance of safety, which led most public figures to adopt a tolerant attitude toward the operations of private bankers, including many firms operating on a small scale. In connection with negotiations over an extension of the charter for the Bank of England in 1708, however, the new regulations stipulated that no unchartered business firm with more than six partners was permitted to issue currency anywhere within the empire, thereby excluding large joint-stock enterprises from entering this financial market.

D. M. Joslin estimated that the number of private bankers in London, which stood at 24 in 1725, had risen to 51 by 1776. (4) Private banks typically held greater deposit than currency liabilities, and specie reserves were normally more than adequate to permit continuous conversion. Only five bankruptcies among London's private bankers occurred between 1745 and 1771, and there is no indication that the holders of private monies by these five firms ever suffered any serious losses. Until the credit crisis of 1772, which came late in the North American colonial era, few Scottish banks had failed. (5) The outstanding record of private bankers in supporting the value of their currency issues led policy makers in Great Britain to look favourably on paper money supported by specie reserves in the first six decades of the eighteenth century.

On the other hand, English political leaders were nearly unanimous in their opposition to the emission of inconvertible fiat currencies by governmental bodies. Their views reflected prevailing monetary theories and were buttressed by historical precedent. The prime objection to fiat monies was the danger of a steady and irreversible depreciation, which could arise because of over-issue and inadequate backing. The irregular discoveries of gold and silver set reasonably finite limits on monetary stocks consisting of coins minted from precious metals as well as currency issues supported by adequate reserves of specie, whereas huge volumes of fiat paper in denominations, large and small, could be printed by irresponsible governments within days. Without effective controls, the temptation to resort to the printing press to acquire spending power, rather than through the mechanism of taxation or public borrowing, was viewed as simply too great for any government to resist once the barrier had been breached. Over-issue led invariably to depreciation, which cheated lenders, unduly rewarded borrowers, and left a nation's financial system in disarray.

Moreover, recent experiences in Europe supported what prevailing theories about fiat monies had predicted. The only sustained government experiment in the issuance of non-metallic monies by the English crown in the seventeenth century had ended disastrously. Starting in 1667, during the reign of Charles II, the Exchequer began emitting what soon became negotiable orders; large denomination orders were issued to persons making specie loans, while amounts as low as £1 to £5 went to purchase routine supplies. These so-called Exchequer Orders were tax anticipation notes, meaning that as taxes were subsequently collected, the outstanding orders were scheduled for redemption in the exact sequence as originally issued. The orders carried an interest rate component and thus increased in redemption value over time. Since the orders were easily transferable, they became a convenient medium of exchange--in other words, paper money. (6)

Exchequer Orders held their value relative to coin for several years. The initial series were redeemed according to plan, and the holders of orders still in circulation remained confidant about their ultimate redemption in specie. But the crown was pressed for additional financing to support military spending. As a convenient alternative to raising taxes, more paper was issued, and the redemption of prior orders began to run behind schedule. Once public doubts had arisen, the paper began passing at discounts vis-a-vis specie. In 1672, only five years after the inauguration of the program, the Exchequer suddenly stopped payment on most of its interest bearing orders. Estimates of the aggregate sums outstanding range from £1.3 to £2.25 million. Most of the suspended orders were held by persons of substantial wealth who presumably held them as an investment vehicle; two goldsmiths alone accounted for approximately 60 per cent of the total. How many orders actually circulated as part of the money supply is unknown, but this failed experiment with a variation of fiat currency had a powerful influence on the attitudes of later generations.

The lessons learned under Charles II confirmed the suspicions of critics about the dangers of experiments with fiat monies. Without any means of converting the Exchequer Orders into specie at face value upon demand, holders were completely dependent on the resolve of the crown to collect sufficient taxes in the future, and, second, to use those revenues to redeem debt obligations on schedule. The stoppage of payments in 1672 was proof enough of the inherent dangers for the vast majority in Parliament; thereafter members were adamantly opposed to any scheme designed to permit the emission of any financial instrument which might function as fiat paper. Despite a shortage of silver coins of intermediate values to promote the convenient exchange of goods and services in eighteenth-century England, Parliament held to a strictly metallic standard.

The prejudices against paper money were reinforced by the financial scandal in France linked to the infamous Scotsman, John Law. After gaining the confidence of the regent for Louis XV, Law was permitted to open a chartered bank in 1716 to aid the government in financing its outstanding debt. He eventually issued an enormous volume of paper notes supposedly backed in full by specie resting in the bank's vaults; but, in truth, the vaults were virtually empty. The whole scheme finally collapsed in 1720, disrupting temporarily the French financial system and its national economy. (7)

Because of the fiascoes in England in 1672 and France in 1720, objections in Parliament were so great that members never gave serious consideration to any proposal for the emission of any form of fiat currency in the home economy or any British dominion. Ample reservations existed about the propriety and practicality of the unproven system of fiat currency. Some 'persons held very strong views--arguing that all paper money, including convertible notes as well as fiat paper, was an evil concept which contradicted every established principle of nature, the will of God, or higher authority in general. Morality and economics were frequently intermixed in discussion of monetary affairs in general, and with reference to fiat paper in particular. When paper money in small to intermediate denominations finally entered the English economy, it was issued strictly by private banks, and not by Parliament. Indeed, the English public did not commonly hold paper money until very late in the eighteenth century, many decades after its widespread acceptance as a convenient medium of exchange in several North American colonies and Scotland.

North American Colonies

Public attitudes toward the issuance of fiat monies by governmental units were radically different in the 13 colonies than in England. In North America, pragmatism and a fair degree of self-restraint triumphed over theoretical abstractions and moralistic pronouncements in most colonies. Based on their own experiences, the colonists in over half the North American provinces concluded that fiat currency, when properly backed either by public taxation or private mortgages, provided a useful supplement to the money stock. It augmented, but never permanently displaced, the foreign coins, mainly Spanish in origin, which circulated among the population. All 13 colonies experimented with some form of fiat currency. Despite instances of heavy depreciation in five colonies, all of which occurred during the first half of the eighteenth century, nine legislatures continued to emit paper money until the outbreak of the American rebellion in the 1770s. Moreover, seven state legislatures remained active in monetary affairs in the 1780s--until ratification of the Constitution outlawed new issues of fiat monies by state governments in the U.S. federal system. (8)

The conflicts surrounding fiat currency in the colonial era pitted the Board of Trade in London, which claimed the authority to disallow any local acts that violated English law or its interpretation of parliamentary intent, against separate and distinct provincial legislatures. (9) After the Exchequer's stoppage in 1672, the membership of the Board of Trade reflected the strong reservations of parliamentary leaders about the propriety of fiat monies at home and abroad. In later years, board members were pressured to uphold their convictions by British mercantile creditors who were becoming increasingly fearful about the exchange risks associated with debt collections in colonies where fiat monies had legal tender status. Accordingly, Parliament passed two acts, one in 1751 and a second in 1764, which limited the powers of colonial legislatures to issue fresh emissions of currency. The latter act, and the board's efforts to enforce it, sparked heated political opposition in North America. Beyond New England, colonial leaders viewed the legitimacy of fiat money in an entirely different light, and they increasingly resented the interference of English officials in this sphere of their domestic affairs.

The initial emission of fiat currency, typically called 'bills of credit' in this era, came in Massachusetts in 1690. The treasury was short of funds to cover the salaries of soldiers returning from a military campaign, and the legislature resorted to the printing press as an expedient. Over the next few years, these paper monies were retired on schedule through tax collections. The success of the first paper money scheme encouraged the Massachusetts legislature to repeat the experiment again and again over the next half century, and other colonies soon became imitators. When Virginia joined the ranks in 1755, every colony had become involved in the process of issuing and redeeming fiat currency. Whenever any of the provincial legislatures authorized a fresh currency emission, it usually specified the future redemption date, ranging from two to 20 years depending upon a host of considerations. Currency issues were retired either in stages or all at once in the maturation year.

Colonial currency was invariably designated as legal tender in the payment of provincial taxes and sometimes in the settlement of private debts. There was little uniformity regarding the terms and conditions of consecutive issues even within a single colony; some included an interest rate component, others had none. Currency was issued in a range of denominations, from large bills like £20 colonial down to amounts as low as one shilling in four colonies. (10) Over half the bills in circulation were for amounts less than ten shillings, which made them widely accessible and convenient for routine purchases of everyday items. [In this respect, the colonies mirrored Scotland where banknotes in small denominations circulated widely as well.] The currency issued in one colony frequently spilled over the borders into neighboring colonies, where it was accepted on a voluntary basis and valued at prevailing exchange rates. For example, a merchant active in the city of New York, in addition to possessing quantities of Spanish, Portuguese, Dutch, and English coins, might also hold in his cash box the currencies of New York, Pennsylvania, and New Jersey.

Colonial currency fell into two broad categories. What distinguished the two were differing backing techniques, meaning the mechanisms by which they supposedly were to maintain their face value relative to coin, bullion, and foreign exchange. In one category were essentially tax anticipation notes like those first issued in Massachusetts in 1690. The provincial legislatures issued currency with the explicit proviso that outstanding sums would be fully retired from proceeds of future tax collections. Some emissions stipulated the payment of interest. (The interest-bearing bills of credit were similar in character to the Exchequer Orders issued in the reign of Charles II.) A final extinction date ranging from two to 20 years was established for each authorized series. When legislatures acted responsibly by moderating the volume of paper in circulation and diligently followed the redemption schedules, the value of their currencies remained fairly stable for decades--with Connecticut the sole exception because of unusual circumstances. (11) New York, Pennsylvania, New Jersey, Maryland and Virginia all had excellent records of paper money price stability.

The first Massachusetts issue had been prompted by a financial emergency, but colonial legislatures in subsequent decades discovered new reasons for emitting fiat paper. An emergency or minor fiscal crisis was not a prerequisite for legislative action after 1710. Some issues were authorized simply to provide the population with monies in small, convenient denominations--for example, in Maryland in the 1730s--or because voters decided to delay the imposition and collection of taxes for a few additional years. In Pennsylvania in the 1720s, the legislature, in a move foreshadowing the techniques of Keynesian deficit spending, voted to emit fiat currency in an effort to stimulate local demand and reverse an economic downturn. (12) The local economy, in fact, revived soon thereafter, and legislative supporters of the currency emission claimed at least partial credit for the favourable outcome. The need to finance military adven-ures, mainly against Indian tribes on the frontier or French forces in Canada, continued to be cited as the prime justification for the authorization of new emissions of fiat currency in most colonies. Nonetheless, in regions where fiat currency was still legally permissible after mid-century, it remained a vital component of the money stock irrespective of prevailing military or political considerations.

The American experience with fiat paper was less than perfect, however, and during the first half of the century some currencies lost purchasing power and steadily depreciated. Several colonies became increasingly lax about retiring outstanding currency. Previous emissions were simply rolled over and kept in circulation because citizens instructed their representatives not to vote the required taxes. In these instances the value of paper money depreciated sharply and irreversibly in relation to coins and financial instruments denominated in sound foreign monies such as sterling bills of exchange. The main offenders were the four New England colonies--Massachusetts, Connecticut, New Hampshire, and Rhode Island--from 1730 to 1750, plus the Carolinas (North and South were then a united province) from 1710 to 1725. Their performances paralleled what skeptics in England had predicted about the likely outcome of risky experiments involving fiat currencies. Parliamentary restrictions were therefore imposed. South Carolina was allowed to maintain indefinitely the volume of paper circulating as of 1731, but it was not permitted to add any new monies--except temporary emissions during wartime emergencies.

With passage of the Currency Act 1751, Parliament likewise outlawed any new emissions of fiat monies in New England; currency issues already outstanding were permitted to circulate until their scheduled maturity dates, however. (13) To facilitate a speedy transition from paper to hard money, Parliament paid a substantial subsidy--mostly in Spanish coin--to reimburse the colonies for expenses incurred in recent military campaigns against the French in Canada. To permit some flexibility in managing periodic budget deficits, the New England colonies were allowed to issue treasury notes paying up to the legal interest rate and maturing in two years or less. The vast majority of these notes were held as short-term investments and did not circulate as currency, according to Leslie Brock, the most dedicated scholar of colonial monetary systems. (14) After mid-century the four New England colonies reverted to monetary systems based primarily on coinage until the rebellion. Meanwhile, the other nine colonies in the middle and southern regions retained the privilege of maintaining fiat currency as a component of their money stock, although every new legislative act was routinely subject to review by the Board of Trade and Privy Council in London and possible disallowance. (15)

In the second monetary category was currency issued through the auspices of governmental loan offices, which functioned as agencies of the provincial legislatures. These offices were usually called land banks by most contemporaries, but the name was an unfortunate misnomer according to modern standards because they neither accepted deposits nor performed a range of financial services. Instead, these governmental agencies granted mortgage loans to citizens with sufficient equity in real properties. (16) In making these loans, they issued freshly printed currency, which was often indistinguishable in design from tax anticipation notes--the alternative form of fiat currency described above. In authorizing a new emission of currency, legislatures frequently allocated a certain sum to meet the recurring expenditures of government and a complementary amount for issuance through the loan office. In most colonies both forms of fiat currency circulated in tandem throughout the provincial economy.

Colonial borrowers were typically eligible to borrow amounts ranging up to one-half of the market value of land and one-third of the market value of residences. The latter provision allowed some artisans to obtain loans, although the vast majority of borrowers were yeoman farmers and owners of large agricultural estates. No restrictions were placed on the use of borrowed funds; most borrowers used the proceeds to invest in other productive assets, but they were free to spend the money on high living and luxury goods as well.

To guarantee wide access to credit facilities, the legislatures placed limits on how much money an individual could borrow from the loan office. In New York, for example, the minimum loan was £25 colonial up to maximum of' £I00 colonial. Most colonies had similar programs designed to prevent a few wealthy persons from depleting the pool of loanable funds. Loan terms typically ran from eight to 12 years for initial borrowers, with amortization schedules stipulating annual installments of interest and principal. The currency collected to cover the repayment of principal was either retired from circulation or re-loaned to other eligible borrowers. (17)

This mechanism of issuance was highly conducive to the prevention of monetary depreciation, since in the absence of a collapse in real estate values, which never happened in the colonies on a grand scale, the currency was amply secured by private mortgages. Meanwhile, the currency was in steady demand because borrowers were required to make annual payments consisting of accrued interest plus a fraction of the principal to the loan office. The responsibility for repayment of the loans, and thereby the retirement of outstanding currency, rested on the shoulders of private parties, not on the will of the elected legislators to approve the collection of new taxes. If a debtor failed to repay an outstanding mortgage, the loan office foreclosed, sold the property, and used the proceeds to sink the paper money. Defaults were low and losses rare, with the exception of the operations of loan offices in South Carolina and Rhode Island prior to 1750, where hundreds of borrowcrs conspired to evade repayment. Elsewhere, however, this form of asset-backed currency generally had an outstanding record in terms of maintaining its value relative to specie and other sterling substitutes.

In addition to injecting a reliable currency into the overall money stock, these mortgage loans generated a steady stream of interest income for provincial governments. Interest rates varied among the 13 colonies, climbing as high as

12.5 per cent in the Carolinas early in the eighteenth century. In the middle colonies, government loans carried interest rates from 5 to 6 per cent, which were extremely low rates for a region chronically short of long-term capital. In Connecticut the rates fell to as low as 3 per cent in 1740. (18) The low rates on public funds reflected, in part, religious concerns about usury; in most colonies the legal maximum on private loans, irrespective of the length of maturity dates, was restricted to 5 to 8 per cent. The legislatures welcomed these interest revenues as a supplement to tax collections. In several colonies--including New Jersey, Pennsylvania, and New York--interest revenues from their loan offices covered nearly all provincial expenditures in some years. As a result, the tax burden imposed on the general population by their legislatures was slight or even zero, in certain provinces for years. (19)

PRIVATE MONEY INITIATIVES

Although the 13 colonial legislatures were far and away the overwhelming issuers of currency, in order to lay claim to a reasonable degree of comprehensive coverage, we should also mention a few abortive initiatives by private parties. None of these private monetary experiments were sustained. Indeed, one of the most lingering and perplexing mysteries relating to colonial financial history, generally speaking, is why no individual issuers--or partnerships with up to six members as permitted by British statute law dating back to 1708--ever developed a long-term commitment to the issuance of monies convertible into coinage upon demand? (20) Why did no American counterparts of English private issuers arise in the leading American port cities--Philadelphia, New York, Boston, Newport, and Charleston? In London, not only did firms, which had evolved from goldsmiths, engage in this activity, but also sundry mercantile firms sometimes participated in private currency issuance as a sideline--a profitable means of employing capital and diversifying their business interests.

Several possible explanations have been offered to account for the American entrepreneurial failure. Some have suggested that there was too little hard money in the colonies to support a convertible currency or, alternatively, that private parties had insufficient capital resources to enter the private banking field. Neither argument holds up to scrutiny. Substantial amounts of specie routinely circulated throughout the economy with the exception of a few crisis years, and merchants and other potential bankers faced no formidable obstacles in adjusting their asset portfolios to include adequate specie reserves. Most firms failed to accumulate hoards of specie not because of its scarcity but because it was a sterile asset without earning power. Moreover, entrance into the banking field did not require a large capital--indeed no minimum was necessary either from a legal or practical standpoint. So long as a private party maintained sufficient reserves against outstanding currency liabilities, the banking sector could be entered on a small scale and then expanded gradually over time, increasing in unison with the enhanced reputation of these private monies and the issuer's asset base. Numerous Philadelphia merchants, plus merchants in other urban centers, appear to have possessed the acumen to have diversified their business activities into a broader range of financial services, including private currency issue, yet to date none have been identified as making a significant commitment to the banking field.

On three separate occasions, large groups of merchants acting in concert did create private mechanisms for issuing paper obligations which contemporaries believed had the potential of circulating as a medium of exchange. All were relatively short-lived experiments. One arose in Massachusetts in 1733, when negotiations between Governor Jonathan Belcher and the colonial legislature over a bill to authorize the emission of additional public monies had stalled. In response, numerous Boston merchants agreed among themselves to issue up to £100,000 in private note obligations redeemable in three stages over 10 years and compounding in value at the rate of 6 per cent per annum. The merchants planned to introduce the notes into the economy by offering them to creditors willing to accept the paper voluntarily in the settlement of outstanding debts and by lending them to persons offering good security. Belcher protested the actions of the merchants and questioned their legality, but the colony's attorney general ruled in December 1735 that the notes did not violate any British laws, including the statute restricting currency issuance to private unincorporated firms with six principals or less. Surviving samples indicate that, while the notes often listed three to six signatures, their redemption in specie was not the joint responsibility of all the merchants who had agreed to co-operate in establishing the terms of issuance. Since the Boston merchants had never formed a joint-stock company with transferable shares, they likewise were not governed by the terms of the Bubble Act of 1720.

Because the notes compounded at 6 per cent interest, their value soon rose to a premium vis-a-vis the outstanding public monies. The vast majority were soon hoarded and held as investments until their redemption dates. (21) Given these circumstances, the Boston merchants' notes do not seem to meet the criteria for classification as a circulating currency. They became instead an innovative and unusual source of intermediate and long-term financing for the merchant issuers, who were responsible for their redemption in stages--three-tenths after three years, another three-tenths after six years, and four-tenths in the tenth year. Their characteristics suggest that these notes were forerunners of the commercial paper that became a steady source of funding for many firms in the larger commercial centers in the nineteenth century. In short, these instruments broadened the scope of local financial markets, but they did not provide a private substitute for governmental fiat issues.

Less than a decade later, also in Massachusetts, two separate groups of investors made formal application to the legislature for charters to create private banks with the authority to issue currencies backed by two different sets of assets. Several hundred citizens from across the colony, led by mercantile organizers in the eastern towns, but including a number of persons of moderate landed wealth, sought permission to create a private land bank. (22) The currency was to be secured by loans against mortgaged property, and its mode of operations were designed to resemble very closely the public land offices which had functioned for several decades. The second group composed largely of a rival group of Boston merchants, generally more wealthy than the first, proposed to issue currency to be supported through the gradual accumulation of a specie fund over a period of 15 years to provide the means for redemption.

The legislature granted the two charters in 1740, and company officials promptly issued around £49,000 against mortgaged real estate and roughly £120,000 against the projected silver pool. Within weeks, Governor William Shirley, who had only recently taken office, suspended the charter bill, dissolved the bank, and promptly submitted the whole issue to imperial officials for resolution. Shirley was on solid ground in challenging the legitimacy of the whole project since Parliament had reserved for itself the authority to grant charter powers to business enterprises, and just to close any loopholes, it formally extended the Bubble Act to the colonies in 1741. By June 1742 two-thirds of the land bank currency and nearly three-fifths of the specie bank currency had been recalled, and commissioners were appointed to oversee the steady withdrawal of the remainder. (23)

The third instance of a collective private initiative on the monetary front occurred in Connecticut in 1732. A group of over 170 persons, drawn from 53 towns, was associated with the New London Society for Trade and Commerce. According to historian Bruce Stark, the members 'did not differ markedly from the rest of the population'; over 70 per cent with identifiable occupations were farmers--with merchants, ship captains, artisans, lawyers, and physicians accounting for the remainder. (24) Sponsors received formal permission from the legislature to establish a joint-stock company under a charter reasonably similar to those granted to parishes in the Congregational church, the dominant religion in the colony. Adopting an expansive view of the latitude expressed in the charter terms, the company's elected officers quickly moved to create a private land bank. They made plans for the issuance of up to £30,000 secured by first mortgages against the lands of borrowers, many of whom where simultaneously stockholders.

The New London Society issued about £15,000 between October 1732 and January 1733. These bills had no built-in interest rate component and therefore circulated as money just as the issuers had intended. But this monetary experiment stalled in mid-January 1733. Critics alleged that the society was exceeding its charter powers. In response to rising complaints, the legislature prohibited the issuance of any additional monies on the grounds that the enabling legislation had not granted the society the explicit right to print its own currency. In a counter effort designed to resolve the controversial affair, the legislature authorized the issuance of £56,000 in currency through the public loan office, with the stipulation that up to £15,000 be made available to members of the New Haven Society for the purpose of calling in the outstanding circulation. The society's leadership accepted these terms, and the private bank began calling in its monies and wound up its affairs over the next few years. Thus ended perhaps the boldest venture by a private firm to establish a competitive currency in the colonial era. The plan was killed by internal economic and political rivalries, although it seems doubtful that the original legislation, even if allowed to stand in Connecticut, would have survived a thorough review by the Board of Trade in London since the whole scheme appears to have been in direct conflict with provisions of the Bubble Act and possibly the 1708 statute regarding the issuance of currency by unchartered firms with multiple partners.

CONFLICT WITH BOARD OF TRADE

One of the major disputes between the North American legislatures and the Board of Trade in London during the two decades before the general rebellion centered on provisions in currency legislation related to the settlement of private debts. Colonial proponents of legal tender status for private debts claimed the requirement was necessary to maintain currency values, and they often prevailed in legislative debates. Although members of the board were always skeptical about legislative acts calling for the fresh issuance of fiat currency, they were generally willing to approve, albeit reluctantly, colonial legislation which stipulated legal tender status for public payments to tax collectors and governmental loan offices. But the board raised strong objections to provisions calling for legal tender status in private transactions, especially among debtors and creditors.

The board was highly responsive to the concerns of English merchants who conducted substantial trade with the colonies based on the extension of credit for as long as 18 to 24 months. (25) As the volume of Anglo-American trade grew after mid-century, English merchants became ever more fearful about being forced to accept payment for past-due debts in colonial currencies which fluctuated in value. Or stated in slightly more technical terms, English creditors were increasingly reluctant to assume the perceived risks associated with transactions denominated in colonial currencies. They preferred payment in specie or its equivalents--coinage or reliable bills of exchange drawn in sterling on accounts maintained in England.

This problem was difficult to assess and resolve because different colonies had different experiences in regard to the amplitude of fluctuations in currency values. Moreover, the attitudes of English creditor shifted from year to year as well. When the values of colonial currencies were trending downward, English anxieties heightened; but when news arrived in London confirming the rebound in currency values, the merchants' concerns abated. As a consequence of these events, uncertainties and inconsistencies governed decision-making. The Board of Trade had hoped to formulate policies with universal applicability but different financial realities in individual colonies at different times made the achievement of that goal impossible. (26)

When the board finally decided to take action, it moved in a heavy-handed manner. Under pressure from English creditors active in the American trade who wanted ironclad protection from potential losses arising from fluctuating currency values in North America, the board induced Parliament to pass the Currency Act of 1764. The Act forbade new paper emissions, which included any legal tender provisions whatsoever, private, or public. The members' biases against any form of fiat currency were fully evident in drafting this Act. The new law applied to the nine colonies outside of New England where new paper money issues were still permissible after 1751. (27)

The colonial legislatures effected by this legislation were indignant. They objected because, in most cases, their currency issues had been managed responsibly for decades and none had experienced irreversible depreciation. Currency values had sometimes fallen but invariably rebounded. Second, they saw no logical reason for denying legal tender status for public transactions since private creditors, including London merchants, were not threatened by such provisions. The Currency Act of 1764 was viewed as nothing less than an attempt to curtail the use of fiat currency, which ran contrary to the wishes of colonial voters, and their leaders reacted defiantly. Some colonial leaders later charged that it was all part of a conspiratorial British 'plot' to exert increasingly greater control over events in North America.

Over the next decade, the legislatures continued to pass legislation authorizing issuance of new currency with legal tender provisions irrespective of Parliament's prohibition. By threatening to refuse payment of annual salaries, the legislatures coerced their respective royal governors into submitting new currency laws to the Board of Trade for approval. The board predictably disallowed some acts, but after listening to special pleadings of colonial agents stationed in London, it reluctantly let others stand. In the early 1770s, for example, the board permitted both Pennsylvania and New York to emit currencies that were designated as legal tender in public payments.

The prolonged controversy was finally resolved in 1773. Upon the board's recommendation, Parliament amended the law to allow the continued issuance of fiat currency with legal tender status in all transactions involving local and provincial governments, but not in private transactions. British creditors voiced no objections to this alteration in the statute since they remained fully protected from the risks of fluctuating currency rates in the colonies. In retrospect, the extension of the law to public sector payments in 1764 had served no useful purpose, and wiser heads sponsored its deletion. The English effort to root out the heresy of fiat paper and thereby purify the North American financial system was perhaps a well intentioned paternalistic policy, but it proved extremely unpopular in the colonies.

Some colonists wanted wholesale repeal of the 1764 Act, but most were willing to settle for an easing of its harsh terms. (28) Yet it took nearly a decade of unproductive wrangling to accomplish that end. The issue was difficult to resolve because imperial officials and colonial leaders possessed radically divergent opinions about the propriety of fiat currency. The contest of wills, which raged concurrently with even more heated debates over the new taxes prescribed in the Stamp and Townshend Acts, left many leaders on both sides suspicious about the motivations of their transatlantic adversaries. With the benefit of two centuries of hindsight and a clearer understanding of how monetary affairs unfolded in the colonies, it seems fair to conclude that the Board of Trade's reservations about the currency emissions of the middle and southern colonies in third quarter of the eighteenth century were overdrawn and exaggerated. Contrary to English expectations, all nine colonies had managed their currency issues exceedingly well after 1750; none had suffered irreversible depreciation. Their legislatures had exercised restraint in authorizing new issues, and in no case had Gresham's Law taken effect--that is, fiat currency had not driven coinage out of circulation since paper and coin remained complementary components of the overall money stock. Tax revenues were collected on a regular basis to sink the colonies' tax-anticipating notes, while individual borrowers paid off their mortgage notes in timely fashion and provided the funds to redeem the currency issued through government loan offices. Occasionally, English mercantile creditors suffered minor losses before the mid-1760s because of the volatility of currency rates over a period of several years, but colonial courts usually took into account changes in the market value of monies when adjudicating cases related to private debts long past due. Nevertheless, English fears of potential losses in distant markets were genuine, and the compromise solution reached in 1773 was prudent and sensible under the circumstances.

Although most English critics condemned the American attachment to fiat paper, almost coincidental with independence, Adam Smith offered a more sympathetic view in the text of his famous inquiry into the true wealth of nations. First, Smith argued that the use of fiat currency was a choice deliberately made by the colonists rather than an unwanted outcome necessitated by the scarcity of metals--an argument that many contemporaries had erroneously advanced. The substitution of paper for coinage was a perfectly rational decision, Smith asserted, because it allowed the colonies to optimize the economic returns on the resources at their disposal; in other words, they could make a partial substitution of specie with paper and thereby export a portion of their hard monies overseas to acquire other more productive assets. Smith was reluctant to endorse fiat currency as a superior mechanism to private paper backed by specie reserves, yet he readily admitted that several North American colonies had behaved responsibly in managing their unorthodox monetary systems. He expressed admiration for those legislatures which had derived an interest revenue from granting well-secured mortgage loans to citizens. (29)

Ironically, the political and military events in the 1770s and 1780s that resulted in independence from Great Britain also forced Americans to reassess their attitudes toward the inclusion of fiat currency in the money stock. Over half of the war costs were financed by the issuance of fiat currencies by the Continental Congress and the individual states. The various fiat monies generally held their value during the early years of the war, but after 1776 they depreciated at accelerating rates. The nominal value of new currency issued between 1774 and 1779 exceeded the value of the coinage in circulation at the start of the war, and Gresham's Law went into operation. Coins were hoarded or exported. By 1780 the market exchange rate between currency and specie was 100:1 and a year later the wartime issues had become virtually worthless.

This negative experience with fiat currency during wartime conditions altered American opinions about its merits. Although seven states reissued paper money in modest amounts after the signing of the Treaty of Paris in 1783, and most of these post-war issues resisted steady depreciation, the drafters of the Constitution in 1787 voted to deny state governments the privilege of emitting fiat currency either through the device of tax anticipation notes or the operations of mortgage loan offices. Currencies already emitted were permitted to remain in circulation until their respective expiration dates in the 1790s or early in the next century. But the American experiment with fiat paper had temporarily ended--not to be revived again until the Civil War emergency led both the Union and Confederate governments once again into the realm of unconvertible paper money.

As a consequence, British and American attitudes regarding the proper composition of the money stock had more in common during the last decade of the eighteenth century than at any date since 1690. In both nations the money supply consisted of coinage as well paper monies issued by private and chartered banks. During the 1780s three state-chartered commercial banks were founded in the United States in Philadelphia, New York, and Boston; in the 1790s the First Bank of the United States received a charter from Congress with the privilege of opening branch offices throughout the nation. By 1800 nearly 30 state-chartered banks were in operation, and during the next decade and one half over 200 additional state-chartered banks opened their doors. Across the Atlantic Ocean, the Bank of England maintained its position as the leading supplier of paper money in Great Britain, and with the addition of the £5 banknote to its denominational structure in the early 1790s, its currency circulated much more widely among the middle classes. In Scotland, mean-while, 18 banks of issue continued to print banknotes in amounts as small as £1 as they had done for decades. J. Clapham estimated the number of private bankers in London at the turn of the century at 'nearly seventy', while the number of country bankers in England and Wales had climbed to 370, according to L.S. Pressnell. (30)

CONCLUSION

Public attitudes about the legitimacy of fiat currency in Great Britain and its North American colonies were sharply at variance in the eighteenth century. Political and business leaders in Britain were generally receptive to paper monies continuously convertible into specie whether issued by chartered banks or private firms with unlimited liability. But they drew the line at the prospect of the government emitting a circulating paper supported either by future taxation or private mortgages. Given the failed financial experiments with fiat currencies under two kings, Charles II and Louis XV of France, the tenuous backing for these monies appeared too risky for British sensibilities. That negative outlook was reflected in the rulings and legislative initiatives of members of the Board of Trade who had primary responsibility for economic affairs in the colonies.

In British dominions in North America, however, colonial leaders experienced surprising success with a system of fiat currency, especially in the region from New York to North Carolina. No banks emerged in the colonies to issue paper money convertible into specie on a sustained basis; thus that form of paper money never became a viable option in the American context. Instead the colonists supplemented the supply of coinage, which was mostly Spanish in origin, with emissions of fiat currency by governmental units. During the first half of the century, the record was uneven. The four New England colonies plus South Carolina had successful financial regimes for several decades, but the temptation to forestall collection of the taxes required to support monetary values finally proved too great. These colonies were unable to hold the financial reins in check, eventually succumbing to ruinous currency depreciation. Events in those five colonies corresponded with the expectations of European critics of fiat monies. Parliament's passage of the Currency Act 1751 moved the New England colonies back toward a hard-money standard, where they remained until the 1770s.

Eight other colonies managed their fiat emissions much more effectively, however, and none fell victim to irrepressible depreciation. These governments were genuine innovators in the persistent use of inconvertible public monies. Their fiat currency was not only a useful medium of exchange but also a reasonably reliable store of value over the long run. Fiat monies entered the money stock in two different ways and were supported in the financial markets by two distinct backing systems. Tax anticipation issues, some with maturity dates as distant as 10 to 20 years, were emitted directly by colonial treasuries and later redeemed from public revenues. Government loan offices--usually called land banks in the eighteenth century--issued currency to citizens mortgaging their properties for periods up to 15 years, and principal repayments, typically amortized over the life of the loan, provided the mechanism for retiring the paper. If borrowers defaulted, the property was sold and the proceeds were used to accomplish the same purpose. Meanwhile, the annual interest payments on these mortgage loans was often sufficient to make a substantial dent in provincial budgets, which were low since Parliament provided most of the funds required to defend the Empire on land and at sea, including the North American continent and North Atlantic Ocean.

Despite the solid record of these eight colonies, the Board of Trade--its members philosophically opposed to fiat currency and under pressure from London merchants worried about credit risks associated with paper money--maneuvered through Parliament the Currency Act of 1764, which outlawed future emissions of fiat monies. Already in a rebellious mood, the colonists protested vehemently. Their legislatures ignored the new regulations, authorized new emissions, and then bullied their governors into recommending approval to the Board of Trade. The controversy lasted until 1773, when a compromise was negotiated which allowed the colonies to continue issuing fiat paper so long as it had no legal tender status in private debts.

On the eve of the War for Independence, fiat currency remained extremely popular in more than half the North American colonies. In several regions it had been a component of the money stock for nearly half a century. It is not surprising, therefore, that the Continental Congress and the new states relied heavily on fiat currency to finance the war effort. But on this occasion the sums issued were too great and the taxes imposed too low. Without adequate backing, the massive wartime issues succumbed to a persistent depreciation, carrying their relative values down to virtually zero by 1781. Despite these problems, currency finance provided most of the purchasing power necessary for the American military to wage an ultimately successful war over six long years. Nonetheless, this episode discredited fiat paper in the minds of many of its former supporters. Although seven state governments revived their currency systems in the 1780s, and they experienced only modest depreciation, the new U.S. Constitution eliminated fiat currency as a future option for state and local governmental units. Meanwhile, banking institutions were established for the first time on the North American continent in the 1780s, and they issued notes convertible into specie upon demand. Before the end of the century, the new nation had chartered the First Bank of the United States, modeled on the Bank of England, and the several states had chartered nearly 30 additional private banks.

Oddly, stark Anglo-American differences over the composition of the money stock, which had divided Crown and colonies for over half a century before the American rebellion, dissipated in the post-war era. The colonies had refused to conform to British expectations regarding the role of fiat currency in their respective economies. But once free and independent, and given the experiences of wartime finance, the new American Constitution drafted in 1787 reflected the more conservative attitudes that had prevailed in Parliament throughout the eighteenth century. Fiat currency disappeared from the American financial system, and it was not reintroduced until the Civil War emergency nearly three-quarters of a century later. By the 1790s American and British theory and practice were finally in accord regarding the legitimacy of only two forms of circulating money: coinage and banknotes supported by specie reserves. Yet, the American colonies had demonstrated the viability of a monetary system based on fiat currency. Their activities foreshadowed the abandonment of the gold standard in the twentieth century, and the adoption of fiat currency as the universal standard in the modern world.

Notes

1. Comparative studies of monetary systems in Europe and North America in the eighteenth century are rare. The only published essay to my knowledge is in Spanish by the American economic historian Eugene White, '? Fueron inflacionaries las finanzas estatles en el siglo XVIII? Una nueva interpretacion de los vales reales', *Revista de Historia Economica,* Ano V. No.3 (1987), pp. 509-26. That article was preceded by the author's unpublished manuscript, 'Inflationary Finance in the 18th Century: A Comparative Study of Colonial America, Spain and France' (1986), which is available upon request by writing to Economics Department, Rutgers University, New Brunswick, NJ, USA 08903-5055.
2. Clapham, *The Bank of England: Vol. I, 1694-1797* (Cambridge, 1966 ed.), pp. 1-52; S.G. Checkland, *Scottish Banking: A History, 1695-1973* (Glasgow, 1975), pp. 1-135; C. W. Munn, 'The Emergence of Joint-Stock Banking in the British Isles: A Comparative Approach', in R.P.T. Davenport-Hines and Geoffrey Jones (eds.), *The End of Insularity: Essays in Comparative Business History* (1988), pp. 69-83.
3. Some scholars argue that limited liability chartered banks were de facto sounder than private banks with unlimited liability; see J. Carr, S. Glied and F. Mathewson, 'Unlimited Liability and Free Banking in Scotland: A Note', *Journal of Economic History*, Vol. XLIX (1989), pp. 974-8.
4. D.M. Joslin, 'London Private Bankers, 1720-1785', *Economic History Review*, 2 series, Vol. VII (1954), pp. 167-86
5. Checkland, *Scottish Banking*, Table 2, pp. 134-5.
6. Sir Albert Feavearyear, *The Pound Sterling: The History of English Money*, 2nd revised edition by E. V. Morgan (Oxford, 1963), pp. 111-16; R.D. Richards, *The Early History of Banking in England* (1929); K. Horsefield, 'The "Stop of the Exchequer" Revisited', *Economic History Review*, 2nd series, Vol. XXXV (1982), pp. 511-28.
7. The best analysis of the Law scandal is L. Neal and E. Schubert, 'The First Rational Bubbles: A New Look at the Mississippi and South Sea Schemes', University of Illinois working paper no.1188, Sept. 1985; see also Neal, *The Rise of Financial Capitalism: International Capital Markets in the Age of Reason* (New York, 1990), Chs. 4-5. A lively account is found in J. K. Galbraith's *Money: Whence It Came, Where It Went* (Boston, 1975), pp. 27-34; also see C. Kindleberger, *A Financial History of Western Europe* (1984), pp. 96-8. For general information on colonial finance in the eighteenth century, the following studies are helpful: L. Brock, *The Currency of the American Colonies, 1700-1764: A Study in Colonial Finance and Imperial Relations* (New York, 1975), a reprint of his 1941 dissertation; E.J. Ferguson, 'Currency Finance: An Interpretation of Colonial Monetary Practices', *William and Mary Quarterly*, 3rd series, Vol. X (1953), pp. 153-80; J.R. Hanson, 'Money in the American Economy', *Economic Inquiry*, Vol. XVII (1979), pp. 281-6; *idem*, 'Small Notes in the American Colonies', *Explorations in Economic History*, Vol. XVII (1980), pp. 411-20; E.J. Perkins, *The Economy of Colonial America*, (New York, 2nd ed. 1988), pp. 163-88; T. Thayer, 'The Land Bank System in the American Colonies', *Journal of Economic History*, Vol. XIII (1953), pp. 145-59; R. Weiss, 'The Issue of Paper Money in the American Colonies, 1720 -1774', *Journal of Economic History*, Vol. XXX (1970), pp. 770-84; R.C. West, 'Money in the Colonial American Economy', *Economic Inquiry*, Vol. XVI (1978), pp. 1-15; and E. Wicker, 'Colonial Monetary Standards Contrasted: Evidence from the Seven Years' War', *Journal of Economic History*, Vol. XLV (1985), pp. 860-84.
9. Older accounts of American monetary and political history stressed internal class con-

flicts--debtors versus creditors--but more recent studies have exploded the myth of a citizenry divided by class status. Members of all occupational groups in the colonies, including most merchants, supported the concept of including some type of fiat currency in the money stock although they may have differed at times over the exact terms of issuance and redemption.

10. Colonial pounds were not the equivalent of sterling pounds in England. The colonists rated Spanish coins, and other foreign coins, at values higher than their respective mint ratios in England in order to discourage coinage exports. The same principle of over-valuation applied to fiat monies; their values corresponded with the ratings assigned to foreign coins, and, to make the story even more complicated, those ratings varied from colony to colony. For example, at the official par, £100 in England translated into £133.33 colonial in Massachusetts, £166.67 colonial in Maryland, and £700 colonial in South Carolina in the mid-eighteenth century. No public or private institutions tried to maintain fixed exchange rates among currency, coin, and foreign exchange. The only fixed standard was the rate at which colonial governments would accept monies in tax and mortgage 'payments as well as other miscellaneous transactions with the general public.

11. Average yearly exchange rates for colonial monies during the eighteenth century are listed in J. McCusker, *Money and Exchange in Europe and America, 1600-1775* (Chapel Hill, 1978). In the first half of the eighteenth century, the Connecticut legislature exercised reasonable restraint in its issuance policy but the currency depreciated heavily nonetheless because so much intermingling had occurred with the monies of Massachusetts and Rhode Island, where self-restraint was not practiced. Connecticut was tainted by the excesses of its immediate neighbors, and the colony was prevented from issuing new paper by the Currency Act of 1751.

12. R. Lester, 'Currency Issues to Overcome Depressions in Pennsylvania, 1723 and 1729', *Journal of Political Economy* (1938), pp. 324-75.

13. This information comes from a microfilm copy of an incomplete, but nonetheless very lengthy, unpublished manuscript recently deposited in the archives of the Alderman Library, University of Virginia: L. Brock, 'Manuscript Draft for an Unfinished Book on Currency in Colonial America'. The author's plan was to carry forward his monetary history from 1764, where his earlier work left off, through the 1770s. In addition, the manuscript contains a long chapter on Massachusetts finance in the 1730s.

14. Brock, *Currency of the American Colonies*, p. 274.

15. The size of the permanent paper money issue in South Carolina was frozen after 1731; the proclamation rate was set at 7:1 vis-a-vis sterling and it remained fixed at that rate until the rebellion.

16. In the London market, many private bankers held mortgage assets, according to Joslin, 'Private Bankers', p. 176

17. Sums reloaned to new borrowers were always for progressively shorter periods of time, an arrangement necessary to make the maturity dates of new loans coincide with the assigned expiration date of a specific currency emission. Assume, for example, the legislature had authorized a currency emission with a life of 10 years. Loans made in the third year after passage were limited to seven years, loans in the sixth year after passage were limited to a four-year term, and loans in the eighth year matured in only two years. The principal of every outstanding loan associated with a specific issue of currency came due in the final year irrespective of when the loan was contracted. When the currency authorization for an existing loan office expired, a new authorization often followed within a year or two.

18. B. Stark, 'The New London Society and Connecticut Politics, 1732-1740', *Connecticut History*, Vol. XXV (1984), pp. 1-21.
19. M. Schweitzer, *Custom and Contract: Household, Government, and the Economy in Colonial Pennsylvania* (New York, 1987); T.L. Purvis, Proprietors, *Patronage, and Paper Money: Legislative Politics in New Jersey, 1703-1776* (New Brunswick, NJ, 1986).
20. Instances of merchants issuing 'IOUs' or various forms of credit vouchers that later circulated among the populace as a medium of exchange, especially in remote rural areas, have sometimes been cited as evidence of the existence of competitive monies issued by private individuals in the seventeenth and eighteenth centuries. But, in my view, the overall effect of these activities has been exaggerated and, irrespective of the circumstances, the conclusions drawn can be highly misleading. So far as I know, the volume of private paper was always small relative to the size of the aggregate money stock. Few, if any, issuers maintained specie reserves and promised convertibility; and, most damning in this context, no issuer expanded these alleged private monetary operations over the decades and emerged as the equivalent of English private bankers, who were typically called merchant-bankers by residents of North America. Some colonial merchants and shopkeepers probably did experiment with the issuance of limited volumes of financial instruments which approached the status of money or at least near-monies--and given the shortage of capital and the absence of legal prohibitions against private issues--some experimentation seems almost inevitable. But the question remains: why did a valuable and frequently very profitable financial service based on lending currency against specie reserves never develop more fully before independence? In theory, both private and public monies could have circulated simultaneously with no negative consequences; the only necessary condition was that no fixed exchange rate be established by law--thereby permitting routine swaps at fluctuating market prices.
21. A. McFarland Davis, 'Currency and Banking in the Providence of Massachusetts-Bay', *Publications of the American Economic Association*, 3rd series, Vol. I No. 4 (Dec. 1900), pp. 1-445, and continued in Vol. II No.2 (May 1901), pp.1-332. Although technically an article, the overall length is longer than most books. This turn-of-the-century economic historian produced some the earliest and most detailed accounts of the financial history of colonial New England. For the author's discussion of specie and land banks, see Vol. II, pp.102-29.
22. G.A. Billias, 'The Massachusetts Land Bankers of 1740', *University of Maine Studies*, 2nd series (1959), pp. 1-53. Billias studied the social origins of the sponsors and discovered, contrary to the assertions of previous scholars, that they were not poor and middling farmers but mostly persons of substantial wealth, including several Boston merchants.
23. Davis, 'Currency and Banking', Vol. II, pp. 130-67. The specie bank scheme seems at first glance to duplicate reasonably closely the type of private banks which British opinion makers found unobjectionable. Yet the terminology employed by the colonists was deceptive, and it disguised some critical differences. The issuers did not promise convertibility from the outset nor at any time for the next decade and one half. Instead, the plan called for accumulating the specie required to back the currency over the life of the issue and then drawing on the fund for redemption at the maturity date. A comparable system was adopted in Maryland to support that colony's public monies, although the fund accumulated was not specie but stock of the Bank of England, which could, of course, have always been sold for specie since active markets existed.
24. Stark, 'New London Society', pp. 1-21.

25. For information on the growth of trade and credit, see J. Price, *Capital and Credit in British Overseas Trade: The View from the Chesapeake, 1700~1776* (Cambridge, MA, 1980).
26. For a discussion of these shifts in British mercantile attitudes, see J. Ernst, *Money and Politics in America, 1755-1775* (Chapel Hill, 1973). In recent years a sharp debate has emerged among several monetary historians regarding whether specie flows, reflecting theories related to the quantity theory of money, or effective backing systems were responsible for maintaining currency values. Ron Michener argues the former position in 'Fixed Exchange Rates and the Quantity Theory in Colonial America', in K. Brunner and A.H. Meltzer (eds.), Empirical Studies of Velocity, Real Exchange Rates, Unemployment and Productivity (Amsterdam, 1987), pp. 233-307, and 'Backing Theories and the Currencies of Eighteenth-Century America: A Comment', Journal of Economic History, Vol. 48 (1988), pp. 682-92; Bruce Smith supports the backing hypothesis in 'American Colonial Monetary Regimes: The Failure of the Quantity Theory and Some Evidence in Favor of an Alternative View' , Canadian Journal of Economics, Vol. XVII (1985), pp. 531-65; 'Some Colonial Evidence on Two Theories of Money: Maryland and the Carolinas', *Journal of Political Economy*, Vol. .XCIII (1985), pp. 1178-1211; and 'The Relationship between Money and Prices: Some Historical Evidence Reconsidered', Quarterly Review: Federal Reserve Bank of Minneapolis, Vol. 12 (Summer 1988), pp. 18-32. On balance, I am in agreement with Smith; this essay therefore reflects the outlook of scholars supporting the so-called 'backing' theory in determining currency values.
27. J.P. Greene and R. Jellison, 'The Currency Act ofl764 in Imperial-Colonial Relations, 1764-1776', *William and Mary Quarterly*, Vol.18 (1961), pp. 48S-518; J. Ernst, 'Genesis of the Currency Act of 1764: Virginia Paper Money and the Protection of British Investments', *William and Mary Quarterly*, Vol.22 (1965), pp. 33-74.
28. Two chapters in Brock's 'Manuscript Draft for Unfinished Book' are devoted to the unsuccessful colonial effort to obtain the repeal of the 1764 act.
29. Adam Smith, *An Inquiry into the Nature of Causes of the Wealth of Nations*, (1776); see his discussion of colonial finance in chapter III, entitled 'Of Public Debts', in book V. At one point in the contest between crown and colonies in the prewar decade, Benjamin Franklin offered a novel suggestion regarding the possible establishment of a currency-issuing continental loan office under direct parliamentary control. Franklin suggested that the interest earned on colonial mortgages could then be used to offset a portion of British defense expenditures in North America, thereby reducing the need for generating tax revenues in the colonies. The idea was never given serious consideration, however, because of the board's bias against fiat currency and the political fear that the continental financial institution with branches in all 13 colonies might serve to unite them to an even greater extent than already existed.
30. J. Clapham, *Bank of England* (Cambridge, 1948), Vol. I, p. 48; L.S. Pressnell, *Country Banking in the Industrial Revolution* (Oxford, 1956), p. 11, and C.P. Kindle-berger, *A Financial History of Western Europe* (1984), p. 83.

Chapter Four

Madison's Debt Discrimination Proposal Revisited: The Application of Present Value Financial Analysis

This paper employs a modern financial analysis technique to offer a fresh perspective on an old historical controversy: the public debate in the early 1790s over granting belated monetary compensation to the original holders of federal debt certificates who had sold their claims to investors in the mid-1780s. My goals are twofold. The first goal is to introduce historians to the application of "present value" financial analysis, which is designed to foster a greater understanding of past events involving either the payment, or alternatively, the receipt of monies at future dates. Put simply, money transferred a year from now, and in all future years, is inherently worth less than the same denominated amount received today. The reason for the difference in market valuation is that a dollar received today can be conveniently invested in a savings account, and its value one year later will reflect the benefit of interest earnings. If the interest rate paid on savings is 3 percent annually, a dollar deposited today will be worth $1.03 in twelve months and $1.06 after two years. Nothing complex here; everyone knows this basic principle of compounding interest, but what follows in the next paragraph is probably less familiar to historians.

This same process also works in reverse, so to speak, in evaluating the present value of monies that we might expect to receive, not today, but at some future date. Let us assume that a debtor agrees to sign a formal note promising to pay the holder the sum of one dollar two years hence. What is the probable market value of the promissory note on the initial signing date? The correct answer is 94 cents given the same prevailing annual interest rate of three percent cited above. Suppose we advance the maturity date on the promissory note to ten years. On the signing date the discounted present value of the note falls to a mere 74 cents. As the maturity date lengthens, the present value of the promissory note steadily

*Previously unpublished manuscript. It was submitted in various drafts to the editors of the *William and Mary Quarterly* and the *Journal of Early Republic*, but it never got past the scrutiny of hostile referees.

declines. If we stretch out the maturity date to 30 years, the present value falls to 41 cents. Why 41 cents? At this point we return to the principle of compounding interest. If we deposit 41 cents in a savings account, after 30 years the accumulated total will be – you guessed it – one dollar. Compounding and discounting are the same processes of addition and subtraction that financial experts use in evaluating financial transactions in all monetary units, in all locations, and all time periods.

The second goal of this paper is to apply these financial principles to the controversy surrounding James Madison's proposal to discriminate between the original and the subsequent final holders of federal debt certificates in funding the overhanging indebtedness linked to the War for Independence. (1) Madison argued that the original certificate owners, who typically had sold years earlier at discounted prices, should receive at least partial reimbursement for their losses and the final holders, in turn, should receive something less than face value. On this issue Madison and Secretary of the Treasury Alexander Hamilton were at odds. (2) Since most historians of the early national period are already familiar with key issues at stake, I propose to lay out the facts expeditiously and then proceed with my revisionist analysis. Hamilton proposed to exchange new federal bonds for all wartime debt obligations at face value. He additionally proposed that the certificate holders on the stipulated exchange date were to receive all the financial benefits of ownership. Hamilton's outlook was basically in harmony with prevailing British law on property rights in financial securities.

In the ensuing House debates, Madison opposed the funding plan of the treasury secretary. He believed that, irrespective of past legal traditions, the plan favored too strongly the wealthy classes, and thus it was inappropriate for a new republican government. Madison outlined an alternative compensation package. He wanted to share the financial benefits more broadly, both by social class and geography. The final holders would receive the prevailing market prices for debt certificates in the months leading up to the ratification of the Constitution, and the original holders would receive the difference between that market price and face value. In anticipation of the creation of a new national government with stronger taxing power, the demand for debt certificates had risen from their former lows to somewhere in the range of seventy-five to eighty percent of face value in the late 1780s.

Madison concentrated on the issue of fairness and equity rather than legal precedents. Why, he asked rhetorically, would the federal government allow speculative investors to reap huge gains, while absolutely nothing was done to compensate, at least partially, those loyal citizens who had decided to sell their financial assets at rock bottom prices just a few years earlier? In formulating his argument, Madison took a straightforward, common sense approach. He portrayed citizens who had sold at deep discounts as the innocent victims of temporarily unfavorable market conditions.

We are now prepared to focus on the main thrust of this discussion. I will argue that we should reassess the degree of alleged injustices and extent of speculative gains by applying the modern techniques of present value financial analysis. After the proper calculations are performed, the results will demonstrate that both contemporaries and subsequent historians have overstated the true benefits to debt purchasers and the real losses of the original sellers. (3) Before proceeding too far, we should recognize that without the demand created by investors in government obligations, the prices of government securities would almost certainly have fallen even further. Receiving a mere 15 to 20 cents on the dollar may seem at first glance an inequitable price for anxious sellers, but it still remains superior to receiving nothing at all. Continental paper money fell to near zero after 1781 because of a hyperinflationary oversupply and a lack of confidence and demand. In our own era, the prices of the securities of numerous "dot.com" firms plummeted to zero after 2001, and many will doubtless never recover.

In all financial calculations, past and present, the timing of payments is invariably reflected in market prices. Present value tables, to which I was first exposed as an MBA student over four decades ago, reveal that a given amount of money received in an earlier period is invariably valued more highly than the same amount promised at a later date. (4) The underlying reason for the difference is that proceeds of an earlier period can always be used to earn interest or profits on its reinvestment in some business or agricultural project or from a simple deposit in a bank savings account.

When sellers of federal debt certificates in the early and mid-1780s received cash proceeds from investors, they had the option of using the monies for immediate investment in other income-producing assets. The seller might acquire livestock, a spinning wheel, a butter churn, extra seed for planting, or make a host of economic improvements in their properties. Assuming the seller could earn a five percent return over a period of eight years – 1783 to 1791 — every dollar initially invested would have grown in value to $1.49, or a gain just shy of fifty percent. This timing factor needs to be considered because it reduces rather dramatically the net losses incurred by the original sellers of debt certificates. (5)

Meanwhile, the investors in debt certificates had their funds tied up in mostly unproductive assets. Some states temporarily assumed the obligations of the federal government and made interest payments to local citizens in the late 1780s, but it seems fair to assume that the overall cash flow to investors was less than one percent of the total face value of outstanding federal obligations. The vast majority of investors owned what today we would classify as something similar to "junk bonds." Interest payments were small and irregular at best, and these certificates had no defined maturity dates. (In modern times, it is not unusual for the outstanding junk bonds of a struggling corporation to trade at discounts of 50, 75, and even 95 percent below face value.)

Given the uncertainties about the timing of future payments of interest and principal, any rational investor would have calculated a very low present value for federal debt certificates in the early and mid-1780s. If a group of urban merchants interested in speculating in debt certificates sought to generate an annual return of 10 percent on their invested funds and they believed interest payments would not commence for another eight years, then they would have refused to pay more than 40 percent of face value. Investors seeking a fifteen percent annual return over the same period would have offered no more than 25 percent of face value. If prospective investors concluded the process of strengthening the nation's financial affairs would take more than eight years, their offers would have been progressively lowered to reflect the probability of additional delays.

In addition to their worries about the date when interest payments might be initiated, investors were likewise concerned about the "political" risk, namely their fear that the principal of the outstanding debt might be partially repudiated. Madison's discrimination proposal to issue a proportion of the newly issued government bonds to the original debt holders in the early 1780s, if it had passed, would have reduced the returns to investors. Thus, the risk of delayed payments of interest and principal plus the risk of political alterations in the final funding process were major factors influencing the prevailing market prices for debt certificates.

Under these circumstances it is impossible to believe that any investor would have been willing to settle for anything less than the prospect of a minimal 15 percent return on a speculative investment in debt certificates. Therefore, a market price of 25 cents on the dollar was probably the "present value" ceiling for federal debt certificates at any date prior to 1786. Given the fact that many investors were probably unwilling to go forward without the prospect of a potential 20 to 25 percent return on investments in such questionable assets, it is not surprising that market prices frequently fell below 15 cents on the dollar. Indeed, the majority of wealthy urban merchants in the nation's port cities were unwilling to participate in these speculative transactions at any price whatsoever because they prudently perceived the high risks of long delays in realizing any tangible returns.

As it happened, investors were quite lucky that the convention to amend the Articles of Confederation met as early as it did in 1787 and that a central government with the power of taxation assumed office as soon as it did. If the process had taken another decade, most investors in debt certificates would have experienced losses irrespective of the terms of the refunding plan. The present value of one dollar discounted at the rate of 15 percent over 20 years is roughly 4 cents. At a discounted rate of 20 percent over two decades, the present value of one dollar shrinks to about a penny. As savants often remind us, "timing is everything" and it rings true not just in life, but also in assessing every financial transaction with future payments and those with the prospects of future income flows.

I am now prepared to argue that most sellers of federal debt certificates, and particularly those who sold at 20 cents or more on the dollar, probably received generous terms for their paper assets (really junk bonds). Depending on the date they sold, the transaction price, and how they used the proceeds of the sale, some sellers came out ahead, while others suffered only modest losses. In turn, depending on purchase date, prices paid, and the level of risk deemed appropriate for their personal business strategies, some investors were satisfied with the final returns on their investment, while others regretted their speculative binges. In the latter group were merchants who concluded that they could likely earn profits of 10 percent annually, with less risk and with the advantage of compounding, in their traditional business activities.

Rather than a case of greedy speculators taking advantage of unsophisticated holders of financial instruments, the net result, when present value calculations and the timing of cash flows are taken into account, approximates more closely a zero sum game. If speculators in the early 1780s as a group came out ahead a decade later, it was only a marginal advantage. Moreover, it was most likely not uniformly favorable for every investor. Many merchants, in retrospect, would have done just as well or better by employing their capital resources in routine mercantile transactions.

Bottom line. Every textbook that has depicted investors in federal debt certificates as rapacious speculators and, in turn, portrayed impoverished sellers as victims of a massive swindle now requires drastic revision. The truth is less dramatic in tone, and less a story about a clash between competing social classes. I estimate that most buyers of federal debt obligations in the early to mid-1780s had realized financial returns of 10 to 15 percent per annum in Hamilton's overall debt refunding program. This rate of profit was modest given the multitude of risks associated with their speculative activities. As late as 1786, these questionable paper assets had an extremely uncertain future. The lesson to be leaned from this financial exercise is that the application of "present value" methodologies can enhance our understanding of the amplitude of the gains and losses linked to transactions with lengthy intervals between the initial investment and the realization of tangible cash inflows.

Historians should henceforth remember that all monies promised, anticipated, or actually transferred in future years must be valued at progressively differing amounts. The value of a specific amount transferred ten years later is almost always lower than the same amount transferred only five years later. The only exception to this general rule would occur in those rare historical periods when deflation is prevalent and interest rates are abnormally low. (6) In addition to the timing factor, the present value of future flows is affected by the percentage rate chosen for the discounting calculations. The higher the applied discount rate, the lower the present value of future flows. Any historian seeking clarification of these analytical tools should be able to obtain guidance from colleagues in economics departments and business schools.

Notes

1. The standard reference is E. James Ferguson, *The Power of the Purse: A History of American Public Finance, 1776-1790* (Chapel Hill: University of North Carolina Press, 1961). See also chapters 7-11 in my volume, *American Public Finance and Financial Services, 1700-1815* (Columbus: Ohio State University Press, 1994).
2. The conflict between Madison and Hamilton, and their respective followers, is discussed in many standard works, but I recommend, in particular, Lance Banning, "The Hamiltonian Madison," *Virginia Magazine of History and Biography* (1984), 3-28.
3. The most recent publication to deal with these issues is Woody Holton, "'From the Labors of Others': The War Bonds Controversy and the Origins of the Constitution in New England," *William and Mary Quarterly* (2004), 271-316. Holton reasserted the traditional wisdom that one of the consequences of the adoption of a new national government was to "enrich bondholders."
4. When I took a position at the Chase Manhattan Bank's credit department in 1963, few of the senior lending officers were familiar with present value analytical techniques. These tools were cutting edge for bankers a half century ago. Thus, it is not surprising that most historians are likewise unfamiliar with these financial tools today.
5. It should be noted, in passing, that the Hamiltonians failed to use this argument to justify funding the debt at face value for the final certificate holders. If the proceeds of the sale were invested in assets that returned 10 percent annually, their value would have more than doubled in the next eight years.
6. Japan in the period 1990 to 2005 might qualify as special case where price deflation and low interest rates could produce expected higher values for monies transferred in future years. Present value financial tools could still be employed to estimate those future values, however.

Chapter Five

Jeffersonian Principles and the Shaping of American Financial Services, 1790 - 1815

How many of you in the course of grading final exams have discovered that some grand theme that you thought you had made perfectly clear in your classroom lectures never really got through clearly and distinctly to your eager students? Somehow you failed to put enough emphasis on your sweeping interpretive framework. The same thing can happen to authors, and it happened to me soon after the publication, in 1994, of my book on the evolution of the nation's emerging financial system in the period from 1700 to 1815. (1)

I thought I had made it plain as day that--contrary to all previous historical accounts--I believed the U.S. financial system reflected, on balance, mainly the outlook of Thomas Jefferson and his Republican allies rather than the biases of Alexander Hamilton and his Federalist followers. But I must have done an extremely poor job in advancing my key argument because none of the book reviewers mentioned my bold assertion about the preeminence of Jeffersonian influences. I thought I was advancing a revolutionary concept and mounting a serious challenge to historiographical trends that had prevailed for decades, but my revisionist interpretation was hardly noticed.

Richard Sylla, a professor of financial history at New York University, in his review in the *Journal of Economic History* probably came the closest of all my reviewers to identifying my Jeffersonian bias. (2) He correctly observed that I had presented somewhat ambiguous views on Alexander Hamilton's role in shaping the nation's financial system in the 1790s. Nonetheless, whereas Sylla criticized several other aspects of my analysis, he never stated that I was wrong about the Jeffersonian impact. Maybe Sylla, in a generous mood, decided that he would not wish to accuse a fellow financial historian of proposing such an outlandish and heretical hypothesis. Or maybe, more likely, I simply failed to make sufficiently plain my intention to boost the Jeffersonian banner.

*Previously unpublished paper delivered at the annual meeting of the Society for the History of the Early American Republic, Nashville, TN, 1996.

So much attention has been given to Treasury Secretary Hamilton over the decades that we now need a very explicit and unequivocal statement about the powerful role of Jeffersonian principles in shaping the nation's overall financial system. By overall, I mean to include the several states as well as a host of unchartered firms operating independently of governmental regulation. Since I made such an unimpressive case for Jeffersonian origins, let me make another effort to present a stronger case in the following paragraphs.

Before we can begin the process, we must first downgrade Hamilton's influence from something truly monumental to something more life-size and realistic. This deflation is necessary in order to give others--Jeffersonians in particular – a chance for the spotlight. Hamilton has received almost all the credit, or alternatively the damnation, for shaping the U.S. financial system because of his highly visible position as Treasury Secretary in Washington's first administration and the forcefulness of his ideas and personality. In truth, Hamilton's ideas were largely derivative of Robert Morris's earlier concepts, but the lack of time and space will not allow the pursuit of that argument in this context. The fundamental principle of Hamilton's program was the centralization of financial power at the national level and into the hands of the wealthy elite. (3)

Let me cite quickly two of the key reasons that Hamilton's role in the evolution of the financial system has dominated our historiography. First, the traditional focus was usually on national issues – the First Bank of the United States and the congressional funding of the overhanging war debt – rather than on a series of less publicized and less controversial developments at the state and local level. Second, historians have tended to concentrate their eyes on the period form 1789 to 1795 when Secretary Hamilton had the greatest impact on the American financial system.

To challenge this prevailing historiography, I will argue that the long-term evolution of the financial system was more in accord with Jeffersonian principles both with respect to the structure of the system and, correspondingly, the access of citizens to a wide range of financial services. Jefferson believed in two basic ideas: 1) a sustained debt repayment program and 2) a decentralized banking system with a strong element of local control. The final result reflected these overriding concepts. Jeffersonian principles are fairly obscure, I suspect, because they emanated not exclusively from Thomas Jefferson himself but from broad groups tightly linked to the anti-Federalist coalition. Many citizens were convinced that financial corruption in London circles had contributed, in large part, to the breakdown in political relations between England and its colonies. Jeffersonian Republicans wanted to prevent the same incestuous climate from emerging in the new nation.

With respect to the First Bank, effective limitations were placed on its power to centralize economic power and to corrupt the body politic from the very outset. The congressional charter contained one provision that made it a radically different institution from its so-called model--the Bank of England. The First Bank was not allowed to add any government bonds to its portfolio above the $8 million authorized for acceptance when individuals purchased its initial offering of common stock. Given that the national debt in 1790 was in the neighborhood of $80 million, the maximum amount of the debt that the bank could ever hold was no more than 10 percent. This critical restriction meant that, unlike the cozy relationship between the Parliamentary Exchequer and the Bank of England, the U.S. Treasury could not use the First Bank as a convenient outlet for raising new long-term capital, and thereby expanding the size of the national debt.

During the eighteenth century the British national debt had risen steadily in order to finance a series of overseas military campaigns, and the Bank of England had regularly accommodated the Exchequer in financing budget deficits through the direct purchase of numerous fresh issues of government bonds running into the millions of pounds. Indeed, the Bank of England had been created in the late seventeenth century for the explicit purpose of assisting Parliament in floating new debt issues. But its American counterpart, created a century later, was absolutely forbidden by the terms of its charter from engaging in any similar debt flotation activities. For this reason alone, the traditional depiction of the First Bank as an institution closely modeled on the Bank of England is highly misleading. The First Bank was permitted to make short-term loans to the federal government, but it could not add any long-term debt to its initial asset portfolio.

Moreover, at the initial gathering of the First Bank's board of directors, which included investors from several states, the members voted to authorize the establishment of a network of branch offices in major commercial centers beyond Philadelphia. The Bank of England, in contrast, had no branch offices. The vote to create a branch network was a decentralizing initiative that reflected Jeffersonian principles. Secretary Hamilton opposed decentralization, but he had not effective means of blocking the vote because four-fifths of the bank stock was in the hands of private individuals. Over the next two decades, increasing portions of its $10 million capital was allocated to the branch offices, and its loan portfolio became more geographically diverse. After Jefferson assumed the presidency in 1801, the federal government ran substantial budget surpluses, and the Treasury no longer relied on the First Bank for short-term financing. By its second decade of operations, the First Bank made loans strictly to borrowers in the private sector – mainly to urban merchants.

As a consequence of the restrictions on the purchase of long-term government bonds and decision to open branch offices in other cities, Philadelphia never had the opportunity to replicate the centralizing role of London in the British Isles. By the late eighteenth century, London was not only the preeminent financial center of the British Empire but of western Europe in general. (4) Philadelphia began as the new nation's leading financial center, yet its position steadily eroded. By the 1820s, New York City was the nation's leading money center. Meanwhile, the nation's political capital had moved to Washington, D.C., and it never rose to anything much more than an insignificant financial outpost compared to Baltimore, Philadelphia, New York, and Boston. Washington and London were two very, very different cities, and the lack of a community of influential bankers in the District of Columbia was a prime example of their stark contrast.

Under Jeffersonian rule, opportunities abounded for hundreds of new firms to enter the exploding American financial services sector. Generally speaking, financial services matured in advance of improvements in the nation's transportation and manufacturing sectors. Commercial banks with state charters popped up in a diverse group of towns and cities; over 100 state banks were operating by 1810. These local financial institutions were created by various groups of private investors, including both Federalists and Republicans. Some banks catered to a wide range of customers, and to indicate their open-door policies, they inserted the words "farmers" and "mechanics" in bank titles. What emerged, in perfect harmony with Jeffersonian principles of local control, was an exceedingly atomistic commercial banking system unlike any other banking system in the world, past or present, in terms of its decentralized character.

The period from 1790 to 1815 also witnessed the rapid growth of an American marine and fire insurance sector. The capital invested in these enterprises reached into the millions of dollars. Fire insurance companies served thousands of citizens in both urban and rural markets, and the premiums were low – only slightly higher than the percentage rates we pay today. Around half the fire insurance companies were organized as mutual non-profits, which meant that the policyholders were simultaneously investors and customers. Again, this innovative ownership pattern was fully in accord with Jeffersonian principles of widespread citizen participation in the financial and economic systems.

Lastly, in this celebration of Jeffersonian themes, we should recognize that, after the election of 1800, the new president and Treasury Secretary Albert Gallatin sustained and accelerated a debt retirement program designed to retire the nation's outstanding obligations during the lifetime of a single generation. This redemption plan ran completely counter to the professed Hamiltonian ideal of perpetual national indebtedness. Great Britain and the other major power in western Europe never paid off more than a small fraction of their respective national debt in the nineteenth century. Although the Louisiana Purchase and the costs associated with the War of 1812 temporarily sidetracked the vigorous retirement program, President Andrew Jackson finally achieved the Jeffersonian goal of paying down the national debt to zero.

To conclude, we need a major reinterpretation of the nation's financial history in the early national period. The prevailing interpretive framework tends to run as follows: the Jeffersonian Republicans, with prodding from Secretary of the Treasurer Albert Gallatin, came in time to accept Hamiltonian principles. In my view that outlook is inaccurate and inappropriate. Instead, the record shows that the Jeffersonians resisted the Hamilton's initiatives from the outset. Through various means, they undermined and undercut the Federalist financial program in the early 1790s. The financial system deviated sharply from the British model when the legislation creating the Bank of the United States passed the Congress. Unlike the Bank of England, the First Bank was not permitted to acquire additional government long-term debt after receiving the initial $8 million from private stockholders. Thus, its potential role in promoting excessive militarism and further debt expansion was effectively thwarted. At the very first meeting of the board of directors, members voted to establish a system of branch offices, which decentralized the bank's capital resources and its loan portfolio. After 1800 the institution was not a government bank in any way, shape, or form, but rather a large commercial bank that competed actively for the business of private customers with numerous state banks in the major port cities. (5) As the years passed, the First Bank steadily lost market share in terms of loans and deposits.

Overall the U.S. financial system functioned more in conformity with Jeffersonian ideals than with Hamilton's Anglican aspirations. My research suggests that Joyce Appleby was correct in identifying the commercial and market orientation of most Jeffersonians. (6) Within that context, I want to add that they had few objections to the expansion of financial services so long as the institutional providers were widely dispersed and both commercial banks and insurance companies were owned and managed by local residents.

It's high time we started revising the chapters on American financial history in the textbooks assigned in the U.S. survey courses to reflect more accurately the influence and impact of Jeffersonian financial principles.

Notes

1. Edwin J. Perkins, *American Public Finance and Financial Services, 1700–1815* (Columbus: Ohio State University Press, 1994).
2. Richard Sylla, "Three Centuries of Finance and Monetary Control in America," book review in *Journal of Economic History* (1995), 902-907.
3. Donald Swanson, *The Origins of Hamilton's Financial Policies* (Gainesville, University of Florida Press, 1963).
4. Larry Neal, *The Rise of Financial Capitalism: International Capital Markets in the Age of Reason* (New York: Cambridge University Press, 1990). See also David Hancock, *Citizens of the World* (Cambridge University Press, 1995.)
5. After 1800 the First Bank became an intermediary that accepted monies from customs houses for the federal government and loaned out a portion of these deposits to the private sector.
6. This paper and much of my research in the late 1980s and early 1990s was inspired by a formal lecture that Joyce Appleby gave before a fairly large audience at the Huntington Library in San Marino, California

Chapter Six

Lost Opportunities for Compromise in the Bank War: A Reassessment of Jackson's Veto Message

The confrontation between President Andrew Jackson and supporters of the bill to recharter the Second Bank of the United States in 1832 is among the most frequently researched episodes in American history. And deservedly so, for the outcome of the battle over the bank had a profound effect on the institutional development of the nation's financial system. In the decades that followed, the issue became so controversial and divisive that it defied political solution until the creation of the Federal Reserve Bank in the twentieth century.

One thrust of scholarship has attempted to assess whether Jackson's attacks on the bank were warranted by the facts or were rather mainly reflections of his pronounced biases against banks and paper money. (1) Although Jackson and the supporters of the Second Bank have both earned their share of defenders and detractors over the years, the modern judgment of economic historians is overwhelmingly favorable toward the bank. The argue that the bank performed its tasks in a manner beneficial to the stability of the economy, especially after 1823, and that it therefore did not deserve the fate it met at the hands of an aroused president (2)

This paper accepts the validity of the arguments favoring the continuance of the Second Bank, but it uses that position simply as a point of departure for a thorough review of a series of substantial objections to provisions of the charter bill as outlined in the presidential veto message of 1832. (3) Jackson expressed opposition to the bank on two levels. First, he objected to the bank on an abstract plane for using its alleged monopoly power to create class and regional divisions within society. On another level, he cited at least seven specific reservations about the terms of recharter and discussed each at length. Even if most of his objections were based on questionable judgments, it does not necessarily follow that a bank bill drafted to satisfy the bulk of his complaints would have

*Reprinted by permission of the *Business History Review*. "Lost Opportunities for Compromise in the Bank War: A Reassessment of Jackson's Veto Message," by Edwin J. Perkins, Winter, 1987.

been unworkable.

My analysis of the contested provisions indicates that the supporters of the bank could have acceded to numerous alterations to the charter terms without emasculating the institution. In truth, the bank's allies could have acquiesced to almost all of Jackson's preferences without drastically transforming the structure or operations of the bank. If they were genuinely concerned about sustaining the bank in order to stabilize the U.S. financial system and promote the general welfare, then their failure to seek a negotiated compromise in the face of determined opposition was not only impolitic but shortsighted as well.

The events leading up the presidential veto are well known and can be briefly summarized. Jackson fired the first volley in the battle over the Second Bank in his state of the union message to Congress in 1832. Acknowledging the existence of a campaign to renew the charter of the bank several years in advance of its scheduled expiration in 1836, the president put its supporters on notice by reviving the old question about its constitutionality and by charging that the bank had "failed in the great end of establishing a uniform and sound currency. (4) In subsequent messages, he recommended that Congress consider, in the years ahead, either substantial modifications in the terms of any new charter for the existing bank or alternative plans for an entirely new institution wholly owned by the federal government. (5) Although Jackson expressed reservations about the structure and operations of the Second Bank, he did not sound dogmatic or uncompromising in his public statements. In private letters and conversations with friends and important political leaders, however, Jackson made no secret of his antagonism toward the bank and its powerful and equally strong-willed president, Nicholas Biddle. (6)

Fully cognizant of the president's general opposition to the Second Bank, Biddle pondered the opportune time to introduce the recharter issue into the political arena. Under the influence of congressional leaders such as Daniel Webster and Henry Clay, Biddle was persuaded to force the matter in the election year of 1832. (7) A clear majority of the members of both houses favored recharter. Bank supporters believed that Jackson would be extremely reluctant to veto a recharter bill, because, being an astute politician, he would not want to jeopardize his chances for reelection in the fall. Moreover, if the bill was withheld for consideration until after the election and Jackson was victorious, he might be much less hesitant to act decisively against the bank in his second, and presumably last, term in office. Thus, Biddle finally decided that a push for recharter was the wisest course of action

FIRST OPPORTUNITY FOR COMPROMISE

In preparing the campaign to clear the way for passage in 1831, Biddle tried to enlist the aid of cabinet members who were already avowed supporters of the bank. Foremost was Secretary of the Treasury Louis McLane. He was the most knowledgeable about the operations of the Second Bank, and Biddle viewed him as a key man in the effort to gain Jackson's ascent to the continuance of the institution. McLane was one of the few men in public life who was able to disagree with the president on important matters and still retain his friendship. But on the bank issue, McLane could make little headway with Jackson, and the two men finally agreed to disagree about the merits of the Second Bank. (9)

Soon after the submission of the recharter bill to Congress in January 1832, Biddle made another attempt to secure the president's support or at least his pledge not to impede the progress of the legislation. His approach was again not direct but through another friendly intermediary, Secretary of State Edward Livingston. In late February, Livingston reported that as a result of conversations with Jackson and other cabinet officers, he believed the president was firmly committed to only four modifications in the terms of the charter. (1O) The first two issues related to the government's participation in the ownership and management of the institution. Henceforth Jackson wanted no government investment in the stock of the bank; but he requested that U.S. presidents continue the appointment of directors to the parent board in Philadelphia and additionally at least one director to the local board of each branch office. Over the years Jackson had become convinced that some branches engaged peri-oically in partisan politics, and the last proposal was probably designed to provide the executive branch with a permanent watchdog on the activities of the local offices.

The other two alterations dealt with the bank's real estate holdings and its liability for taxes assessed by! the states on banking facilities. The president asked that the bank set a limit on the length of time it could hold real estate obtained as a result of defaults on mortgage loans. During the aftermath of the Panic of 1819, the Second Bank had acquired through foreclosure a substantial amount of land in the western states, particularly in the Cincinnati area, and it had continued to maintain ownership long after property prices had recovered sufficiently to cover any losses. Jackson claimed that the bank was participating in real estate speculation, and he wanted to place a time limit on how long the bank could withhold from the market a given piece of property.

Jackson's last critical modification request was that the Second Bank pay local taxes on its branch properties at the same rate used in taxing the property of state banks. The president's intention was to create explicit legislation designed to slip through the loophole left purposely open by Chief Justice John Marshall in his opinion supporting the Supreme Court's decision in the case of *McCulloch vs. Maryland.* The justices had ruled in 1819 that the states had no power to tax the banknotes issued by an institution possessing a federal charter or, indeed, any aspect of its normal business operations. The Chief Justice added, however, that the ruling "does not extend to a tax paid on real property of the bank, in common with other real property within the State." (11) Many historians, including myself, have misinterpreted this episode by assuming that Jackson's aim was to issue a new challenge to the Court by asking Congress to pass explicit legislation focusing on an issue that he knew full well had already been declared unconstitutional, namely state taxation of the federal government.

But Jackson in fact was not behaving in a combative manner vis-a-vis the Supreme Court. Rather, he wanted to insert a clause in the charter that conformed to Marshall's statement about the probable legality of state taxation of the *real* property of a corporation chartered by the federal government. Jackson was convinced that the Second Bank maintained an unfair competitive advantage over the state banks because of its apparent complete exemption from state and local taxation. His plan was to place all banking institutions on a more equal standing. He could not accomplish that goal completely, but by making the Second Bank clearly liable for the payment of real estate taxes on its branch offices at the same rate paid by other business enterprises in a given state, Jackson could move a step further in that direction.

Biddle readily agreed in correspondence with his chief Washington lobbyist, Charles Ingersoll, to all four of Jackson's reported requests for alterations in the charter terms: "In truth I believe there is no change desired by the President which would not be immediately assented to by the Bank." (12) Given Jackson's well-known aversion to the bank, Biddle was doubtless surprised at the mildness of the president's initial demands. For a brief time, he was lulled into believing that the recharter bill, with only a few slight modifications, might sail through Congress without presidential opposition.

During the last two weeks in February 1832, however, the bank's congressional opponents decided to pursue a strategy of obstruction and delay. Citing the circulation of a number of rumors about possible misconduct and suspected violations of the charter, Senator Thomas Hart Benton of Missouri and Representative Augustin Clayton of Georgia led the movement for a congressional investigation of the bank's policies and procedures. The initiation of formal investigations was a favored tactic of the anti-bank contingent. In 1819, for example, the release of a report by a House subcommittee had precipitated the resignation of the institution's first president, William Jones. In this instance, Jackson let it be known that he was averse to any congressional action on the recharter bill until a full investigation of all charges had been completed. There the matter rested during March and April.

By mid-May the investigating committee had failed to uncover any information that seriously discredited the bank, and the recharter issue moved again into the political limelight. Meanwhile, Jackson had hardened his opposition to the Second Bank, and he demanded nothing less than withdrawal of the bill. Assured by Henry Clay and Daniel Webster that they had sufficient votes to pass the legislation handily despite the president's attitude, Biddle resolved to avoid any postponement. Before presentation to the Senate, the managers of the bank bill added a few new amendments to the original charter, which were apparently designed to satisfy some of the previous critics.

In his detailed study of the Second Bank in 1903, the economic historian Ralph Catterall claimed that the goal was to make the bill "as unobjectionable to the president as possible, in the hope that his assent might be secured." (13) Yet a review of the amendments reveals that only one of the four minimum requirements attributed to Jackson in February 1832 was covered in the revised bill. In this case, as in many others, Catterall's biases against Jackson led him to distort the historical record and to mislead scores of later historians.

The proposed new charter forbade the bank to hold real estate acquired as the result of defaulted mortgages for a period longer than five years, a provision that was in line with Jackson's demands. But the bill ignored completely Jackson's views in regard to government ownership of bank stock, the power of the president to appoint directors to the boards of the branch offices, and finally the local taxation of the branches at the same rates prevailing for state-chartered banks. Here was the first missed opportunity for sensible compromise.

SECOND OPPORTUNITY FOR COMPROMISE

After months of informal discussions and negotiations between Biddle's intermediaries and Jackson, the bill presented to the Senate for action in late May contained little to assuage a suspicious and hostile president. The bank faction was not intent on seeking any sort of compromise; it believed it had the votes to recharter the Second Bank without any substantial alterations in the existing charter. Jackson viewed the bill as a congressional challenge to his political power, which, of course, it was.

During the floor debate in the Senate, Benton emerged as the chief spokesman for the administration. He and several colleagues offered a series of amendments to the recharter bill. At this juncture the managers of the legislation had another genuine opportunity to disarm doubters and to appease the president. They rejected that opportunity, however. All but one of the opponents' amendments were voted down. The only amendment approved gave Congress the authority to prohibit the issuance of banknotes in sums below $20.

Four of the rejected proposals dealt with issues that were subsequently cited in the presidential veto message as major deficiencies in the terms of recharter. The allies of the administration had proposed the following: 1) that the bank surrender its privileged position as the only possible holder of a national charter; 2) that foreigners be ineligible to own bank stock; 3) that the bank be required to accept banknotes in the payments of debts from individual citizens under the same rules applicable to state-chartered banks; and, finally, 4) that branch properties should be subject to taxation by the states.

In his history of the Second Bank, Catterall asserted that the rejected amendments were offered "mainly with the purpose of embarrassing the bank and assisting Jackson in the coming campaign" and that opponents "contemplated no fixed plan of improving the bank as a financial concern." (14) Catterall's judgment was probably correct about the merits of the proposals. On the other hand, if the pro-bank forces, in the interest of promoting political harmony, had accepted all of them, the impact on the operations of the bank would have been minimal. The fundamental issue for bank supporters was--or should have been--not whether the proposed amendments would make the bank a stronger institution, but whether they would have caused considerable harm. The failure of Biddle and his congressional allies to seek an accommodation with opponents by acceding to a series of fairly modest alterations in the charter terms during the critical Senate debate was a serious tactical error.

VETO MESSAGE: ANALYSIS OF SPECIFIC OBJECTIONS

The recharter bill passed the House and Senate by majorities of 55 and 60 percent, respectively. On 10 July Jackson returned it, accompanied by his famous veto message, written in collaboration with his close friends and advisers, Amos Kendall and Roger Taney. Most historical accounts have concentrated on the rhetorical aspects of the veto message. In his recent interpretative biography of Jackson, James Curtis described the document as cast "in the language of social apocalypse." The trio of writers of the veto message depicted the bank as "an engine of aristocracy, the symbol of special privilege, and the cause of the nation's discontent." (15) Robert Remini described it as "a powerful and dramatic polemic, cleverly written to appeal to the great masses of people and to convince them of the truth of its arguments." (16)

But the message contained more than hyperbole. In addition to challenging the constitutionality of the bank, Jackson cited numerous specific objections to the terms of recharter. My analysis of these presidential complaints reveals that bank proponents could have conceded six points with little fear about the net effect on bank operations. On one issue, they could not have capitulated completely to Jackson's wishes without undermining the institution, but ample room existed for a compromise solution. In retrospect, only the issue of the bank's constitutionality remained non-negotiable.

One of the key issues that disturbed Jackson and his advisers was the Second Bank's privileged status. Except for a provision allowing banking capital inside the District of Columbia to expand up to a limit of $6 million, the bill prohibited Congress from chartering any competitive national banks with the authority to establish a network of interstate branches. The bills creating the national banks in 1792 and 1816 had extended those rights and privileges over a period of twenty years. Supporters of the bank were well aware of Jackson's sensitivity to the special privileges issue, and in a small effort to placate him, they had reduced the length of the proposed charter renewal to only fifteen years. In return for its exclusive status, the bank was scheduled to pay the federal government a $3 million bonus, at the rate of $200,000 per year over the life of the charter.

Although the bonus would have provided the government with additional revenue, Jackson objected. "The bonus which is extracted from the bank is a confession," he charged, "that the powers granted . . . are greater than are necessary." (17) The insinuation was that the payment was nothing less than a bribe offered for acquiring monopoly privileges. Actually state legislatures routinely collected bonuses from banks seeking charters, even without monopoly powers. The bonus was primarily payment for the acquisition of corporate status and the provision of limited liability for investors in bank stock. How critical was the granting of exclusive status to the bank? In truth, it was largely superfluous. The likelihood that Congress and later presidents would have subsequently agreed to authorize the formation of a number of competing national banks in the period from 1836 to 1851 was extremely remote. No major political figure in either party was advocating multiple charters at the national level. Moreover, even if a competing bank had succeeded in obtaining a national charter, there is no reason to believe that its existence would have threatened the viability of the Second Bank. The Second Bank profited from its close association with the federal government, but it was by no means strictly a government bank. The largest revenues came from interest on commercial loans in the private sector, where the bank competed for business with hundreds of state-chartered institutions.

The complete elimination of exclusive charter rights from the recharter bill would not have seriously threatened the position of the bank. By dropping the request for exclusivity, bank supporters could have also argued for a reduction in the size of the charter bonus, or perhaps its removal. A smaller bonus would have improved the net profits of the institution. For Jackson, the absolute denial of national charter rights to any other proposed financial institution and the $3 million bonus offered to guarantee complete protection from potential competition represented disturbing symbols of the power of an aristocratic, moneyed elite to corrupt the political system. By excluding them from a revised recharter bill, proponents could have satisfied two of the president's strongest objections in rather painless fashion.

FOREIGN STOCKHOLDERS

Jackson was almost equally disturbed about the presence of a substantial number of foreign stockholders. By 1832 they held about one quarter of the outstanding shares of the Second Bank. The president charged that foreign investors held an unfair advantage because their overseas residence exempted them from property taxes on bank stock, on which some states had assessed their citizens at rates of up to one percent annually. As a result of these tax differentials, the veto message claimed, bank stock "will be worth 10 or 15 percent more to foreigners than to citizens of the United States." (18) Of course, Jackson and his co-authors had no knowledge of market prices for bank stock in Europe, nor did they know whether foreign governments imposed similar property taxes on the overseas holdings of their own citizens. Moreover, from a strictly financial standpoint the whole argument was completely irrelevant in this context. The important point was Jackson's conviction that foreigners were somehow profiting handsomely at the expense of American borrowers. The complaint was based on xenophobia, not on rational financial considerations--which is why subsequent attempts at logical refutation proved futile.

Jackson also feared that foreigners might become unwitting accomplices in a scheme hatched by a small group of American stockholders to gain absolute control over the bank. Under the terms of the existing charter, foreigners were ineligible to vote their shares at the annual meetings of stockholders. With from one-third to one-fourth of the stock excluded from the vote, it created a great "temptation to designing men to secure that control in their own hands by monopolizing the remaining stock." (19) Under those circumstances, a small clique would be in a position to reelect themselves into office year after year. Jackson concluded: "It is easy to conceive that great evils to our country and its institutions might flow from such a concentration of power in the hands of a few men irresponsible to the people." (20) The existence of a large block of non-voting stock simply increased the likelihood of this outcome. Of course there was no evidence that any such problem had ever materialized in the previous three decades of operations of both the first and se«ond national banks, or was even remotely probable in the future. Again, however, Jackson was more interested in possibilities than realistic probabilities.

The solution to the difficulties allegedly caused by foreign ownership was as simple as it was obvious. The recharter bill could have been amended to prohibit foreign stockholders in the Second Bank after 1836. The negative impact on the bank would have been marginal at best. Sufficient funds were available in the United States to support the capital of the institution. Restricting the sale of stock to U.S. citizens probably would have reduced slightly the price at which this gilt-edge issue traded in the stock market, but it is doubtful that prices would have fallen below the par value of $100 because the Second Bank had paid a steady dividend after 1823. With four years to transfer about $8 million in stock to American owners, foreigners would not have been forced to resort to panic sales. Most important, however, changes in the market value of bank stock after its initial issue date in 1816 had absolutely no effect on the operations of the Second Bank or on its capital structure--and would have had no effect in future years. Thus a ban on foreign ownership of bank stock would not have penalized the institution in any significant manner, yet it would surely have aided in the appeasement of Jackson.

DISCRIMINATION AGAINST PRIVATE CITIZENS

The veto message also chided the Second Bank because, in its relationships with borrowers, the institution sometimes granted privileges to state-chartered banks that it denied to private citizens. The issue in question related to the policy guiding a given branch in accepting or rejecting from customers the banknotes issued by other offices in the Second Bank's extensive branch system. In transactions involving the repayment of debts by other banks, the Second Bank accepted at par (face value) the banknotes issued by any of its various branches. For private citizens, however, the rules were different. If an individual or business firm wanted to repay a similar debt, a given branch legitimacy of that particular form of taxation on the bank's real property holdings across the states. The president believed that the Second Bank was a legitimate target for state taxation. He would have preferred to make the accepted only its own banknotes and rejected those issued by distant offices within the system.

Customers holding banknotes from other branch offices were forced to exchange them for local banknotes with brokerage houses, which charged a modest commission for their services. Thus, private borrowers discharging their debts to the bank occasionally found that their overall expense, because of the cost of currency conversion, was often one or two percent higher than the expense incurred by the state banks. Jackson viewed it as a problem of equity: "This boon conceded to the State banks, although not unjust in itself, is most odious because it does not measure out equal justice to the high and the low, the rich and the poor." (21) The fact that the Second Bank never made loans to the low and the poor did not, of course, deter Jackson in offering his criticism of the institution.

The question of favoritism toward state banks and discrimination against private citizens was strictly a peripheral matter. From the perspective of the bank, its policy on the handling of bank notes issued by distant branches could easily have been altered without any major ramifications. If Jackson saw the problem as important, then a resolution to pacify him would not have been difficult to work out. The recharter bill could have included a provision stipulating that the bank would henceforth extend similar rules to both private citizens and the state banks in the collection of its debts. This point of contention, like its predecessors, was not an issue over which bank supporters should have risked the continuance of the institution.

STATE TAXATION OF U.S. GOVERNMENT AGENCIES

Another objection to the terms of recharter cited in the veto message related to the power of states to tax the branches of the Second Bank. With his eye firmly focused on the fairness doctrine, the president was irritated because the Second Bank was seemingly exempt from local taxation while competitive state banks remained liable for taxes on property and capital. In the Supreme Court's ruling in 1819 in the famous case of McCulloch vs. Maryland, Chief Justice Marshall had declared that the state had no power to tax the operations of a superior political power, namely, the federal government, because the taxation power implied the power to destroy. But Marshall also made it very clear in the formal opinion that the Court's decision was narrowly drawn. He indicated that the states would be within their powers in assessing taxes on the real property--land and buildings--of chartered corporations and agencies of the federal government, or in this case the branch offices of the Second Bank. (22) Jackson simply wanted a clause in the recharter bill acknowledging the Second Bank liable for all forms of state taxation, but since the Supreme Court had closed the door on taxing its notes or operations, he was prepared to take the only avenue still available. In the veto message the president expressed profound disappointment that the recharter bill remained silent about the taxation issue. My analysis of the situation suggests that there were no economic realities that should have prevented his opponents from acceding to the president's will on this matter.

The president may have thought that he had been deceived on this issue. The inclusion of a provision in the recharter bill stipulating that the Second Bank would henceforth be liable for property taxes at the same rates applicable to state-chartered banks was one of the four minimal changes Jackson had listed as necessary to secure his support in February 1832. Secretary of State Livingston had informed Ingersoll, Biddle's chief Washington agent, of the president's demands, and Biddle acceded to them in a letter to Ingersoll on 25 February. (23) Presumably Ingersoll informed Livingston, who would then, in turn, have told the president that Biddle had agreed to the inclusion of a provision ending the Second Bank's tax-exempt status.

Why Biddle subsequently reneged on his assurance of support for the presidential program is unknown. Payment of nondiscriminatory real estate taxes on the branch offices would not have threatened the profitability of the Second Bank. Given their knowledge of the president's outlook on this issue several months prior to the drafting of the final recharter bill, it is difficult to understand why the bank contingent dismissed his request in such a cavalier manner. In so doing, they also undermined the reliability and credibility of Nicholas Biddle.

THE ISSUE OF OVERCAPITALIZATION

Jackson raised one complaint about the terms of recharter that analysis reveals could not have been fully satisfied without damaging the institution, but this was an issue on which ample ground existed for a negotiated compromise. The president asserted that the size of the bank as reflected in its capitalization of $35 million was unnecessarily large. The First Bank of the United States, he noted, had functioned effectively and served the requirements of the federal government with a capital of only $10 million. The successor bank was therefore overcapitalized by $25 million, or over 200 percent. To support his contention, Jackson pointed to the size of the national debt, which had risen substantially during the War of 1812 but was, in 1832, on the verge of extinction. "The public debt which existed during the period of the old bank and on the establishment of the new has been nearly paid off, and our revenue will soon be reduced." As a consequence, the government foresaw a diminishing reliance on the bank to provide public services. The additional $25 million in capital authorized in 1816 would, Jackson claimed, serve only "private purposes" during the proposed recharter period.

The president failed to take into account the substantial growth of the economy since 1792. Indeed, largely as the result of population growth, the relative roles of the two national banks in the U.S. economy were roughly equivalent. If its capital were reduced to the previous level of $10 million, the Second Bank undoubtedly would have experienced difficulties in maintaining branches throughout the nation. At the same time, there was merit to the president's argument about the likelihood of reduced government reliance on the bank for collecting revenues and paying off the national debt.

The perfect opportunity existed for a compromise solution. Bank supporters might have proposed a reduction in capitalization of perhaps one-quarter to one-third or to $26 or $23 million. Even then the Second Bank would have been, by far, the largest financial institution in the nation. In 1832, for example, a bank of that size would have still contained over 15 percent of the total paid-in capital in the U.S. banking system. (24) A reduction of $8 million could conceivably have come from the retirement of the outstanding stock held by overseas investors, thereby reducing the size of the institution and simultaneously eliminating the allegedly pernicious role of foreigners in the affairs of the bank. A smaller bank would probably have maintained fewer branch offices and thus would have appeared to be a less imposing institution.

A more modest capital structure might well have diminished the bank's capacity for exercising influence over the U.S. financial system. Yet, under the circumstances, the possibility of operating a smaller institution should not have been rejected out of hand; there was nothing sacred about a capitalization of $35 million. A reduction of one-third to one-fourth in the size of the Second Bank would also have aided in thwarting the allegations about the exercise of monopoly power. In light of Jackson's vociferous objections to the continuance of the Second Bank with its existing capital, an offer to reduce the figure to a more acceptable level would have been a logical and prudent response to the veto message of July 1832.

THE CONSTITUTIONAL ISSUE

Only one of Jackson's specific allegations left no margin for appeasement: the assertion that the legislation creating the national bank was unconstitutional. The constitutionality of the national bank had been controversial as far back as the early 1790s, and the question had remained alive over the decades. Alexander Hamilton and his allies had claimed that the authority to establish the bank rested on the doctrine of implied powers, and the Supreme Court had upheld that view. Nonetheless, advocates of strict interpretation and states' rights remained skeptical about the propriety of the national bank, and in 1811 they had sufficient strength in Congress to defeat the attempt to recharter the First Bank of the United States. (25) Thus the president's attitude toward the constitutional issue was not an isolated opinion, but one he shared with a distinguished group of predecessors, among them Thomas Jefferson, and many contemporaries. (26) In the veto message, he stated that the Supreme Court did not possess sole authority to decide on the constitutionality of legislation: "It is as much the duty of the House of Representatives, of the Senate, and of the President." (27) Therefore, he was only carrying out the responsibilities of office.

For our purposes a discussion of the constitutionality debate is unnecessary. The significant point is the pro-bank faction's lack of maneuvering room on this issue. Biddle and his allies were in no position to accede to the president's opinions, nor was there any basis for seeking a compromise solution. Only by altering the provisions of the recharter bill to conform with Jackson's other objections did the bank's advocates have any hope of persuading him that a restructured Second Bank was a different type of institution, one that was constitutional in principle.

LACK OF EXECUTIVE CONSULTATION

The president's final complaint was not directed at the terms of recharter but addressed the failure of bank proponents to solicit his active participation in the process of drafting legislation. The bank was clearly a division of the executive branch, yet the initiative for recharter had come exclusively from outsiders. On the two other occasions when a national bank had received a congressional charter, in 1792 and 1816, presidents George Washington and James Madison and their respective secretaries of the treasury, Alexander Hamilton and Alexander Dallas, had been closely associated with the formulation of bank legislation. In this instance, however, the executive branch was merely a passive participant. "Neither upon the propriety of the present action nor upon the provisions of this act was the Executive consulted. It had no opportunity to say that it neither needs or ,wants an agent clothed with such powers and favored by such exemptions." (28) Jackson probably exaggerated the absence of opportunities for executive participation in drafting the recharter bill, since he revealed no inclination to become involved. But past performance aside, the remedy for this problem was readily at hand. In the days following the veto, bank supporters could have responded positively and invited executive participation. Moreover, if they had chosen to begin direct discussions with the president, an appropriate agenda for negotiations was already laid out in the text of the veto message.

NO COMPROMISE: THE POLITICS OF CONFRONTATION

Rather than taking seriously the presidents arguments about defects in the recharter bill and using them as a vehicle for a possible compromise, his opponents mounted instead a frontal attack on his position. Adopting the same argumentative style as Jackson and his co-authors, Biddle and other bank supporters set out to override the veto. They chided Jackson for introducing inflammatory language into the debate, such as the unsupported charges that the bank set class against class, section against section, and foreigners against citizens. They devised formidable arguments to contradict every objection that Jackson and his speechwriters had raised in the veto message. (29) Supremely confident of the force of their logic, bank partisans set out to win the debate on its own merits, letting the facts speak for themselves. In perhaps the greatest folly of all, Biddle arranged to have the veto message reprinted in large quantities and distributed across the nation. (30) Meanwhile, they never paused to consider a strategy of meeting the vast majority of Jackson's objections--irrespective of the merits of his arguments--and possibly saving the institution in a slightly modified form. Bank supporters were so locked into maintaining the status quo that they utterly failed to weigh properly alternative means of achieving most of their goals.

Unfortunately for the bank, some of the leading political figures sponsoring the recharter bill did not rate the continuance of the institution as their top priority. For them, the defeat of Jackson in the upcoming presidential election held precedence over all other considerations. Many promoters of Henry Clay's candidacy actually welcomed the veto of the recharter bill because they believed it could be used to defeat Jackson in the November election. (31) Jackson explained the situation succinctly to Martin Van Buren. The Bank is trying to kill me.... but I will kill it." (32) And Clay as well, he might have added. Partisan battles and the striving for political advantage virtually precluded any effort to explore all the implications of the veto message.

Nicholas Biddle, the bank's proud and overbearing president, must also share the blame for failing to contemplate exactly how little damage the institution would incur by bowing to Jackson's prejudices. He permitted his political allies to place their own ambitions above the salvation of the bank. He made no effort to reopen a dialogue with the president, either directly or through emissaries such as McLane or Livingston, after the release of the veto message. Biddle failed to perceive that the power to dictate the terms of any successful recharter bill had shifted from the pro-bank faction to its opponents. Moreover, he chose to ignore the extent to which his continuance as the chief executive of the bank had become a divisive issue. At the very least, he could have pledged to step down when the recharter bill was scheduled to take effect in 1836, Instead Biddle permitted his standing as chief executive to take precedence over the perpetuation of the bank and the public welfare. Given the rivalry that had emerged between these two powerful and obstinate figures, Biddle's offer to resign, immediately or at some future date, would appear to have been a prerequisite for initiating a renewed drive to recharter the bank on the general conditions laid out by Jackson.

CONCLUSION

Although no historian can claim with certainty that Jackson could have been persuaded by tactful and skillful negotiation to agree to the recharter of the national bank in an altered form, it is, nonetheless, worthwhile to examine thoroughly the concessions that might have placated him and to assess their probable impact. With the publication of the veto message, his objections became a part of the public record. As the preceding analysis reveals, most of these complaints were not so outrageous or impractical that they could not have been relatively easily satisfied. Exaggerated arguments do not invariably lead to untenable solutions.

The following alterations in the recharter terms would have met most of Jackson's stated objections: an end to the exclusive charter privileges of the bank and a paring down of the bonus; the termination of the eligibility of foreigners to remain as stockholders; an equalization of policy toward state banks and private citizens in the acceptance of banknotes offered in the payment of debts; a clear statement indicating that the bank would be subject to state taxation of its *real* property; and finally a reduction in the capitalization of the bank. Of course a revised bill tailored to appease the president might still have been rejected on constitutional grounds, since compromise on that issue was impossible. On the other hand, if Biddle and the pro-bank faction had capitulated on the vast majority of the disputed provisions, Jackson would have had the opportunity to proclaim a great victory for the people, and he could have forseeably signed a thoroughly revised recharter bill.

Supporters of the bank who sincerely believed the continuance of the institution was in the national interest were a majority in Congress in 1832. But through arrogance and disregard for the opinions of the president, their leaders proceeded in 1831 to devise a strategy for recharter in isolation from the executive branch. After Jackson called for an investigation of the bank and postponement of the vote in spring 1832, Biddle and his allies completely abandoned all efforts to seek an accommodation with their opponents. (33) When spokesmen for the administration introduced a series of relatively mild amendments to alter the recharter terms along the lines later spelled out in the veto message, the pro-bank majority promptly voted them down. Bank supporters wanted the continuance of the institution on their own terms, and they were willing to risk an all-or-nothing fight to the finish. (34)

Regardless of the extent of their misjudgment prior to the introduction of the bill into Congress and their mishandling of the legislation when amendments were offered, the behavior of the pro-bank faction was irresponsible after the publication of the veto message. Angered and blinded by the distortions and hyperbole of the Jacksonian rhetoric, they failed to take seriously few, if any, of the seven very specific objections to the terms of recharter and to reflect on whether common ground existed for a compromise that might preserve the bank in slightly altered form. Instead they engaged in the politics of confrontation. They lost the vote to override the presidential veto; and Jackson's subsequent reelection sealed the fate of a large national bank with an extensive branch system for the next three-quarters of a century.

To date, most historical accounts have assigned President Andrew Jackson and a few of his key advisers the overwhelming responsibility for destroying the Second Bank of the United States. But that judgment is too one-sided and requires substantial modification. A more balanced approach that places an even greater responsibility on the shoulders of its supporters is more consistent with the evidence. They, after all, had the most to lose if recharter was denied. The pro-bank faction had three distinct opportunities for compromise: in early 1832 while the recharter bill was still being drafted; during the Senate debate in May over amendments sponsored by spokesmen for the administration; and finally in the months after the veto message had become a public document. All were lost, however.

Bank supporters erred because they refused to consider objectively revisions in the charter terms proposed by the president, his closest advisers, and spokesmen for the administration in Congress. Those alterations might have sustained the bank in a modified but clearly recognizable form. The unwillingness of Biddle and his allies to explore avenues of compromise based on the president's stated objections was a strategic error of enormous magnitude with lasting implications.

Notes

1. The literature on Jackson and issue of banking is vast. A representative sample of a few important books includes: Bray Hammond, *Banks and Politics from the Revolution to the Civil War* (Princeton, NJ, 1957); Arthur Schlesinger, Jr., *The Age of Jackson* (Boston, 1945); John McFaul, *The Politics of Jacksonian Finance* (Ithaca, NY, 1972); James Sharp, *The Jacksonians versus the Banks: Politics in the States after the Panic of 1837* (New York, 1970); William Shade, *Banks or No Banks: The Money Issue in Western Politics* (Detroit, MI, 1972); and Edward Pessen, *Jacksonian America: Society, Personality, and Politics* (Homewood, IL, 1969). The best account of the contest between Jackson and the Second Bank remains Robert Remini's *Andrew Jackson and the Bank War* (New York, 1967). Remini covers much of the same territory in volume two of *Andrew Jackson and the Course of American Freedom* (New York, 1981), 331-73.
2. See, for example, Walter B. Smith, *Economics of the Second Bank of the United States* (Cambridge, MA, 1953); Fritz Redlich, *The Molding of American Banking*, 2nd ed. (New York, 1968). I, 96-151; and Richard Timberlake, *The Origins of Central Banking in the United States* (Cambridge, MA, 1978). Every textbook written by an economic historian over the last quarter century, and their have been many, including my own, offers a generally favorable assessment of the performance of the bank under the leadership of Nicholas Biddle.
3. Andrew Jackson, "Veto Message." 10 July 1832, House Miscellaneous Documents, 53rd Congress, 2nd sess. (Washington, DC, 1893-1894), 2: 576-91. The complete text of the message, plus excerpts from books and articles, are in *Jackson vs. Biddle's Bank,* ed.

George Rogers Taylor, 2nd. ed. (Lexington, MA, 1973), 10-29
4. Jackson, "State of the Union Address," Dec. 1829, in *Messages and Papers of the Presidents*, ed. James Richardson (Washington, DC, 1896-1890), 2: 462.
5. "Plan for a National Bank," in Amos Kendall to Jackson, 20 Nov. 1829, box 1, file 16, Tennessee Library and Archives, Nashville. Larry Schweikart provides an in-depth analysis of the favorable attitudes of Jackson and his followers regarding the prospect of greater centralization of the banking system in his highly revisionist manuscript, "Jacksonian Ideology, Hard Money, and 'Central Banking': A Reappraisal," forthcoming in *The Historian*.
6. An excellent source of material related to Jackson's attitudes and opinions from a participant in these events is James Hamilton, *Reminiscences* (New York, 1869).
7. For an analysis of political considerations, see Hammond, *Bank and Politics*, 325-450, and Thomas Govan, *Nicholas Biddle: Nationalist and Public Banker, 1786-1844* (Chicago, 1959), 169-204.
8. Jean Wilburn, *Biddle's Bank: The Crucial Years* (New York, 1967), reveals the extent of the broad Congressional support for the bank in 1832.
9. For McLane's limited role in the bank war, see John Munroe, *Louis McLane: Federalist and Jacksonian* (New Brunswick, NJ, 1973), 317-50.
10. Ralph Catterall, *The Second Bank of the United States* (Chicago, 1903), 224-28.
11. McCulloch vs. Maryland, 4 Wheaton, 316. For a detailed analysis of the complex legal issues, see Leonard Baker, *John Marshall: A Life in Law* (New York, 1974), 588-620; the quotation is found on p. 603. A misleading account of the implications of the court decision, which implies that federal government agencies were thereafter exempt from all state and local taxation, is in Hammond, *Banks and Politics*, 262-68.
12. Biddle to Charles Ingersoll, 26 Feb. 1832, in *The Correspondence of Nicholas Biddle*, ed. Reginald McCrane (Boston, 1919), 185-86.
13. Catterall, *Second Bank*, 233.
14. *Ibid.*, 234.
15. James C. Curtis, *Andrew Jackson and the Search for Vindication* (Boston, 1976), 130. Perhaps the strongest emphasis on the social implications is found in Schlesinger, *Age of Jackson*, chaps. 7-10.
16. Remini, *Jackson and the Bank War*, 82; Richard Latner, *The Presidency of Andrew Jackson: White House Politics, 1829-1837* (Athens, GA, 1979), 111-23, argues that the main concern of the drafters of the message was not the absence of absolute equality, "but special privilege, monopoly, and the abuse of government powers" (p. 118).
17. Jackson, "Veto Message."
18. *Ibid.*
19. *Ibid.*
20. *Ibid.*
21. *Ibid.*
22. *McCulloch vs. Maryland*; Baker, *John Marshall*, 23.
23. Biddle to Ingersoll, 20 Feb. 1832.
24. This estimate is based on my analysis of date in J. Van Fenstermaker, *The Development of American Commercial Banking, 1782-1837* (Kent, OH, 1965). 65-69
25. Hammond, *Banks and Politics*, 197-226.
26. In 1803 Jefferson described the First Bank as an institution "of the most deadly hostility against the principles and form of our Constitution." He also spoke of the nation as functioning "under the vassalage" of the bank. Jefferson to Gallatin, 13 Dec. 1803, in *The Writings of Thomas Jefferson*, ed. H. A. Washington (New York, 1846), 4:519.

27. Jackson, "Veto Message."
28. *Ibid.*
29. Daniel Webster, speech to Senate on bank bill, 11 July 1832, *The Writings and Speeches of Daniel Webster* (Boston, 1903), 6: 149-180. Excerpts of Webster's address are reprinted in Taylor, ed., *Jackson vs. Biddle's Bank*, 34-43.
30. Catterall, *Second Bank*, 240-41. Despite his biases against Jackson, Catterall concluded that the reaction of the bank's supporters to the veto message was "ludicrous and almost pathetic."
31. Biddle's initial reaction was optimistic since he believed the exaggerated language was all that "the friends of the Bank and the country could desire." Biddle to Henry Clay, 1 Aug. 1832, in *The Life Correspondence and Speeches of Henry Clay*, ed. Calvin Colton (New York, 1857), 4: 341.
32. Martin Van Buren, *Autobiography*, ed. John C. Fitzpatrick (Washington, DC, 1920), 625.
33. Both Robert Remini and James Curtis suggest that prior to the summer of 1832 Jackson might have been amenable to a genuine compromise, but the implacability of his opponents stirred his combative nature; see Remini, *Jackson and the Bank War*, 43, and Curtis, *Andrew Jackson*, 121-29.
34. Biddle told a correspondent in discussing Jackson's attitude toward the institution: "I will not give way an inch in what concerns the independence of the Bank to please all the Administrations, past, present, or future." Biddle to Dickens. 16 Sept. 1829, in McCrane, ed.,, *Biddle*, 75-76.

Chapter Seven

Managing a Dollar-Sterling Exchange Account: Brown, Shipley & Co. in the 1850s

"We aim and with perfect right – at the rank and position equal to the Barings, but it is impossible that we can maintain it, if we are to be in the discount market week by week...whereas they never discount and are known to have always large sums lying at call." (1) That was the pessimistic assessment of the situation by the resident managers of Brown, Shipley & Co. in their letter of 9 February 1855, to their partners in the firm's New York branch. If the house was to achieve parity with Baring Brothers & Co., the Liverpool partners added, it would have to make sweeping changes in the firm's capital structure. These changes would reduce the size of the partnership's investments in American railroad securities and concurrently increase the overall liquidity of the English branch. This transatlantic debate about the proper allocation of the partnership's financial resources was one of the matters causing divisiveness within the House of Brown around the mid-century. The resolution of this dispute over the firm's strategy is among the several topics discussed in the following examination of the role played by the Liverpool branch in the management of the Browns' Anglo-American foreign exchange operations.

By the 1850's, the House of Brown was the dominant firm in the U.S. foreign exchange market. (2) Its assumption of a position of leadership was due in large part to the firm's unique organizational structure. In the United States the house created a series of outlets in all the major northern and southern ports, while in Liverpool it possessed a branch office of unparalleled importance. (3) Indeed, the House of Brown was the only one of the great nineteenth-century merchant-banking firms to function under a genuinely transatlantic pattern of ownership. Whereas the Barings, George Peabody, and other merchant-bankers conducted foreign exchange operations in the United States primarily through a chain of independent businessmen acting in an agency capacity, the House of Brown had approximately the same number of full partners on both sides of the Atlantic. (4)

*Reprinted from the British journal, *Business History* (January 1974), pp. 48-64.

In that sense, the Browns formed the only true Anglo-American partnership, and this unity of purpose gave the house a competitive advantage in the operation of a dollar-sterling exchange account.

In the years preceding the American Civil War, the Browns' foreign exchange operations were a highly seasonal activity. (5) The effective performance of this business function relied heavily on interbranch cooperation. From approximately May to November, the firm's offices in Baltimore, Philadelphia, Boston, and New York were predominantly sellers of sterling to American importers. The cash inflow generated by these sterling sales was temporarily invested in short-term commercial paper in the New York money market. In the late autumn, when the cotton crop Began moving to the English market, the short--term investments were gradually liquidated, and the funds were made available to the firm's southern outlets. It was the duty of the southern representatives to purchase sterling bills at seasonally low prices and remit them to the Liverpool branch for collection. These remittances were needed to cover the previously overdrawn accounts of the firm's northern branches. The seasonal cycle was then complete.

Although some of the responsibilities for managing the firm's foreign exchange activities were shared jointly by the Liverpool and New York branches, each office was also charged with a certain number of specific tasks. One of the prime responsibilities of the English house was to accept, upon presentation, the sterling bills sold by the firm's U.S. outlets and to arrange for their later payment. Equally important, however, was its participation in the correspondingly reverse process--that is, the house presented for acceptance the covering bills on other payees which were regularly remitted for collection by the American representatives. (6) In the short run, the associated inflow and outflow of cash was rarely in equilibrium. As a result, the Liverpool managers were expected to regulate their position in the English money market with skill whether they faced a cash deficit or a periodic surplus. In addition, they maintained credit files on a diversity of British payees frequently named by bill drawers in the United States. Their information on the standing of these payees guided the American representatives in their daily purchasing activities. Indeed, it was absolutely critical to their success in the field. The degree of risk inherent in a given firm's foreign exchange operations was determined principally by the quality of credit information flowing from one's English representatives.

The New York partners, on the other hand, were generally responsible for directing and coordinating the buying and selling activities of the American outlets. From an operational standpoint, they established the firm's quoted selling rates and communicated all the adjustments in those rates to the various offices via the telegraph. In addition, the New York partners managed the investment of cash seasonally accumulated in the northern branches and later oversaw the transfer of those funds to the southern outlets. At the same time, they usually consulted their Liverpool counterparts before making a decision to cover a deficit balance in the exchange account with specie or merchandize shipments in place of the normal remittances of sterling bills. (7)

Since adjustments in the exchange account were possible on a weekly or even a daily basis, the Liverpool and New York offices continually discussed market tactics in the interbranch correspondence. In this planning process, the role of the Liverpool partners was essentially an advisory one because the actual implementation of shifts in the firm's position had to be initiated on the American side, where sterling bills were bought and sold. In the meantime, the mix of sterling debits and credits converging on the Liverpool branch in any given week was difficult to foresee. Therefore, the resident partners, who were Francis Hamilton and Mark Collet in the fifties, had the strictly operational task of managing the English account in light of the latest transatlantic advices of bill sales and purchases. (8) In sum, the major responsibility for meeting the firm's financial obligations was placed squarely on the shoulders of the Liverpool partners. When the firm's plans went awry, it was they who felt the pressure most intensely.

Since they were regularly burdened with the task of financing the seasonal deficit during the autumn and early winter months, it is little wonder that Collet and Hamilton were consistent advocates of a strengthening in the branch's overall liquidity. In a letter to the New York office in February 1852, the Liverpool managers discussed the procedures that were customarily followed in raising the funds to replenish a temporarily weakened cash balance. Inasmuch as the letter was written during the height of the buying season in the southern ports, Collet and Hamilton began by urging the New York partners to keep them 'well supplied' with bill remittances over the next few months. Because the American branches were slow in covering their overdrawn accounts, the Liverpool partners were quite concerned about the reasons for the general delay. Collet and Hamilton expressed a great interest in working their way back to a position where they would not have to discount any acceptances that had not been held by the branch for a minimum of twenty to thirty days. (9) 'All we wish to avoid is to be obliged habitually to convert our remittances immediately after they are accepted, as it might be construed as arising from a paucity of means, of which we would not even wish to be suspected', they explained. (10)

In a broad statement of their basic managerial philosophy, Hamilton and Collet also articulated for their New York counterparts their own attitude about raising funds through borrowing against the firm's security holdings:

> With regard to borrowing on Stock we should be decidedly averse to resorting to such a course, if we had to do it in the open market, & nothing short of necessity would induce us to take a step so unusual for a House occupying the position we do; but so long as we can get any advance upon them we may want, from our own Bankers, who know our circumstances & position, we should simply consult our own convenience in using these securities or not; but even with our Bankers

> we should first exhaust our Bills - as being the usual, recognized & legitimate mode of raising money . . . (11)

Throughout the 1850's, the Liverpool partners argued in favor of a reallocation of capital resources away from allegedly speculative investments in American securities and into more liquid assets that would build up the working capital and secondary reserves of the house. Although the Browns did not actually use the modem terminology in their correspondence, they did distinguish between capital that was 'available' for use in their normal business transactions and that which was 'locked up' n real estate, steamship lines, and railroad issues. Any outside investment was considered to be 'locked up' by the Liverpool partners if they felt it could not be used as a source of ready cash in a time of need. Thus, only those assets that could serve as collateral for a loan from the most respectable English bankers were qualified for listing among the firm's so-called 'legitimate' reserves. The whole question of the allocation of capital and the nature of the firm's investments was an issue of divisiveness within the partnership for many years because there was no consensus among the members about the real purpose that would be served by maintaining a high degree of liquidity in Liverpool.

The debate over an enlarged working capital for the English branch had two main aspects. It was partly a matter of making adequate preparations for unforeseen financial panics and other emergencies and partly a matter of improving the firm's prestige in the world of international finance. The New York partners favored the allocation of only a moderate amount of the firm's resources to the management of foreign exchange operations. They conceded that the English branch required sufficient funds to maintain solvency and to retain some degree of flexibility in the administration of the firm's sterling account. At the same time, it was felt that a certain amount of pressure was to be periodically expected in Liverpool and a heavy reliance on borrowed funds, whether obtained directly from other banking houses or in the open market, was predictable. Since large deficits were only a seasonal phenomenon, the New York partners saw no reason for keeping a large portfolio of cash or near cash assets at the service of the Liverpool office on a year-round basis. They believed the holding of large cash balances was too costly in terms of the potential foregone profits from alternative investment channels. Moreover, the New York partners had much confidence in the ability of their overseas associates to manage the account proficiently without an excess of reserves.

Mark Collet and Francis Hamilton, on the other hand, had a more ambitious goal. They hoped to elevate the firm (and themselves) to the stature of the House of Baring in the eyes of the commercial world. This could be accomplished, they believed, by keeping sufficient funds available in cash or near cash assets so as to eliminate entirely their reliance on the discount market. In view of their more extensive foreign exchange operations in the American market, however, there was some question in the New York office about whether the Barings' conspicuous liquidity was a valid basis for a realistic comparison of the financial strength of the two houses. All agreed that an extraordinarily liquid position was one of the hallmarks of a great banking enterprise, but many of the American partners did not feel it was an absolute prerequisite for distinguished status. They viewed the Barings' attitude against discounts as an expensive luxury that was not justifiable on the basis of even the most conservative banking principles. (12) Nor were they willing to forego the financial leverage which borrowing in the discount market added to the firm's capital structure.

The whole issue was also clouded because the Liverpool partners did not discuss their needs in terms of specific amounts. As a result, the senior men in New York found it impossible to determine how much working capital was realistically required for the normal functioning of the exchange account and how much was being sought for non-quantifiable factors relating to prestige. In this internal debate which raged for almost an entire decade, the New York position was progressively weakened, however, as their outside investments failed to yield the anticipated returns. The absence of any great success in financial fields beyond the firm's niche of expertise encouraged Collet and Hamilton to marshal, and exploit to the fullest, every conceivable argument in favour of investing more funds in U.S. government bonds and British consols.

Although they failed to attain their maximum goal of avoiding discounts, Hamilton and Collet were able to convince their New York associates to increase steadily the liquidity of the Liverpool branch. The improvement in their position was reflected in a decreasing reliance on discounts for financing during the 1850's. In the first half of the decade, the Liverpool partners often raised from £300,000 to £500,000 per month in the discount market. (13) The vast majority of the loans were negotiated directly with their London bankers, Denison Heywood Kennard & Co. and successor firms. It was their policy to confine most transactions to the private discount market and to avoid, thereby, borrowing in the more publicly visible 'open market' for foreign acceptances. In December 1852, the Liverpool partners reported that they were rarely forced to turn to the open market any more often than 'twice during the year. (14)

Two financial statements from the late fifties are illustrative of the strengthened working capital position of the Liverpool branch. The first shows that the Browns relied on discounted acceptances for only 40 per cent of their requirements during the Panic of 1857--a period when many Anglo-American bankers, including George Peabody, were on the verge of insolvency. Collet and Hamilton broke down their figures for the final quarter of 1857:

In Oct., Nov. & Dec. our payments were		£2,253m
Toward which documents applied		854m
Of these discounts we took from		
Bk of England	129	
Alexanders	170	
Overends	17	

The remaining £518,000 had been supplied by their London bankers, Heywood Kennard & Co. (15)

Another statement prepared one year later summarized the branch's experience over the last half of 1858. In the letter accompanying their presentation the Liverpool managers pointed with pride to the fact that only £40,000 of their borrowing had been in the open market. (16) One part of the summary gave a monthly breakdown of their acceptance payments in thousands of pounds:

July	£ 729	Oct.	£ 465
Aug.	651	Nov.	582
Sept.	607	Dec.	475
	Total		£ 3,509m

This breakdown is especially valuable because, given a two or three month lag, the payment schedule roughly paralleled the earlier pattern of sales of 60 d/s sterling bills by the American offices. Another part of the statement listed the monthly discounts:

July	£ 86,038	Nov.	149,733
Aug. – Oct..	none	Dec.	135,472
		Total	£ 372,263

During the last quarter of 1858, discounts had provided only about 20 per cent of the branch's requirements.

Yet the Liverpool partners also disclosed that there had been times during the year when they had borrowed funds from the Bank of Liverpool which were repayable on demand. The loans were secured by their bills receivable and carried a very favourable interest rate of 0.5 per cent below the current market rate for prime acceptances. The tone of the correspondence seemed to indicate that the arrangement with the Bank of Liverpool was a new departure from the established mode of raising funds. At the same time, it was revealed that Brown, Shipley & Co. had sometimes returned the favour and loaned funds to the bank on call whenever the cash account had shown a temporary surplus. In previous years, the branch had frequently used idle balances to payoff outstanding acceptance liabilities before the normal sixty days had transpired. By paying their obligations in advance, the Liverpool managers were able to liquidate their liabilities at less than their face values, and savings were the equivalent of interest revenue. In other words, the partners occasionally entered the money market on the supply side and discounted bills on themselves for other borrowers. The informal agreement with the Bank of Liverpool thereafter provided an alternative channel for putting idle balances to work, and with the maximum of flexibility.

In reviewing the branch's financial records for 1858, several points are worth a brief analysis. First, it is apparent that the borrowings of £371,000 for the entire second half of the year were even less than the amounts often required in a single month at the beginning of the decade on approximately the same volume of transactions. The schedule of discounts also shows how the deficiencies in the Liverpool account began to build up during the late Autumn and early winter; this was the natural outcome of heavy sterling sales during the preceding months in the United States. Real relief came later in the spring when the remittances of sixty-day bills from the firm's outlets in the South finally began to mature. In 1858 complete coverage of the interbranch account had not occurred until sometime during the month of July.

By the end of the decade, the Liverpool partners had persuaded their counterparts in New York to redirect the firm s resources away from speculative investments and into assets that stressed greater safety and more liquidity. The partnership's involvement with a diversity of outside business interests was sharply reduced, and the movement toward further specialization in dollar-sterling operations and other financial services for the foreign trade sector of the Anglo-American economy was intensified. In August 1958, the New York branch bought $500,000 of U.S. government bonds for a recently created 'reserves fund. (17) When new articles of partnership were drawn up in 1860, they provided for the purchase of £180,000 of Consols for the English Reserve Fund. (18) With the creation of these reserve funds, the firm had assumed more of the attributes of a conservatively and prudently managed banking house. Its impregnable strength was communicated to the broad commercial community through a greater degree of financial independence as evidenced by a lessened reliance on the discount market.

Beyond the management of the sterling account, another major responsibility of Liverpool partners could be broadly described as information gathering In this activity, the scope of their interests was extremely varied. However, most of the information they accumulated can be classified into two main categories: that which was likely to have an affect on the Anglo-American economy generally or an identifiable group of businessmen within the economy and that which was related to the credit standing of individual firms active in the American trade. In the former category, the Liverpool branch communicated to the New York partners virtually every economic and political development in Europe or the British Empire which might have an impact on business conditions or foreign exchange rates. In fact, the actual developments routinely reported were so diverse that they defy characterization. Only a few of the more important topics can be mentioned here. Special significance was usually attributed to large specie shipments, large capital movements, changes in the Bank of England's rediscount rate, the state of the cotton market, major business failures, and war rumors. At the same time, it can be said that the Liverpool partners tended to emphasize those events which were expected to have a detrimental affect on international trade. On those occasions they advised caution and sometimes an actual reduction of sterling sales in the United States.

A series of letters written during the spring of 1854 after the outbreak of the Crimean War illustrate both the range of factors analyzed by the Liverpool partners and the policy recommendations they proposed in response to emerging developments. To explain in narrative form the contents of the letters and the context within which each was written, however, would require a longer exposition than space allows. But the essence of the material can be covered expeditiously, and for our purposes quite adequately, with resort to the capsule summary. (19) Six of the most important notes recorded in the partners' private letterbook from March to June, in 1854, will suffice:

> 25 March 1854 - Collet and Hamilton to Brown Brothers & Co., New York
>
> The Crimean crisis only shows that the best policy is to keep large means in England & not locked up in the U.S. Two main reasons are more safety in case of stringency & greater ease in expanding letter of credit & foreign exchange business.
>
> 27 March 1854 - Collet and Hamilton to William Brown in London
>
> We fear war and high interest rates. We have asked New York to send us enough first class bills so we can stay clear of the discount market or at least not have to rely on it for upwards of £500,000 per month as now. Their sales of exchange should be appropriately limited. We hope our government will keep on friendly footing with the U.S. The government & ministers should not meddle in trade but let it take care of itself or it is sure to involve them in trouble.
>
> 29 March 1854 - Collet and Hamilton to William Brown in London
>
> A review of our financial condition shows £585 m in lockups of one sort or another & only £385 m of available capital. The London bill brokers will do nothing at under 5.5 per cent. With cotton declining in price, we see a disposition of payees to refuse acceptance. We worry about the drain in gold which will no doubt be caused by a foreign war.
>
> 12 May 1854 - Collet and Hamilton to New York
>
> The Bank of England raised its rate 0..5 per cent yesterday to 5.5 per cent. We are glad to learn you are considering borrowing against some of your securities. We would concur in a loan of substance for 12 months even at an interest rate of 7 per cent. The money could be used here as a reserve; our greatest desire is to be prepared.
>
> 30 May 1854 - Collet and Hamilton to New York
>
> There are many houses here who would extend us broad discount facilities, but it is best to prepare for the worst. If, on the other hand, we could come through a crisis with little resort to the open market, it would be a source of much pride. We think you should avoid opening all letters of credit which have the slightest chance of becoming lockups - even with regular customers.

> 9 June 1854 - Collet and Hamilton to New York
> We would not object if you temporarily increased your sales in working a profitable exchange operation so long as it was at a rate that could be covered profitably in gold. if we are short of remittances. We appear to be in good shape this month even without gold.

Despite the urgency of their dispatches, a serious financial crisis was avoided, and by mid-summer it was business as usual. One false alarm did not, however, outweigh the advantages of an almost constant monitoring of new developments in the Anglo-American economy. The value of such information to the organization as a whole was incalculable; in 1857 it helped to bring them through a genuine crisis with ease--so much so in fact that the house achieved the lofty stature which Collet and Hamilton had been so actively seeking.

The most time consuming phase of information gathering was the maintenance of credit files on the host of English firms who were frequently named as payees by American bill drawers. The credit ratings based on these files were disseminated throughout the Browns' banking chain, and the information served to guide the outlets in their purchasing activities. Any significant change in the status of a potential payee was quickly communicated to the various American representatives through the regular correspondence, which the Liverpool branch routinely carried on with all the firm's outlets. By the early fifties, their files included reports on approximately 2,000 names. The list of firms covered ranged from their major competitors in the foreign exchange field to those wholesalers and manufacturers who regularly purchased American raw materials and foodstuffs on their own account. Without up-to-date information, large-scale foreign exchange operations were an extraordinarily risky venture because the purchase of only one or two bad bills drawn in moderate amounts could easily wipe out a whole year's profits.

In assessing a firm's credit position, there were three main considerations. The means, or wealth, of the parties involved was a factor of critical importance. During the second half of the century, more firms began employing the limited partnership form of business organization, and the Browns then had to keep closer track of the exact amount of capital an individual invested in each separate enterprise. A firm's reputation for promptly and judiciously meeting its obligations was almost equally emphasized. The third factor for consideration was a firm's volume of business relative to its estimated resources. Even large businesses with solid reputations might come under unusual scrutiny if they were suspected of 'overtrading'. But the cause of most alterations in a firm's standing was a change in the partnership alignment. Shifts in a firm's membership were common in the commercial community, and keeping apprized of the latest additions and withdrawals was a meticulous task.

The sources of the Liverpool office's credit information are not fully known. Much of it came from the firm's themselves; and more was supplied by their bankers and creditors. Because many names were located outside of Liverpool, the Browns had to rely on correspondents to provide them with a fair amount of their information. One exchange of letters in 1859 with the National Bank of Scotland in Glasgow provides a good example of how credit inquiries were then handled. The correspondence was initiated by Brown, Shipley & Co. on 18 April 1859:

> We shall feel much obliged by your particular confidential report upon the means & present standing of Peter Buchanan & Co. of your city. Your last report marked them '2' which we rather think is not quite equal to the position they at one time held ... The immediate object of our inquiry is to arrive at some amount which we might safely & prudently hold of their acceptances at one time running . . . we should esteem it a favour if you could suggest a line which it would be prudent to keep running ....(20)

The bank's answer was dated 21 April, and it read in part:

> PB &Co. enjoy a good reputation here, we may almost say of undoubted credit. They keep their account here entirely with the Union Bank of Scotland. The business had been well & successfully conducted. We do not know the precise capital of the Coy, but we learn, on very good authority that P.B. is worth £200,000 chiefly in the business. He is a bachelor, cautious to a degree, careful, clear headed & saving. Mr Harris who is also a bachelor, has at least £80,000 in the business. . . We may mention that . . . Drafts pass through our Hands, from time to time, for acceptance on account of one of our Banking Correspondents - the aggregate fluctuating from £3 or £4,000 to £10,000, or thereby, current at a time. . . We have endeavoured to procure & send you as much information as can well be done by Letter - & this we hope may enable you to determine what line it may be prudent for you to keep running.... (21)

Upon receipt, the Liverpool partners made a copy of the letter and sent it to the New York office for reference. On the basis of the 'strength' indicated by the report, they wrote, 'you cannot go wrong with a line of £10,000 (548,000) running'. (22) The suggested limit was only 3 per cent of the reported capital and appeared to them safe enough.

The acceptance line referred to in the correspondence was one of the key managerial tools employed by the Browns' in their foreign exchange activities. The decision to establish revolving lines on British payees was made in response to the economic disturbances of 1847. Because the U.S. economy was not seriously affected by that European recession, the Browns and the other Anglo-American bankers were spared too many setbacks. But the experience frightened the partners, nonetheless, and they were soon examining their overall operations with an eye to improvements. One proposal favourably received was the establishment of definite limits on the amounts of bills that would be purchased in the U.S. on specific payees during any given sixty day period. (23) The plan was expected to act as a check on 'over-expansion' and, at the same time, ensure that the portfolio of acceptances held by the Liverpool branch would be well diversified.

The actual setting of limits, or more accurately guidelines, was a responsbility shared by the two main offices, but in practice the New York partners generally deferred to the judgement of the Liverpool managers. A given line might call for either clean bills or documentary bills depending on a firm's capital, the nature of its transactions, and the extent of its business activity. Some lines were a combination of both--for example, clean bills up to £20,000 and an additional £15,000 with bills of lading attached. As the years passed, the trend among exchange buyers was to insist on the bill of lading in a higher proportion of transactions. Eventually the stigma of inferiority that was originally associated with the documentary bill of exchange dissipated. Finally in the 1860's and 1870's, bills of lading were almost universally required with drafts against the two most important U.S. exports, cotton and breadstuffs.

The guidelines were not always rigidly enforced, and there was generally room for some leeway on individual payees. The identity of the original drawer could also be an important factor in determining the extent of their purchases. In May 1859, for instance, the Liverpool house told the New York office that they would be 'glad to keep as low as possible' certain classes of bills. Among them were Harper & Co. on E. Ridings & Bros, Don Rose on Wm. Anderton, and Thos. Rogers, Jr. & Co. on John Greaves. On the last named, they added the following:

> We have now £40,700 running upon him & he has probably as much or more through other channels, and we do not know how much of his Cotton he holds. Still he ought to be good upon his own means, & we would not imply that you might not take some ore on him with BfLdg from sound drawers, but that you should keep your eye on the line. (24)

The same cautious attitude was exhibited in regulating their holdings against other prominent Anglo-American banking houses as well. The only exception was, of course, the Barings whose bills, in any amount, were never questioned. With George Peabody & Co., on the other hand, they were far more careful. Doubts about the eagerness with which they had taken Peabody's bills arose as early as 1852. At a dinner party given by William Brown in November 1852 Peabody stated to the host that his outstanding acceptances were then approximately £1,000,000 and that they had been as high as £1,200,000. The Liverpool partners relayed the details of the conversation to the New York branch and added a comment of their own, 'It is strange if his engagements are only a million that we should hold one fifth--certainly more than our share'. (25)

One of the most revealing letters written by the Liverpool partners during the late 1850'S concerned the confidentiality of credit information--such as that volunteered by George Peabody. What makes their letter unusually interesting is the information it conveys about the relationship between the partners and their subordinates and agents in other cities. The correspondence dated January 1859 began as follows:

> Your private letter. . . is before us, and we sincerely regret to observe the difference of opinion that still obtains between us, as to the mode of dealing with information about parties communicated to us in confidence, which we transmit to you under the same reserve. We must suppose that it arises from the different footing & understanding upon which such confidential information is given & received on the two sides of the Atlantic, for you are clearly in error when you express your belief that 'Banks & others communicating to us in confidence' facts relating to the means & transactions of parties (of which we could have knowledge thro' no other channel), suppose that we shall communicate the same to all our agents throughout the U. States!

On the contrary, the Liverpool partners wrote, the supposition in England was that they would form their own estimate of the parties based on the information given in confidence, and thereupon give merely instructions about the handling of those bills in question to their agents and subordinates. The facts per se, on the other hand, they could not 'in good faith or honour give . . . a wider circulation' than among the bona fide partners of the firm. This argument, advanced earlier by the New York office, Collet and Hamilton completely rejected:

> The line you draw. . . that all Agents you have. . . are entitled to all the information bearing upon the standing of drawees, that come into your possession, includes not only the Agents themselves, but the clerks. . . in charge during their absence are unknown to us sometimes even by name -- as deserving of the same confidence in the use of such information, as those who are your own partners; this surely is an assumption quite beyond the fact .

Moreover, it was not really necessary for the branch managers to know all the contents of the private correspondence, the Liverpool partners claimed, 'since after all it is you, not they, who regulate the lines you take on these names and the conditions on which they are taken . . .' Although they were, as a rule, fully devoted to the proposition that subordinates should possess all the facts required for the safe conduct of their part of the business, Collet and Hamilton believed that in this instance there had to be some limits. If such limits were not imposed, then they were in danger of eventually losing the confidence of their informants. (26)

The credit files maintained by the Liverpool partners were not exclusively for the benefit of the American outlets. Collet and Hamilton also drew on the information they had accumulated in making decisions about when to release bills of lading on the documentary bills of exchange remitted to them for collection. So long as the Liverpool branch held the bill of lading, the Browns in effect owned the merchandise against which the original sterling bill had been drawn. After receiving a documentary bill of exchange, the Liverpool partners usually had several options at their disposal. If the drawee's credit rating was satisfactory, the B/L was often handed over at the time of acceptance. By accepting the draft, the payee formally and legally acknowledged his financial obligation. If, on the other hand, the drawee's credit standing was questionable, the partners held the bill of lading until the acceptance was actually paid.

The Browns were not the only parties who had a direct stake in the acceptance and payment of a remitted bill of exchange. In the United States, their representatives never bought a bill without the seller's endorsement, and if the bill was ultimately dishonoured, the Browns immediately had recourse to seller for reimbursement of the original purchase price. Therefore, it was as much for the protection of their American customer as for themselves that the Liverpool partners exercised their judgement on the release of a given B/L. In most cases, the U.S. bill sellers left the whole matter to the discretion of the Liverpool partners, but some sellers were permitted to specify that their lien be preserved until final payment was actually made. Although the vast majority of the remitted bills were routinely processed, there was always the risk of non-acceptance or non-payment or both. Regardless of the cause of the irregularity, the Browns invariably acted swiftly and expertly in seeking a solution to the problem. This was a bonus American exporters received when they elected to sell their sterling to the House of Brown.

The amount of time and energy often expended in the collection of one dishonoured bill was sizeable. Inevitably, some English importers failed in the interim between shipment and a bill's expected due date. In other cases, a sharp drop in the price of a commodity frequently induced the drawees to discover excuses for non-acceptance. The most prevalent reason given for non-acceptance of a bill of exchange was the receipt of a cargo of an allegedly inferior grade of cotton or grain. Some situations were not resolved until the Liverpool managers were able to transfer the commodity and the financial obligation to an alternative importer. On other occasions, they sold the cargo outright through local brokers. The best word to describe most of these predicaments would be 'messy'; in settling many of the disagreements between buyer and seller the partners sounded as much like lawyers as bankers.

Some managerial decisions were rarely made without preliminary consultations between the New York and Liverpool branches. One of the more important topics falling within the area of shared responsibility was the coverage of their foreign exchange account through any form of remittance other than the standard bill of exchange. Thus, the senior partners in both branches generally participated in the discussions which--on occasion--led to the partial reimbursement of the Liverpool account with the proceeds from a transatlantic transfer of securities, specie, or merchandise. Of the, three main alternatives to the sterling bill of exchange, specie shipments were by far the most significant because of their frequency and their relationship to movements in the dollar-sterling exchange rate. (27)

By the 1850's, gold shipments from the U.S. to England were a regular feature of the firm's foreign exchange cycle. Most transfers were concentrated in the months from June to November when sterling sales in the United States normally exceeded bill purchases by a wide margin. With a well-timed schedule of shipments, the Liverpool partners were rarely forced to rely heavily on the discount market for financing.

A series of letters addressed to the New York branch by the Liverpool partners in 1859 illustrate the planning of specie transactions. In the first letter, dated 29 April, Collet and Hamilton spoke of their need to begin the seasonal discounting of acceptances within the next two or three weeks. (28) For their maximum convenience in meeting commitments, they suggested a specie shipment in preference to bill remittances. The proceeds of the gold would be used 'to supply our first heavy deficiency in June', they explained. Interestingly enough, no mention was made of how high the sterling premium would have to rise before this alternative method of covering the account would be economically justified. In correspondences one week later, however, the Liverpool partners were more explicit about the conditions under which specie should be shipped. Gold was still their first choice over sterling bills, 'even if you have to send it without profit', but they were 'not yet prepared to ask you to ship any at a loss'. (29)

In two letters written later in 1859, Hamilton and Collet demonstrated that there were many situations in which the relative prices of sterling bills and specie could be a prime consideration in determining the coverage mix. The low costs reportedly incurred by a few of the firm's major competitors on a recent series of specie transfers came up for discussion in the correspondence of 29 July. The freight rate on gold bars by the latest steam-powered screwboats was put at only one-eighth to three-sixteenths of a per cent. If the bars had been bought at par in the United States, Collet and Hamilton noted, the gold remittance would 'stand' at under $4.884 in England and perhaps as little as $4.873, provided the specie had been immediately sold for export to the continent. (30) Maybe, they suggested, the New York partners had been unaware of these low freight rates. Since the firm's American selling rate was most recently reported as $4.906, the Liverpool partners argued that it would be better to send gold than sterling bills whenever the covering rate was in the range of $4.884 to $4.895. (31) Basing their calculations on the most favour-able outcome of a gold shipment, it was estimated that the firm could improve its profit margin on exchange transactions from the normal 0.5 per cent to perhaps 0.68 per cent, an increase of approximately one-third.

In their response the New York partners maintained that they had been deterred from shipping specie by the difficulty of obtaining gold in bar form. And gold coin they did not like to ship 'except at a profit on the worst result of it when melted and sent into the Bank (of England)', which the Liverpool branch had calculated to be $4.895. (32) However, Collet and Hamilton took exception to this statement in their letter of 26 August. It was their opinion that it was 'always worth while to give Specie the preference over Bills when at the worst result of the coin or Bullion you can do as well as with Bills'. (33) On the basis of the behaviour of their American counterparts in the following months, it appears that the arguments of Collet and Hamilton were persuasive. When, in the face of rising demand, the New York partners jumped their selling rate from $4.884 to $4.906 in the last days of October, they did not miss the opportunity to cover a portion of their sales with a transfer of gold. In a letter dated 22 October, the New York branch divulged the details of the shipment to the manager of the Baltimore office:

> We sent per City of Washington $300,000 gold at ½ per cent freight to BS &C which remits us equal to sixty d/s bills at less than 10 per cent, or $4.8841. (34)

A specie shipment at this time of the year had not been originally planned, the New York partners explained a few days later, but the 'early cold snap of weather did not extend far enough south to effect the rate of exchange as we had anticipated, causing a temporary scarcity of bills'. (35) A month later, the firm was actively purchasing sterling in the South at $4.795 or less, and all talk of gold remittances ceased for the next four or five months. For the year as a whole, the New York branch had shipped gold valued at around £600,000 to the Liverpool office. This sum accounted for close to 6 per cent of all the firm's remittances in 1859. (36)

The Browns' correspondence suggests strongly that the gold adjustment mechanism functioned almost exclusively through the foreign exchange dealer. Very few of the firm's customers seem to have initiated their own specie transfers as an alternative to the sterling bill. Although many complained of steep rates and energetically sought out lower prices from competitive dealers, this researcher did not come across a single instance in which a customer threatened to ship gold rather than pay the Browns' rates. Even at a very high premium, sterling sales were often brisk. In fact, it was only during a financial panic that the sterling premium ever climbed high enough in the United States to induce the general public to attempt the settlement of international debts with specie. When this happened in 1857, as it had twenty years earlier, the commercial banks promptly suspended specie payments, and the price of gold was allowed to float upward along with the sterling rate. Any incentive to substitute specie for sterling bills was quickly thwarted. (37)

The gold points, it seems, had no practical relevance to any business group other than the larger foreign exchange dealers like the Barings and the Browns. The costs of smaller, more irregular specie shipments were such that the commercial banks in the United States had invariably suspended payment before the typical merchant found it profitable to forego sterling bills for gold. In sum, it might be said that there were limits to the gold points themselves. A moderately high premium would stimulate an outflow of specie to England by the exchange dealers, but an extremely high sterling rate inevitably led to suspension and a reversion to the bill of exchange.

In the handling of gold shipments, as in the management of their overall dollar-sterling exchange operations, the Browns benefited greatly from the advantages inherent in their organizational structure. The existence of branch offices in both England and the United States was a crucial factor in the firm's success. Of course, the administrative structure alone was not sufficient to boost the Browns to a position of leadership in the Anglo-American foreign exchange market. It also required personnel who were thoroughly trained; who could exercise sound judgement in difficult situations; and who were attuned to the co-operative spirit which permeated the whole organization. In Liverpool, the firm was represented around the mid-century by Francis Hamilton and Mark Collet, two men of extraordinary administrative ability.

During the 1850's, Collet and Hamilton waged a long campaign against the inappropriateness of investments in new ventures beyond the traditional scope of the firm's activities. They continually advocated the allocation of a greater portion of the firm's capital to reserve funds, which would strengthen the partnership's position in the dollar-sterling exchange market. It was not until the next decade, however, that the validity of their point of view was, in a sense, formally recognized. Stewart Brown, one of the senior partners in the New York branch, admitted as much in a letter written in the autumn of 1864. (38) He attributed most of the credit for the firm's splendid position--'having free all our capital'--to the Liverpool partners. There had been a time when a large portion of the partnership assets was locked up in outside investments. It was only after Collet and Hamilton had become active managers in the early fifties, Stewart Brown wrote, that Liverpool had begun 'giving us statements. . . of the active capital in the business showing how small a part of our means were free and urging us not to put out any more in unavailable things however good'. At the time, some of the senior partners in New York had taken 'very unkindly' to some of their recommendations, but they had 'proved to be right'. Moreover, he admitted that they had been right about the handling of the foreign exchange account, although he himself had been among those who were originally 'impatient at their suggestions'.

The leadership exhibited by the managers of Brown, Shipley & Co. in the 1850's and 1860's was, in summary, a crucial factor which explains in large part why the House of Brown was able to maintain a dominant position in the Anglo-American foreign exchange market during the third quarter of the nineteenth century.

Notes

1. Brown, Shipley and Co., Liverpool, to Brown Brothers and Co., New York, 9 February 1855, in Brown, Shipley and Company Papers (Liverpool Public Library); hereafter abbreviated BS&CP. Photocopies of the correspondence can be found in the historical files of Brown Brothers Harriman and Co., New York City.
2. Edwin J. Perkins, 'The House of Brown: America's Foremost International Bankers, 1800-1880' (Unpublished dissertation; Johns Hopkins University, 1972)
3. Aytoun Ellis, *Heir of Adventure: The Story of Brown, Shipley and Co., Merchant Bankers* (London, 1960).
4. Ralph Hidy, *The House of Baring in American Trade and Finance: English Merchant Bankers at Work, 1763-1861* (Cambridge, Mass. 1949), and Muriel Hidy, 'George Peabody: Merchant and Financier, 1839-1854' (Unpublished Ph.D. dissertation, Radcliffe College, Cambridge, Mass., 1939). For information on another important house in the Anglo-American trade, see Sheila Marriner, *Rathbones of Liverpool, 1843-73* (Liverpool, 1961).
5. Arthur H. Cole, 'Seasonal Variation in Sterling Exchange', *Journal of Economic and Business History*, II (1929/30), 203-218.
6. G. H. Conder, 'Bills of Exchange: The Part They Have Played in English Banking, Past and Present', *Journal of the Institute of Bankers* (October, 1889), 415-441; A. P. Usher, 'The Origin of the Bill of Exchange', *Journal of Political Economy* (June, 1914), 566-576.
7. George Goschen, *The Theory of Foreign Exchanges* (London, 1863); Paul Einzig, *The History of Foreign Exchange* (London, 1962).
8. William Brown, who founded the Liverpool office in 1810, spent much of his time after 1840 in London where he served as an M.P.; he died in 1864. Joseph Shipley, who was largely responsible for bringing the house through the panic of 1837, retired from the firm in 1851. Francis Hamilton began his association with the house in an apprentice capacity and was invited to join the partnership in the 1840's. Mark Collet was employed as a sub-manager of the Bank of Liverpool just prior to accepting a partnership in 185I, upon Shipley's retirement.
9. W. T. C. King, *History of the London Discount Market* (London, 1936).
10. Brown, Shipley, and Co., Liverpool to Brown Brothers and Co., New York, 18 February 1852, BS&CP.
11. *Loc. cit.*
12. For a review of the Barings' attitude toward discounting see Ralph Hidy, *House of Baring*, 149.
13. Francis Hamilton to William Brown, 4 June 1852 and 27 March 1854, BS&CP.
14. BS &C, Liverpool to BB &C, New York, 28 December 1852, BS&CP.
15. Ibid., 1 January 1858.
16. *Ibid.*, 1 January 1859.
17. *Ibid.*, 3 August 18S8.
18. James Brown to BB & Co., New York, I3 November 1860; Historical Files (Brown Brothers Harriman and Co., New York).
19. All the letters can be found in the Brown, Shipley and Co. collection at the Liverpool Public Library.
20. BS&C, Liverpool to the National Bank of Scotland, Glasgow, 18 Apri11859, BS& CP.
21. John Hart, Agent, The National Bank of Scotland to BS&C, Liverpool, 2 April 1859,

BS&CP.
22. BS&C, Liverpool to BB&C, New York, 23 April 1859, BS &CP.
23. Stewart Brown, New York to Joseph Shipley, Liverpool, 17 February 1848, BS &CP.
24. BS&C, Liverpool to BB&C, New York, 2 May 1854, BS&CP.
25. *Ibid.*, 25 November 1852.
26. *Ibid.*, 25 January, 1859.
27. Lance Davis and J. R. T. Hughes, 'A Dollar-Sterling Exchange, 1803-1895', *Economic History Review*, XU (1960), 52-78.
28. BS &C, Liverpool to BB &C, New York, 29 April 1859, BS&CP.
29. *Ibid.*, 3 May 1859.
30. The mint par figure, which did not include any transportation costs, was $4.8665 to the pound,
31. As a rule, the Browns purchased sterling bills at $0.025 below their current selling rate; this gave them a 0.5 per cent gross margin on most transactions.
32. The New York partners' remarks were quoted in BS&C, Liverpool to BB&C, New York, 26 August 1859. BS&CP.
33. *Loc. cit.*
34. BB&C, New York to William Graham, Baltimore, 22 October 1859; Brown Brothers and Co. Papers (New York Public Library).
35. *Ibid.*, 25 October 1859.
36. The total amount of sterling and specie remitted in 1859 was £9.92.9,833 or approximately $44.640,000. All the figures are found in BS&C, Liverpool to BB&C, New York, 2.2 February and 24 March, 1860, BS&CP.
37. On this point, see Peter Temin, *The Jacksonian Economy* (New York k, 1969). 145.
38. Stewart Brown, New York to James Brown, visiting in Europe, 27 October 1864, Historical Files (Brown Brothers Harriman and Co.).

Chapter Eight

Tourists and Bankers: Travelers' Checks and the Rise of American Tourism, 1840-1900

The second half of the 19th century witnessed the rise American tourism. Prior to 1850, the number of Americans traveling overseas to view the sights of Europe or to take long restful vacations was relatively small. Even on the largest and fastest sailing packets, quarters were cramped, the food was often unappealing, and the voyage lasted from three to five weeks and sometimes longer, depending on wind and weather. Then improvements in ocean transportation suddenly changed the whole character of overseas travel. First, engineers successfully adapted steam propulsion to ocean-going vessels, then shipping entrepreneurs took advantage of the new technology, and began the construction of completely new ships which naval architects now designed primarily to transport passengers rather than goods. The initiation of regular steamship service between the United States and Europe in the late 1840s brought more spacious and comfortable accommodations, a reasonably palatable cuisine, a generally predictable crossing schedule of 10 to 14 days, and somewhat reduced fares. Upper-class Americans, who could afford the $600 to $900 cost of a three months' vacation in Europe, responded enthusiastically. [5] The number of tourists headed overseas rose from a yearly average of approximately 6,000 in the 1840s to around 30,000 in the late 1850s, and finally grew to 94,000 persons a year in the last decade of the century. [14, 16]

As transportation improved, so too did the ancillary services for the foreign traveler. Guidebooks describing the high spots of European culture as well as handbooks offering practical, down-to-earth advice to the inexperienced tourist proliferated in this era. [9] The package tour, first introduced to the English by Thomas Cook in the 1850s, soon attracted a large number of Americans traveling abroad for the first time. [17] Travel books appearing in the 1860s by William Dean Howells and other less skillful writers whetted the American appetite for foreign adventure and for Old World culture. Howells published his

*Reprinted from *Business and Economic History* (1979), 16-28

Venetian Life in 1866 and followed the next year with *Italian Journeys*; Mark Twain's *Innocents Abroad* reportedly sold 30,000 copies in the first six months after its publication in 1869. [4]

Among the most important of these improved services were expanded financial facilities for the American tourist, particularly the issuance of travelers' letters of credit by the leading international banking houses serving the US market. Over the years these banking firms upgraded their procedures both for issuing traveling credits at home and for handling them overseas. The number of cities in the world where letters of credit were readily accepted grew rapidly after the mid-century. At the same time the cost of this financial service remained low. By making the transfer of dollars to foreign lands easier and by holding down the cost, international bankers aided the movement toward a greater volume of overseas travel.

Moreover, those foreign bankers who acted as correspondents for the leading international houses often performed other services beyond their strictly financial obligations. In order to attract a larger volume of business, the more aggressive correspondents turned their offices into general information centers for wandering Americans. Frequently they acted as overseas post offices for travelers, holding and forwarding their clients' mail. In towns distant from a US consulate, distraught tourists suddenly faced with unexpected problems often sought the aid of the local banker named in their letter of credit. The banking firms participating in this expanded international financial system became in a sense adjunct consulates; they too were prepared to act on behalf of American citizens temporarily away from home. The favors and courtesies extended by foreign bankers were invariably recounted upon a traveler's return to the states, and the confirmation of such reports gave more Americans the courage to embark on transatlantic voyages and the confidence to plan trips to new regions previously considered too remote.

Although the widespread use of travelers' letters of credit carne only in the 19th century, its precursors had been facilitating the transfer of funds over long distances and their conversion into different mediums of exchange for centuries. References to such transactions date back to the ancient world and became more common in the Middle Ages. In its earliest form the letter introduced the visitor to his foreign hosts and vouched for his financial integrity. Normally an important merchant or private banker in the traveler's hometown, or in a nearby commercial center, wrote letters addressed to his counterparts along with the proposed itinerary. These documents became more meaningful to reimburse distant parties for any funds given to the traveler under the terms set forth in the formal letter. As vague introductions matured into firmer guarantees of reimbursement, the main features of the traveler's letter of credit had emerged.

The mechanism of transfer was already fairly well developed by the 16th century. In his *Touring in 1600: A Study of the Development of Travel as a Means of Education*, E. S. Bates, published in 1911, listed the possession of a letter of credit as an alternative to carrying cash and coin on one's person or, more commonly, to having funds sent forward periodically by a friend or merchant residing in the traveler's native town or his main point of departure. Of the three methods of transfer, the letter of credit was the most expensive, Bates explained, although "under favorable circumstances it might cost no more than ten per cent." [1] Still, specific arrangements with foreign bankers and with merchants were necessary far in advance and the number of places such credits could be arranged was limited.

The expansion of the Atlantic economy and the corresponding growth of the great Anglo-American merchant-banking firms such as Baring Bros. & Co. encouraged tourism and created new opportunities for the utilization of travelers' letters of credit. As English bankers acquired an international reputation for financial strength, overseas bankers and foreign exchange dealers readily honored their traveling credits. In the first quarter of the 19th century, the U.S. correspondents of English merchant bankers granted travelers' credits primarily as an accommodation for favored business customers, many of whom simultaneously held commercial letters of credit issued in more substantial sums for buying foreign merchandise. The supplementary credit gave the traveling merchant access to local currency for living expenses and for personal transportation.

It was not until the 1840s that Baring Bros. & Co., the best known Anglo-American merchant-banking firm, found its volume of American traveling credits sufficiently large to justify separate treatment in the bookkeeper's listings of the firm's outstanding credit obligations. [11] Ralph Hidy, the main historian of the House of Baring, analyzed the partners' attitude to this sphere of their business activities. Although the face values of traveling credits were usually small, Hidy revealed, "the labor involved for the Barings was large," since in addition to filling out the various forms, "arrangements for honoring [them]... often had to be made with a score or more houses on the Continent." The remuneration for providing these extra services was very low, however; the normal fee was only 1 percent of the face value of the credit whereas the firm often charged up to 2.5 percent for issuing its profitable commercial letters of credit to importers. Nonetheless, the Barings continued to accommodate customers because "the partners felt it necessary to entertain American travelers and to accord them every courtesy." [11, p. 584]

The Barings' policies show clearly that until mid-century merchant bankers had not viewed the issuance of traveling credits as a profitable activity in its own right. Most bankers hoped that the availability of these credits on very reasonable terms would generate customer goodwill and eventually induce businessmen to direct to them other transactions which were genuinely profitable, such as the issuance of commercial letters of credit or transactions involving foreign exchange.

One of the new financial techniques aiding tourists was the introduction of "circular" letters of credit. The issuing house granted a traveler's credit immediately upon application, and it gave customers a list indicating the names of banking firms in other cities that had agreed in advance to provide local funds upon presentation of the credit document and proper identification. Thereafter, the traveler could plan a long trip without making extensive financial arrangements with overseas bankers prior to departure. The "indication list" was typically printed on the back of the circular credit, and by referring to it along the way travelers could manage their finances more efficiently and with greater convenience. These foreign correspondents usually charged a moderate fee for handling each transaction; in some regions they made an additional profit from the conversion of British pounds into the local currency. When circular letters of credit commonly came into use is difficult to pin down, but a list of correspondents drawn up in 1851 by the House of Brown, an Anglo-American merchant-banking firm which rose to challenge Baring Bros. & Co., contained the names of bankers in 75 cities in Europe, the Levant (Middle East), and India. [15]

The whole market for traveling credits changed dramatically soon after the Cunard Line, in 1848, and the Collins Line, in 1850, began regular steamship service from New York and Boston to Liverpool using new vessels designed to carry 160 to 220 regular passengers in reasonable comfort and up to 40 servants. [5] Other steamship lines offered transatlantic service to France and Germany, usually with a short stopover in Southampton. The number of passengers increased fivefold over the previous decade; many travelers were genuine tourists, not merely businessmen journeying abroad to buy foreign merchandise. "The expense not being more and probably less than traveling in this Country; many are induced to take a Sea voyage," a Brown partner observed in 1855. [2] So many went abroad, in fact, that American tourist expenditures overseas rose from a yearly average of $4.2 million in the 1840s to $21.4 million in the 1850s. [14]

The Brown partners were apparently the first merchant-bankers to appreciate fully the new opportunities in the travelers' credit field. The House of Brown was a geographically dispersed Anglo-American merchant-banking firm which, unlike its competitors, conducted business in the United States mostly through its own branch offices rather than through a chain of independent agents. In addition to offices in New York, Boston, Philadelphia, Baltimore, Mobile, and New Orleans, the Browns also maintained a branch in Liverpool and, after 1863, in London. By the 1840s, the Brown firm had supplanted the Barings as the leading issuer of commercial letters of credit in the American market. Yet the partners had shown little interest in expanding the issuance of traveling credits. Profits were negligible, if they existed at all, and the Browns were not as concerned about making a favorable impression on social, economic, and political elites such as the Barings and George Peabody. [10] Moreover, the firm's English partners disliked the practice of lavishly entertaining and personally catering to the needs of visiting Americans.

The increased number of travelers in the 1850s caused the Browns to reassess their strategies. As the demand for financial services grew, it occurred to some of the partners that with a sufficient volume of travelers' credits and a few slight alterations in their terms of issuance, the business might become genuinely profitable. Thus the Browns devoted new energy to this sphere of their activities, and within a few decades the firm had become the acknowledged leader in the traveling credit field.

One new procedure, which aided tourists and was instrumental in catapulting the Browns into a position of leadership in the field, was the implementation of a plan, in 1859, to expedite the issuance of traveling credits in the United States. Previously, the Browns and most other Anglo-American merchant bankers had required customers to stop by their English offices after the ship's arrival and fill out various forms and documents. Thus, American travelers could only make preliminary arrangements in their port of departure--usually New York; the official paraphernalia was picked up after arriving in England. At the very least, this added step was an inconvenience for some travelers. For the Browns, prior to 1860, it meant that the volume of business was limited to those Americans who planned an initial stop in Liverpool. Those tourists planning to proceed directly to the continent could not be adequately served under this system.

The new procedures were outlined in November 1859: "We have now commenced to issue circular credits here for European travelers," the New York partners announced to the Baltimore branch manager. "We will furnish them to you . . .. upon your giving us the following particulars--the name of the party... by which conveyance he goes out, four separate copies of his signature, .. the amount, and how long you wish it to remain in force." If the time was short, the New York office instructed the branch manager to handle travelers' credits as in the past--that is, to fill out the preliminary forms for the Liverpool partners and to let them "make up the circulars on the other side." [2]

The Liverpool partners optimistically predicted that the improved service would stimulate an increased volume of activity. In correspondence with the New York office in February 1860, they emphasized the potentially large market for travelers' credits. "The totals are small compared to the amount that must be spent by travelers in Europe," they observed; "but as 1859 shows an increase over 1858, so we trust there will soon be a steady and progressive increase, when the additional facilities of your present system of circular credits becomes known." [3] In 1859 the Brown firm had issued travelers credits amounting to $1,225,290--a figure which accounted for 4.6 percent of American tourist expenditures in that year. If the cost of ocean transportation, or approximately $200 per passenger, is deducted from the expenditure figure of $26 million, which seems appropriate, since most Americans undoubtedly purchased a round-trip ticket before departure, then the Browns' share of the potential traveler's letter of credit market was just over 6 percent.

The forecast of improved business proved accurate. American tourists liked the more convenient system of full issuance prior to sailing, and they increasingly used the Browns' circular credits. In 1868 the firm issued $4.8 million--a rising figure that now accounted for approximately 25 percent of the travelers' credits issued in the United States. [3] (1) Indeed, the business expanded so rapidly that the partners became concerned about the large number of foreign bankers requesting placement on the firm's official list of overseas correspondents. In January 1868 the partners managing the new London branch acknowledged that many foreign bankers were already offering service to holders of the firm's travelers' credit on a volunteer basis. When such hospitality was verified by returning American tourists, it put "pressure" on the Browns to add the name to their list of official correspondents.

Nonetheless the London partners disapproved of the efforts of so many foreign bankers to work their way onto the firm's indication list. They felt there was something demeaning about pushing too hard for new business. Moreover, they suspected that "many houses want to get on the list because it appears as if we are in fact *recommending* them & use it to their own advantage." [3] The London partners believed there was still merit in the policy of limiting the number of banking houses in any given city to one or two names. As far as they could determine, tourists were already receiving adequate service, and additional correspondents were not required. They thought, too, that spreading the available business thinly among a host of correspondents would unnecessarily damage these banking houses that had been "our long time friends in these cities." Despite their caution, the Browns had correspondents in over 240 cities throughout the world by 1873 and multiple listings in 59 of those locations. This proliferation of outlets where traveling credits were honored presumably was experienced by other international banking houses as well, and the net effect was to create a more favorable climate for tourism everywhere.

By the late 1860s the Brown partners felt they were making real inroads on the leading position of Baring Bros. & Co. in the travelers' credit field. The London partners offered a partial explanation for the declining influence of the Barings in May 1868. Although their main rivals still retained the edge, the London partners believed they had detected signs of slippage:

> Mr. Russell Sturgis' intimate personal knowledge of so many Americans gives Messrs. Barings an advantage.... but as he has given up the general & almost indiscriminate entertaining & since no other partner... has taken it up, there will less opportunity to maintain personal intercourse, and less room, on the part of travelers to make invidious comparisons in this respect.

Meanwhile, they had done their best to live down their earlier reputation for indifference about this sphere of the business. "We have taken great pains & we think not unsuccessfully to give every possible business attention & facilities to travelers, and frequently receive cordial recognitions for them," the London managers boasted in correspondence with their partners in New York. [3]

After the mid-century, the Browns' strategy was to put the issuance of travelers' credits on a more business-like basis and their approach was more conducive to handling a large volume of transactions in a less personal but more efficient manner. Their positive initiatives came only after there were clear signs that the demand for travelers' credits was rising and that this demand stemmed primarily from tourists who normally cared little for personal contact with the firm's senior partners. The typical tourist did not expect to be wined and dined upon arriving in England; all he wanted was a means of transferring monetary assets overseas that was safe convenient and widely accepted. The Browns' systematic and more efficient method of handling traveling credits was in greater harmony with mass tourism and contributed to its growth.

Popular handbooks for tourists often advised readers about financial matters, and they invariably recommended the circular travelers' credit issued by prominent international banking houses. The most comprehensive publication of its day, Harper's *Handbook for Travelers in Europe and the East*, told its readers in 1873 to deal only with "bankers whose credit stands so high that their names are honored at Paris and Damascus, at Cairo and Vienna, with the same confidence as in New York." [6] In some parts of the world--notably the Black Sea area, Constantinoble. Damascus, and Jerusalem--the handbook's author, W. Pembroke Fetridge, even suggested that travelers might have better luck carrying travelers' credits drawn in French francs on Paris bankers than credits drawn in British pounds, the currency traditionally used by Americans visiting abroad.

Travel writers echoed the advice about the value of travelers' credits. In his Abroad Again; or a Fresh Foray in Foreign Lands, published in 1877, Curtis Guild explained for the edification of the novice exactly how the letter of credit mechanism operated overseas; how for example, a banker in one city deducted the amount of his payment from the funds then available so that future bankers would immediately know the traveler's current financial status. "All bankers on the continent receive tourists politely, have withdrawing room and English and American papers, English-speaking clerks, and a register of tourists in town, for the convenience of those whose drafts they cash," Guild wrote assuredly. "They also receive the letters and papers of the tourists." Bankers on the continent were "courteous and civil," he added, "having learned that the American, if humored, will spend money liberally." [17, p. 32] (2)

According to Guild, the Barings' reputation for catering primarily to VIPs while snubbing the typical tourist was common knowledge. "The banker in England," he informed his American audience, "is considered of the highest grade in the business social circle; only the true blood of nobility is above him." But among the great bankers of London like the Barings and Rothschilds, "there is an impression," the author continued, "that Americans are an inferior race and should be treated accordingly." Americans could pay them back for their alleged arrogance by declining to use their travelers' credits. Some international banking firms were, on the other hand, best avoided because their office facilities in London were substandard. Guild cited MacCalmont Bros. & Co. as one firm with international standing which nonetheless maintained deplorable facilities; its location was bad, the counter space was inadequate, and the waiting room was a matchbox. This inferior firm offered none of the amenities that tourists normally expected by the late 1870s. [7, p. 35]

A second wave of American tourists flocked to Europe in the mid-1880s. The number of yearly tourists passed the 100,000 mark for the first time in 1885; on average 93,600 persons a year crossed the Atlantic in the last decade and half of the century, whereas the average figure had been only 52,600 in the previous fifteen-year period. [16] The steamship had become a floating luxury hotel. It provided not merely transportation but offered a holiday atmosphere throughout the voyage. Indeed, competition between the major shipping lines centered on the provision of extra service and frills. The meals were lavish. Depending on the vessel, passengers had access to smoking rooms, music rooms, libraries, or gymnasiums. To entertain its passengers, the Hamburg-American Line introduced nightly band concerts. Driven by twin-screw propellers, these ocean liners normally made the transatlantic trip in seven days or less. Whole families now went abroad for the summer as a matter of course; a European honeymoon became a common occurrence for upper class Americans. [5]

Meanwhile the issuers of travelers' credits had altered the pricing system. Indeed, international bankers had radically restructured the fee schedule. In the past, many merchant bankers had charged a fee of 1 percent on the face value of the credit but had simultaneously allowed customers to earn interest ranging from 4 percent to 5 percent on the funds deposited with the firm at the time of issuance. By the late 1870s, however, both the initial fee and the interest allowance were completely eliminated on most credits. Tourists now received travelers' credits that were nominally free of charge. Under this arrangement, international bankers actually covered their costs solely from the use of a customer's funds during the interval between the initial deposit and the final payment of the checks or drafts drawn against the credit--a period normally running two to four months. (3) The "no fee-no interest" plan remained in force for a decade or more. Yet credit issuers found it impossible to earn an adequate profit under these terms, and most firms reimposed an issuance fee of up to 1 percent in the 1890s.

The entry of the American Express Company into the field was the most significant development in the last decade of the century. The inauguration of financial services for the foreign traveler was an outgrowth of the firm's money order business in the domestic market. American Express, which was originally begun as one of the nation's earliest fast freight companies, initiated the sale of money orders, usually in amounts of $5 and $10, in 1882. Within a few years it had built a large network of sales locations including not only railroad stations but also drug stores and other retail outlets. During a visit to Europe in 1890, the firm's president, J. C. Fargo, found the traditional letter of credit mechanism somewhat unsatisfactory because he could obtain funds only at the offices of foreign banks, and many banks had limited banking hours. Upon his return to New York, Fargo urged his associates to introduce a new, more convenient financial system for overseas travelers modeled on the firm's already successful money order business. [8]

The American Express system for transferring funds abroad had several distinctive features. First, the firm issued travelers' checks rather than letters of credit. These checks could be negotiated at any time and at any place where they were accepted. The firm issued checks with the predetermined value of one currency in terms of other currencies printed boldly on the face. This feature eliminated the uncertainty in the traveler's mind about the precise proceeds of his checks in Europe's leading currencies on any given day. The application of predetermined exchange rates to travelers' checks was possible because of the great degree of monetary stability existing under the gold standard mechanism then in operation. The new checks were issued under the unique double-signature system of identification. Each document was signed by the purchaser at the sales point and again later in the presence of the person cashing it. This method of identification worked so satisfactorily that it is almost universally in use today.

American Express also expanded the number of locations where the checks could be negotiated. Whereas most banking houses had relied on overseas correspondents to handle their traveling credits, American Express promoted its checks not only among foreign bankers but with railroads, steamship lines, and hotels throughout the continent. Tourists soon discovered that they could cash their checks in the evenings and on weekends as well as during normal banking hours. The firm also opened branch offices overseas to serve its customers better. A Paris office opened in 1895, and others followed in London, Liverpool, Hamburg, Bremen, Le Havre, and elsewhere. The firm encouraged visitors to use its branch offices as forwarding points for mail and baggage. The American Express travelers' checks were an instantaneous success with tourists; sales reached $6 million by the turn of the century and rose steadily thereafter. (4)

Other firms, including the industry leader, the House of Brown, quickly carne out with similar forms of travelers' checks. [13] The traveler's check was especially convenient for carrying cash in relatively small amounts--that is, $100 or less; and the tourist was guaranteed against loss from misplacement or theft. The Brown firm sometimes issued travelers' letters of credit and travelers' checks in tandem, with the former for substantial sums of money and the latter for lesser amounts.

In spite of the increasing popularity of travelers' checks, some tourists still found the letter of credit a useful financial document. Mary Cadwalader Jones, the author of *European Travel for Women*, recommended use of the standard letter of credit although it cost 1 percent of the face value of the credit against a fee of only 0.5 percent for travelers' checks. "It is a sort of general introduction from the banker who issues it to all his correspondents," she wrote in 1905. In case of an accident or an arrest for breaking a minor ordinance, "a banker in good standing may be quite as useful as the resident consul," the author advised her readers. [12] Comments like the preceding illuminate the broad role of the foreign banker in fostering tourism and underline the great degree of confidence that travel writers had in the performance of the international financial system.

To the 19th century tourist, a letter of credit was almost a passport. It identified the traveler as the valued customer of an esteemed banking house; it entitled the holder automatically to the consideration and protection normally accorded to all persons who carried similar financial documents. The letter of credit was internationally respected; it signified that the traveler had sufficient monetary assets to command the respect of overseas bankers and businessmen. Moreover, in the event a traveler encountered mistreatment at the hands of disrespectful foreigners, the issuing house often had the power to retaliate against the offenders--primarily by blacklisting them and excluding them from participation in similar or related financial transactions in the future.

The international banking system was very interdependent, and those firms that stood at its head possessed a substantial amount of power and influence over their foreign correspondents. By carrying a letter of credit, or later travelers' checks, issued by a prominent banking house, travelers temporarily transferred to themselves some of the power and prestige associated with that banking firm. Such financial documents provided tourists with a reassuring affirmation of their own identity and strengthened their ability to cope with the inevitable problems encountered in the course of daily living in a foreign, and at times hostile, atmosphere.

The rise of American tourism in the last half of the 19th century was fundamentally a response to improvements in the comfort and speed of trans-atlantic transportation. (5) But the increasing sophistication of the international financial system was an important complementary factor as well. An efficient mechanism for transferring the traveler's funds overseas provided the underpinning for expanded world travel. The improved financial services of business enterprises significantly decreased the apprehensions of tourists about handling money matters while far away from home. With a letter of credit in hand issued by an important banking house, the tourists felt less vulnerable and thus were more inclined to minimize the risks of overseas travel. By enhancing the safety and convenience factors in their various documents and by expanding the network of cooperating bankers and foreign businessmen, those firms providing financial services for the traveler contributed to the rise of international tourism.

Notes

1. The New York branch issued 73 percent of the total, the Philadelphia branch issued 23 percent, and the remaining 4 percent was issued by other offices in the banking chain. [3]
2. Guild observed that the "annual spring and summer rush of tourists from American to Europe has now become almost an American fashion." The expense was not much more than spending the summer at the "sea-shore" or a "watering-place" in the United States. The package tour was popular, Guild stated; the "cheap excursion system has enabled a large number... of travelers to visit Europe." [7, p. 6]
3. This arrangement was common in Europe some years before its introduction to Ameri-

can tourists. In 1862, the Browns' English partners referred to the "no fee-no interest" system as the "London plan."

4. The $6 million figure represented about 6 percent of the U.S. market in 1900. Brown Brothers & Co. was still the market leader at the turn of the century. American Express apparently passed the Browns in total dollar sales sometime in the 1920s. Citing persistent losses on its travelers' letters of credit operations, the Brown firm creased their issuance in 1947.

5. As a percentage of total U.S. population, the big jump in tourism came in the 1850s, coinciding with the expanded steamship service of the Cunard and Collins lines. In the 1830s about .08 percent of the population went overseas each year, but by the 1850s the percentage had risen to .19 percent. As late as the 1920s, when over 250,000 Americans on average went abroad every year, the percentage was still only .22 percent – or just slightly higher than in the 1850s. A second major shift in travel patterns occurred in the 1950s, coinciding with the growth of air travel.

References

1. E. S. Bates, *Touring in 1600* (Boston: Houghton Mifflin, 1911), p. 346.
2. Brown Brothers & Co. Papers, New York Public Library, correspondence dated 21 June 1885, and 26 November 1859.
3. Brown Brothers Harriman & Co. Papers, New York Historical Society, Correspondence dated 22 February 1860; 23 May 1862; 17 January 1868; and 23 May 1868.
4. James L. Dean, *Howells' Travels Toward Art* (Albuquerque: University of New Mexico Press, 1970).
5. Foster Rhea Dulles, *Americans Abroad: Two Centuries of European Travel* (Ann Arbor: University of Michigan Press, 1964), pp. 43-54 and 102-109.
6. W. Pembroke Fetridge, *Harper's Handbook for Travelers in Europe and The East* (New York: Harper, 1873), p. 6.
7. Curtis Guild, *Abroad Again: or, A Fresh Foray in Foreign Lands* (Boston: Lee and Shepard, 1877), p. 32.
8. Alden Hatch, *American Express: A Century of Service* (Garden City: Doubleday, 1950), pp. 84-102.
9. Christopher Hibbert, *The Grand Tour* (New York: G. P. Putnam, 1969), p. 16.
10. Muriel Hidy, *George Peabody, Merchant and Financier, 1829-1854* (New York: Arno Press, 1978), Ph.D. diss., Radcliffe College, 1939.
11. Ralph Hidy, *The House of Baring in American Trade and Finance* (Cambridge, Harvard University Press, 1949), pp. 135 and 584.
12. Mary Cadwalder Jones, *European Travel for Women* (New York: Macmillan, 1905), p. 23.
13. John Kouwenhoven, *Partners in Banking: An Historical Portrait of a Great Private Bank* (Garden City: Doubleday, 1968), p. 171.
14. Douglass North, "The United States Balance of Payments, 1790-1860," in *Trends in the American Economy in the Nineteenth Century* (Princeton: Princeton University Press, 1960).

Chapter Nine

The Emergence of a Futures Market for Foreign Exchange in the United States

Although financial scholars have cited the development of an active futures market as a clear sign of the maturation of the U.S. foreign exchange market during the second half of the nineteenth century, little evidence has thus far been uncovered on the precise timing of its emergence. An extensive examination of the business records and letter books of the era's leading foreign exchange dealer, Brown Brothers & Co., in New York, and its allied house in Baltimore, Alex. Brown & Sons, however, has unearthed new information, which suggests that such a market was developing in the late 1870's. (1) The firm's records indicate, moreover, that the expanded use of futures contracts coincided closely with other changes in the nature of the foreign exchange market, including an increased volume of trading in other European currencies besides the pound sterling particularly French francs. It is the intention of this paper, first, to identify a tentative date for the emergence of a futures market for foreign exchange in the United States and, second, to offer some hypotheses about the reasons for the timing of its birth.

For several decades the English economist, Paul Einzig, has been the leading historian of forward markets, and a brief review of his research provides a useful background for further analysis. Although documentary evidence of forward exchange transactions survives from the Middle Ages, and exists at periodic intervals thereafter, the formation of organized futures markets came only in the second half of the nineteenth century. (2) The first modern European markets developed in Vienna and Berlin in the 1880's and 1890's, with a keen interest rate arbitrage arising between the two financial centers.

The London forward market was, in contrast, less organized in the late nineteenth century. "The reason for the slow development of the Forward Exchange market in London," Einzig states, "was the practice of British importers and exporters to insist on doing business in terms of sterling." (3) The necessary exchange transactions, whether spot or forward occurred overseas. "Importers and exporters abroad were able to cover their exchange risk in the highly developed forward markets in sterling that existed in their own centres." It was

*Reprinted from *Explorations in Economic History* (1978), 193-211.

a paradoxical situation: "even though sterling was by far the most important international currency and London was by far the most important international financial center, the turnover of the London Foreign Exchange market was distinctly smaller than that of a number of less important international financial centres." (4) Moreover, it was not until after World War I that London became the major European market for foreign exchange futures.

While the instability of the international money market in the postwar period is often cited by monetary theorists as the major cause of the growth of forward transactions in the twentieth century, the main factors accounting for the formation of earlier futures markets on the continent are more obscure. Einzig has hypothesized that "forward dealings between bankers and their customers preceded the development of a market in Forward Exchanges." (5) In the produce trade where profit margins were narrow, merchants frequently covered the exchange risk through forward transactions even on business "between countries with stable currencies." (6) However, another group of financial speculators, who had little connection with the trade sector, also engaged in forward transactions and profited from interest arbitrage. In Europe, Einzig concluded, it is impossible to determine "whether commercial demand for forward facilities was first in the field and the market created for it was used and misused subsequently by speculation, or whether it was, the speculators who created the market, which, once in existence, provided facilities also for genuine trade requirements." (7) But whatever the cause, the expanded use of forward transactions was encouraged by "progress in banking technique and the increase of confidence amidst relatively stable conditions in the second half of the 19th century." (8).

In the United States, he added, "forward dealings must have originated from the exchange fluctuations brought about by the Civil War, but very little has been written about them." It is known however that during the concluding decades of the nineteenth century "American produce exporters covered their exchange risk by selling forward their sterling bills." (9) The business records of the House of Brown reinforce this conclusion about the role of exporters in the creation of the U.S. market. But the same records indicate that the monetary disturbances in the Greenback Era may have done more to retard than to stimulate the development of a forward market for foreign exchange.

The Browns were a family of merchant-bankers who, over the ante-bellum decades, shifted their business activities toward a concentration on the extension of financial services to the American foreign trade sector. (10) In the course of expansion, the House of Brown established wholly-owned branch offices in New York, Philadelphia, Boston, and, most importantly, transatlantic branches in Liverpool and London. After the Civil War the firm also maintained agency agreements with independent businessmen in Baltimore, Charleston, Mobile, Galveston, and New Orleans. The Browns became the dominant firm in the foreign exchange market immediately after the closing of the Second Bank of the United States in 1836, and the house retained a position of leadership throughout the remainder of the century. In the late 1860's, it is estimated that the Browns and their chain of allied firms annually bought and sold approximately 16% of the foreign bills of exchange drawn in the United States. (11) During the last half of the century the market structure became increasingly oligopolistic, with much of the competition coming from the London based firm of Drexel, Morgan & Co., whose partners rank among the most recognizable names in American financial history. (12)

Although most of the Browns' senior partners were located in the main offices in New York and London, the initial stimulus for their entry into the futures market apparently came from the outlet in Baltimore. For almost a quarter of a century, Baltimore had been a minor outpost in the Browns' organizational scheme; in 1860, for example, the branch had generated only 6% of the firm's overall exchange sales. During the late 1870's, however, American agricultural exports to Europe expanded rapidly, and Baltimore was one of the ports that benefited from the increased activity. In the ten years from 1870 to 1880, Baltimore's foreign trade balance shifted from a net import deficit of $5.2 million to a net export surplus of $56.3 million. This reversal was caused by a fivefold increase in the export figure, which rose from $19.9 million in 1870 to $76.2 million in 1880. Wheat shipments to Europe were responsible for almost all of the increase. As a result of this abrupt change in the port's status, the Browns' Baltimore office was suddenly transformed into one of the most vital links in the banking chain.

The Browns were represented in Baltimore through an agency agreement with Alex. Brown & Sons which, despite the similarity in names, was an independent banking firm at this later date. One prominent feature of their association was the operation' of it joint exchange account The agreement called for AB&S and the main organization to share equally in the profits and risks of all the foreign exchange business originating in Baltimore. The basic understanding was that the local office would match its sterling sales to importers with bill purchases from exporters at a margin of 0.5%. However, AB&S was unable to achieve a daily balance in its buying and selling activities, then the New York office was obliged to cover its position, in either direction, at a guaranteed minimum margin of .25%. Another important part of the agreement was the stipulation that the New York office would exercise absolute control over the establishment of the exchange rates at which its allied house did business. Rate changes were sent out over the telegraph whenever necessary, and by the late 1870's, AB&S was receiving instructions from New York on rates as often as two or three times a day.

Because of the huge excess of exports over imports, Baltimore's foreign exchange market was in a permanent state of disequilibrium. The local supply of foreign bills of exchange was almost four times greater than the demand for them. As a result, the main activity of foreign exchange dealers was overwhelmingly the purchasing of bills. The vast majority of the agency's purchases were offset by sales in the New York market, and close coordination via the telegraph became essential to the handling of the joint exchange account.

Although the Browns and their agents enjoyed an upsurge in the volume of business during the late seventies, there was nonetheless one element in the general pattern of grain exports that was not entirely compatible with the partners' traditional strategies and their organizational structure. In the past the Browns had restricted themselves largely to the purchase and sale of bills drawn in sterling. Because of the surge in European demand for American breadstuffs, however, a substantial proportion of the shipments now headed directly for continental ports. (13) Therefore, the bills of exchange created in the export sector were increasingly drawn in currencies other than pounds. Unlike the Barings, Rothschilds, Morgans, and other prominent English bankers, the Browns' London branch had no joint exchange account agreements with banking houses located in any of the major financial centers on the European continent.

The expanded volume of bills drawn in francs on Paris and Antwerp became a progressively serious problem for the Baltimore branch in particular. An early sign of the difficulties ahead appeared in the spring of 1878. In an April letter to the New York office, AB&S reported that one of the port's largest grain shippers, James Knox & Co., had recently received a series of massive orders from Antwerp. Knox & Co. had been instructed by the overseas buyers to draw 60-day sight bills in francs on the Bank of Antwerp. In response to its customer's inquiry about purchasing the bills when drawn, the agency could offer to do no more than follow the standard procedure prescribed by the main Brown organization. That is, AB&S could not purchase the bills outright at a firm rate, but it would accept the drawings as a collection item, with the exact proceeds to be determined later upon final payment in Antwerp or the sale of the bills in the London market. Writing to the New York office, the agency described its response in this way:

> we told him we could only take the bills subject to final adjustment when advised or their 'outturn, not being willing to incur the risk of fluctuation in Continental Exchange (14)

However, as an alternative to an outright purchase, AB&S asked the New York partners how much they might be willing to advance against a given franc bill subject to the eventual proceeds, or as they preferred to call it, the outturn. There was the prospect of a large business in francs, New York was advised, and "we should prefer to control it, if possible, rather than have it go elsewhere--& perhaps divert some of the Sterling bills we do now get."

The competitor AB&S feared most was Drexel, Morgan & Co., in London, and Drexel, Harjes & Co., in Paris. In Baltimore, Robert Garrett & Sons served as the chief representative of the Drexel-Morgan alliance. (15) However, when the volume of exchange drawn by exporters was unusually large, Drexel & Co. in Philadelphia also entered the Baltimore market for its own account via the telegraph. With a branch in Paris and strong connections throughout the continent, the Drexel-Morgan organization was in a favorable position to supplant the Browns as the leading exchange dealers in the Maryland port if the proportion of bills drawn in sterling declined dramatically.

The agency's worst fears were soon confirmed. Although AB&S did manage to obtain the first franc bills drawn by James Knox & Co., after offering a liberal advance, its success was short-lived. When Knox drew another group of bills two weeks later, the Baltimore office wrote the London partners that Drexel & Co. had promptly entered a firm bid for the exchange and taken the business. Because it was anticipated that the Philadelphia house would now become a permanent interloper in the Baltimore market, AB&S was very apprehensive about the future. With the Drexels and Garretts indicating a willingness to purchase francs outright, the Baltimore managers were visibly disturbed:

> We are not likely to get any more of them [francs], and we only hope their loss may not imperial the Sterling drawings of these parties which we heretofore retained. (16)

James Knox & Co. was not, of course, the only shipper to receive a substantial volume of orders for continental delivery. Other grain exporters were soon filling a large number of orders. In a January 1879 review of business prospects for the coming year, AB&S saw little reason for optimism: "this season the bulk of shipments will be in francs, which will very much reduce our sterling bill purchases." Several months later the Baltimore management was actively urging the main organization to form an alliance with one of the important Paris banking houses.

The suggestion was not altogether an unfamiliar idea. The Browns had actually considered expanding the volume of their franc transactions on several occasions in the past, but the impediments in the way of conducting a sizeable and profitable business had always appeared too formidable. In comparison with sterling, the American market for francs had been exceedingly thin. Even in New York the demand for franc bills was unsteady, and it was anticipated that any large purchases of francs would, at times, have to be offset with sales of sterling bills. On one occasion, when the Baltimore agency had purchased francs from a favored customer as an accommodation, it had taken the New York office almost three days to make a covering sale in the same currency. In addition, the senior partners in England objected to handling franc bills through the London office because the collection process was understandably more involved, and because French laws governing bills of exchange were considered too restrictive in certain respects. (17) Thus when news arrived late in January 1879 that the inhibiting French laws on bills of exchange had been relaxed by the General Assembly, the whole question of engaging in franc operations was suddenly brought forward for another review.

Meanwhile, another matter of equally great importance was demanding attention as well. Competitive pressures in Baltimore, and presumably other in markets, were forcing the Browns to examine their response to the growing practice of contracting for bills of exchange to be delivered at future dates. Future markets for actively traded commodities such as grain and cotton were already an established part of the American financial environment by the 1870's, and the financial principles on which a futures contract was based were generally understood in the commercial community. (18) Stated briefly, a contract provided for the setting of a fixed price that would later be applied to bills of exchange delivered by the seller by some date in the reasonably near future.

In the situation at hand, it was primarily grain exporters who hoped to sell their future drawings to foreign exchange dealers such as the Browns. The prime motive of the grain shipper was to avoid the risk of a drop in exchange rates between the date an order was received by cable from across the Atlantic and the date on which the cargo actually left the American port for its overseas destination. By selling an exchange future on the same day as an order was received, the exporter could immediately calculate his profit on a given transaction. The exchange risk normally inherent in fulfilling foreign orders could thereby be completely eliminated since the shipper would not be forced to wait several months before learning what the exact proceeds of his bill would be. With this uncertainty removed, the exporter would be able to extend lower prices to foreign buyers and therefore increase his competitiveness in the transatlantic grain market. For the Browns, however, the only incentive for engaging in such operations seems to have been the protection of their leadership position in the U.S. foreign exchange market from the onslaughts of other dealers.

The first hint of real difficulties in the Baltimore market came in December 1878. In a letter to the New York Office, AB&S casually mentioned that another of the port's important grain dealers, Gill & Fisher, had recently sold to Robert Garrett & Sons a "block of £100,000" with the understanding the bills would "be delivered as the shipments are completed." (19) Within two months, a trend toward an increased volume of futures transactions had definitely emerged, and there were signs that the movement was gaining momentum. Besides the competition from local houses, exchange dealers in New York such as Hallgarten & Co. were regularly quoting rates for futures through Baltimore brokers.

When AB&S brought up the subject in a letter to the Browns' Liverpool office in January 1879, the situation was not encouraging: "We have always declined to name rates for Exchange to be delivered in the future, as we believe is also the case with the New York house, and we do not see how it could be done under our system of closing the account each week." (2O) In another letter to the same party the next month, the Baltimore management elaborated further on its current plight:

> As to your suggestion that we should confer with the New York House in regard to purchasing exchange for future delivery, we

> would say that we have understood that they never make such purchases, and they do not seem to have considered the subject with favor when we have suggested it to them. We would like to be able to meet this desire on the part of shippers but the difficulties that occur to us are that to make sure of a margin in the exchange it would be necessary to sell at once against such time purchases, which meanwhile would leave our account with you short remitted, and involve a charge of interest that we could hardly cover by the rate at which we purchased, as we hear that sales are made at about the rate for immediate delivery... if you think that these difficulties can be overcome or in some way avoided, we will be glad to hear from you, as we (eel that to control our share of the business here we must meet as far as possible what may appear to be the requirements of the trade. (21)

Apparently, the senior Brown partners in New York and London agreed that the problem was a serious one because in the following months a major topic of discussion was the manner in which the contemplated operations in futures could be effectively implemented.

The letters written by the Baltimore agency during this period are unusually interesting because, as seen above, many of the questions it raised were the logical ones that might have occurred to any novice in the futures market. A fundamental issue was exactly how the purchases of exchange for future delivery could be covered with sales at a safe and predictable margin. All the correspondence indicates that there was little demand for futures arising from the import sector of the economy. Somehow, it was obvious, futures purchases would have to be offset by current sales; otherwise, the exchange risk would be forced upon the dealer.

These matters were discussed in a letter from AB&S to the New York office dated April 15, 1879:

> We note your remarks in regard to the purchase of sterling for future delivery, but would ask if it is your idea that we should sell against such purchases at the time . . .Is it your custom, when making such purchases, to give current rates, or are you guided simply by the prospective advance or decline in the market as may appear probable at the time of purchase, and on this basis make the best rate practicable? (22)

The reply AB&S received to these queries has not survived, but when the New York house began the regular quotation of futures rates that summer, the Browns offered to buy bills delivered within one month at the same rate normally paid for 3 day sight bills [the standard short remittance] and to take bills delivered within two months at a rate $.01, or .21% below that. The first regular quotation reaching the Baltimore agency from the New York office on August 14, 1879, listed a rate of $4.79 for September delivery and $4.78 for October delivery. (23)

In the course of establishing ground rules for the new operations, the interest rate to be charged by the Brown's English branches on the anticipated deficit balances in the Baltimore agency's joint account became an issue of contention. Since the agency agreement had taken effect in 1867, the interest had always been stipulated as 5%. Because AB&S had been careful in matching closely sales and purchases, very little interest had ever been assessed against the account. But the basic plan for handling futures transactions called for the Baltimore office to sell an offsetting 3-day sight bill at the same time that it signed a contract to buy a bill drawn in the future. While this procedure assured a satisfactory profit margin of 0.5% on any given transaction, it still left AB&S open to a slight risk in the interest area. If the Baltimore office was unable to earn a 5% or better return on the proceeds of a bill sale during the interval from contract signing to the actual purchase date, then AB&S would not be able to offset fully the interest charges in England.

This topic was the key issue discussed in a letter from AB&S to the New York office dated June 24, 1879. The Baltimore management did not feel it could be absolutely certain of earning any more than a 4% return on short-term investments in the local money market. Either the London branch should lower its rate, the agency argued, or the New York office should assume responsibility for guaranteeing a minimal 5% return on the idle Baltimore balances. Otherwise, the interest charges in England might cancel out part of the normal profit margin on exchange transactions. In fact, it was the opinion of the agency that "these time transactions should be kept entirely separate from the current business." A special account should be set up, AB&S suggested, and "when transactions are finally closed by payment for the bills here, the balance, including such interest as we might be able to earn [should) be then transferred to London." When the New York office balked at any change in the 5% rate, which had been traditionally applied to all debit balances in England for over one-half a century, the Baltimore agency voiced its objections even more strongly. The maintenance of a 5% interest rate on any accounts associated with futures while competitors "are working on the basis of current rates. . . precludes the possibility of business." (24) Eventually, the interest problem was settled to the satisfaction of the main organization and its agent, and the two firms began to participate actively in the developing market for foreign exchange futures.

At the same time the Browns were formulating policies for their entrance into the futures market, the senior partners were also actively engaged in negotiations with bankers in Paris pursuant to the expansion of their trading in francs. No doubt the distressing reports emanating from Baltimore during the first half of 1879 spurred the London partners on in their efforts. In summarizing the situation in Baltimore in a letter to the London office dated April 29, 1879, AB&S made the following statement: "Our principal drawers of Francs, Gill & Fisher, now sell regularly to Drexel & Co. ..... and they and others ... are now getting such very full rates that we could not at present hope to divert the business." Suddenly three months later, AB&S received instructions from the London office to remit all franc bills either advanced against or purchased outright to Comptoir d/ Escompte de Paris. The Baltimore management was clearly surprised by the announcement of the new alliance. "It is the first intimation we have had of any arrangement having been made, and we are quite without instructions of a general character as to the conduct of the business," AB&S' wrote the New York office on July 31. In another letter the next month, the agency reviewed what it understood to be the precise) details of the business arrangement with the Paris house. The main organization and Comptoir d/ Escompte would each take one-half the profit and risk on franc operations. For its own part, AB&S stated, "it will be agreeable to us to do the business here as proposed for one-fourth the profit...and...risk." The Baltimore management felt that it would confine most of its activity to bill purchasing since there was little demand for franc bills from local importers. "We will be glad to receive your quotations for francs as promised," AB&S told the New York office. (25)

AB&S then turned to another topic of significance: namely, the possible purchase of franc bills for future delivery. And for the first time in the Baltimore correspondence, it was suggested that the New York house might, on occasion, be able to offset purchase contracts with corresponding sales of bills for future delivery, in both sterling and francs. In the event sales contracts were actually negotiated, AB&S was worried about what would happen when the delivery dates on sales and purchases did not exactly coincide. The overriding concern was that an exporter might present his bills and demand payment prior to the time that the New York office had collected the cash proceeds from the offsetting sales contract. The question was posed in the following terms: "Are your bills under time sales deliverable at your option with the period stated or would we come under advance for bills under such purchases which may be delivered to us prior to our reimbursement from you?" (26) The response of the New York firm has not survived, but information from outside sources indicates that naming the specific date of delivery within the allotted time span was an option of the customer under both sale and purchase contracts. Thus in those situations where a futures purchase was offset by a futures sale, the dealer was forced to assume the risk of possibly losing a few days of interest.

On top of all the difficulties associated with the expansion of transactions in futures contracts and continental exchange, the Baltimore office, and presumably other outlets in the Brown chain, found itself suffering from increasingly severe price competition. At the beginning of 1879, the difference in the Browns' quoted rates for sterling purchases and sales was 0.5%--or roughly the same differential that had been in force for the last four decades. Sterling rates generally fluctuated in a narrow band around the mint par figure of $4.8665. This meant that the Browns named buying rates were typically $.025 below their current selling rates. During the first half of the year, however, the Baltimore office had difficulty making purchases at the rates dictated by the New York house. Much of the competition came from foreign exchange dealers in New York and Philadelphia, who quoted their rates through local brokers.

The prices they offered were often $.01 to $.015 higher than the Baltimore agency was permitted to go. This meant that some dealers were willing to do business on margins of .25% or less. Concomitantly, many out-of-town dealers were handling transactions in francs at the same low margins previously reserved for sterling. Therefore, when the New York office finally began to send out regular quotations for both francs and futures, AB&S lost many opportunities to purchase bills because it could not meet the higher rates offered by other dealers. It soon became clear that the agency would either have to settle for smaller margins or lose the business entirely.

Neither alternative seemed very attractive. By early April the Baltimore office was already discouraged: "The competition is so great that we have to pay more than formerly, and the heavy concession you make in sales for us leave but little margin to cover risks," AB&S complained to the New York house. (27) The story was much the same in July: "We have had to bid higher than the rates you name for sterling bills," they admitted; "we have had to meet the market or pass the bills, preference having been given us at the same rates." Under the circumstances, this last remark was at least some consolation. And in the months ahead it became, in fact, the basis for new pricing tactics. The previous policy of maintaining a uniform rate structure for all customers was modified. In bidding for the large drawings of the major grain exporters, AB&S extended rates that were competitive with those quoted by out-of-town dealers. At the same time, it continued' to do business with the medium to small customers at the standard 0.5% margin. The effects of a late entry into the market for francs and futures combined with downward pressure on margins showed up in the end of the year earnings figure. AB&S's one-half share in the foreign exchange profits for 1879 was $33,800 compared to $50,300 the year before a drop of just about one-third. In the New York office, profits from foreign exchange operations decreased from $221,700 in 1878 to $176,100 in 1879, or 21%. (28) The sharper decline in the agency's income is a further indication that much of the stimulus for readjustments in the Browns' operating policies came from the Baltimore market. (29)

The year 1879 brought many changes in the Browns' traditional pattern of operation. The swiftness with which change occurred was, in retrospect, particularly notable. Once the Browns recognized the seriousness of the threat to their leadership position in the foreign exchange field, they acted quickly to adjust the range of their services to the demands of the market. The Baltimore agency became concerned about the possible loss of business due to the inadequate facilities of the main organization as early as the spring of 1878, but it was not until the beginning of 1879 that the situation was judged to have reached a critical point. By April the New York office was issuing instructions on the handling of sterling purchased for future delivery. Three months later the formation of an alliance with the French firm, Comptoir d/ Escompte, was announced. In August the purchase of francs for future delivery and the possible sale of futures contracts in both sterling and francs were being discussed. By the end of the year, the House of Brown, the nation's leading dealer, was an active participant in the emerging market for foreign exchange futures.

Despite the richness of the written data, the Browns' records do not indicate any reasons for the sudden appearance of a futures market for bills of exchange. The partners were primarily concerned with formulating a response to the innovative practices of competitors, not an analysis of the causes of their predicament. Although it is beyond the scope of this paper to suggest a comprehensive explanation for the timing of the market's emergence, there are nevertheless some observations which can be made about the circumstances of its birth

From an institutional standpoint, a brief survey of the historical development of the futures contract per se within the borders of the United States may provide enlightenment. The futures contract was an outgrowth of the earlier practice of selling merchandise while it was in transit from one destination to another, or, as the practice was then called, "to arrive." The technique of selling on arrival was perfected in the Chicago grain market during the early 1850's, and it later spread to the nation's other commodity markets. Out of the arrival sale evolved the futures contract. It called for the future delivery of a specific grade of a given commodity within the maximum time specified. The general adoption of this innovative financial device coincided with the formation of organized exchanges for the respective commodities in Chicago, New York, and other commercial centers. The commodity exchanges established uniform grading standards and stipulated the rules under which the regular trading of futures contracts would be conducted. (30)

Although the exact nature of the maturation process is at present undefined, it is nevertheless quite clear that the emergence of a market for foreign exchange futures came only after trading procedures for futures contracts on the commodity exchanges had been refined during the 1860's and 1870's. A futures market for bills of exchange was, then, the final step in the revolution in the marketing and financing of agricultural commodities. This broad relationship deserves special emphasis because, generally speaking, it has not been stressed (or even noted) by those scholars who have made independent studies of futures transactions in the commodities and foreign exchange markets.

In theory, American grain exporters might have avoided using the forward exchange mechanism by following the alternative practice of hedging their position by combining the currency credit markets with the spot markets. (31) However, as Einzig points out, "the extent to which it is possible to go short in a currency by borrowing money and selling the spot exchange is naturally limited by the availability of credit facilities for that purpose." (32) Credit facilities for hedging in foreign currencies, which would have given exporters the alternative of following the credit-spot route, do not seem to have existed in the United States in the late 1870's. The Browns' records contain no references to such transactions. The failure of a speculative market to develop simultaneously can probably be laid to the high cost of obtaining information and prohibitive transaction costs.

A review of the Browns' activities indicates that there were three exogenous developments which could have been responsible, either separately or jointly, for the emergence of a forward market at this time: increasing economies of scale, the transfer of financial technology from the European continent, and the resumption of specie payments by the American banks after January 1, 1879. Another possible influence--a sharp reduction in communication costs--can be eliminated as an important factor since the undersea telegraph cable to Great Britain had become operational thirteen years earlier, in 1866. From 1871 to 1879 the size of the foreign exchange market grew rapidly. Much of the rise in the export sector stemmed from increased European purchases of American agricultural products. The figures in Table I show that while worldwide exports grew by 57% over the eight-year period, exports to Europe expanded at a somewhat higher rate of 70%. Within the European category, the shipment of crude foodstuffs (non-processed agricultural output) was up a dramatic 450%, with almost half of the increase coming in the last two years of the decade. Since there was an approximately corresponding increase in the foreign bills of exchange drawn in the U.S. market, economies of scale in matching buyers and sellers must be considered as a possible encouragement for exchange dealers to engage in forward transactions.

However, a more detailed country-by-country analysis of U.S. foreign trade statistics reveals an important shift in the pattern of exports, which may be far more relevant to our investigation. As the data in Table 2 demonstrates, wheat shipments overseas in 1879 were up 35% over 1878, despite a $13.5 million decline in exports to Great Britain, traditionally the nation's best customer for agricultural products. Meanwhile, wheat shipments to France increased by a tremendous 700% in 1879, and exports to Belgium more than doubled. American grain dealers drew a corresponding volume of franc bills on Paris and Antwerp. It was, therefore, primarily an expansion in the size of the market for continental exchange, rather than for foreign exchange generally, which coincided with the increase in forward transactions. If markets for forward exchange were already a feature of the continental financial environment in the mid-1870's, as Einzig suggests, then the development of a similar market in the United States might be viewed as essentially imitative.

There is further evidence in support of the hypothesis that the practice of negotiating forward exchange contracts had continental origins. It was, after all, those exchange dealers with close contacts in Paris, Antwerp, and other continental cities such as the Drexel-Morgan banking interest, which introduced these innovative techniques to the American market. The Browns, in contrast, lacked a strong network of continental correspondents. The partners' unfamiliarity with the procedures to be followed in organizing facilities for the handling of forward transactions can be explained by the paradoxical failure of London, the world's financial center, to develop an active futures market in the nineteenth century. Thus, there exists a fair amount of largely circumstantial evidence indicating that the financial techniques associated with forward transactions were transferred to the United States from the European continent, and that the stimulus for the transfer was the more than sevenfold increase in the bills of exchange drawn in francs against shipments of wheat to France and Belgium in 1879.

Third, there is the argument that the resumption of specie payments, after a seventeen-year suspension, may have provided the stimulus for the emergence of a futures market. The immediate success of the government's resumption policy encouraged foreign exchange dealers to look forward to an extended period of international monetary stability, during which exchange rates could be expected to fluctuate within a narrow band around mini par. Extreme variations in the rates would be eliminated through the operation of the gold point mechanism. There can be little doubt that this renewed stability contributed to the increasingly severe price competition which the Browns faced in 1879 and which drove profit margins on large transactions down from 0.5% to .25%, and sometimes even less. At the same time, it is also possible that a reduced fear about the amplitude of exchange rate fluctuations encouraged dealers to expand their volume of forward contracts.

However, this conclusion clashes sharply with the general belief that the modern forward market came into existence primarily as a response to the destruction of confidence in foreign exchange rates after World War I. The supposition was that greater uncertainty about the future movement of spot rates, rather than less uncertainty, encouraged forward transactions. How can these apparently contradictory explanations be reconciled? Einzig's research on the emergence of continental markets in the late nineteenth century provides a clue. In that situation, he cited the fundamental stability of the foreign exchange markets in Austria and Germany as a factor in fostering forward transactions. (33) Yet Einzig found it impossible to determine which group--financial speculators or actual merchants involved in the produce trade--was primarily responsible for initiating futures trading in the two countries. It is probable, therefore, that futures markets in foreign exchange have arisen at different times in response to demands from two distinct economic groups, and that monetary stability, rather than instability, was more conducive to the forward operations of one of these groups. The Browns' data indicates strongly that it was grain dealers, not speculators, who provided the stimulus in the U.S. market during the late 1870's.

While it may be argued that the business records of the House of Brown alone are not sufficient to overturn the traditional view of the indispensable role of uncertainty in fostering an active forward market, these records do contain sufficient evidence to reopen the issue for closer examination and to challenge monetary theorists to explain the apparent discrepancies.

Notes

1. Alexander Brown & Sons Papers (Library of Congress) hereafter abbreviated AB&S; and Historical Files--Brown Brothers Harriman & Co. (New York).
2. Paul Einzig, *A Dynamic Theory of Forward Exchange* (London: Macmillan, 1961), pp. 1-11.
3. *Ibid.*, p. 8.
4. Paul Einzig, *The History of Foreign Exchange* (2nd ed. Rev.; London: Macmillan, (1970), p. 183.
5. Einzig, *Dynamic Theory*, p. 7.
6. *Ibid.*, p. 9.
7. *Ibid.*, p. 5.
8. *Ibid.*, p. 6.
9. *Ibid.*, p. 8.
10. There are several books on the Brown family and its business enterprises; the most recent is John Kouwenhoven, *Partners in Banking: An Historical Portrait of a Great Private Bank, Brown Brothers Harriman & Co., 1818-1968* (Garden City, New York, 1968). The most important contribution from the family itself is John Crosby Brown, *A Hundred Years of Merchant Banking* (New York: Doubleday, 1909). For the latest research on this family enterprise, see Edwin J. Perkins, "The House of Brown: America's Foremost International Bankers, 1800-1880" (Unpublished Ph.D. dissertation, Johns Hopkins University, 1972).
11. Perkins, *op.cit.*, p. 588. In 1867 the firm's volume of transactions was in the neighborhood of $90 million in greenback currency.
12. Arthur H. Cole, "Evolution of the Foreign Exchange Market of the United States," *Journal of Economic and Business History*, I (1928/29), pp. 384-421. For more information on these banking families, see Fritz Redlich, *The Molding of American Banking*, (2nd ed.; New York: Johnson Reprint Corp., 1968), passim. Although J. P. Morgan is best known for his activities in the field of investment banking, it is significant that he received his early training in the international trade area.
13. For general information on American agricultural exports in the second half of the nineteenth century, see two important articles by Morton Rothstein: "America in the International Rivalry for the British Wheat Market, 1860-1914," *Mississippi Valley Historical Review* (December, 1960), 401-418, and "The International Market for Agricultural Commodities, 1850-1873," in the Gilchrist and Lewis, ed., *Economic Change in the Civil War Era* (Greenville, Del: Eleutherian Mills-Hagley Foundation, 1966).
14. AB&S, Baltimore, to Brown Brothers & Co., New York, April 11, 1878, AB&SP.
15. Harold A. Williams, *Robert Garrett & Sons, Origin and Development, 1840-1965* (Baltimore, 1965).
16. AB&S, Baltimore, to Brown, Shipley & Co., London, April 23, 1878. AB&SP.
17. French law required the holder of a collateralized franc bill to release the bill of lading for the merchandise to the drawee on the date of formal acceptance. In England, in contrast, holders had the option of holding the bill of lading until the final payment date. The Browns preferred to retain the option in the management of their foreign exchange operations.
18. Harold Woodman, *King Cotton and His Retainers: Financing and Marketing the Cotton Crop of the South, /800-/925* (Lexington:: University of Kentucky Press, 1968).
19. AB&S, Baltimore, to Brown Brothers & Co., New York, December 10, 1878, AB&SP.

2O. AB&S, Baltimore, to Brown, Shipley & Co., Liverpool, January 12, 1879, AB&SP.
21. Ibid.,. February 7, 1879.
22. AB&S, Baltimore, to Brown Brothers & Co., New York, April 15, 1879, AB&SP.
23. Two weeks later, on August 26, the agency agreed to take francs at a rate of 5.3125 for both September and October delivery.
24. AB&S, Baltimore, to Brown Brothers & Co., New York, June 24, 1879, AB&SP.
25. Ibid., August 27, 1879.
26. *Loc. cit.*
27. *Ibid.*, April 5, 1879.
28. The New York figures are found in Brown Brothers & Co. Papers (New York Public Library).
29. Baltimore profits were greater than those of all the other branch outlets combined, including Boston, Philadelphia, and various southern agencies.
30. Pertinent monographs on futures trading in the commodity markets are the following: "American Produce Exchange Markets," *Annals of the American Academy of Political and Social Science*. Vol. 38, No.2 (September, 1911), 319-664; Henry C. Emery, *Speculation on the Stock and Produce Exchanges of the United States* (New York: Columbia University Press. 1896); Stanley Dumbell, "The Origin of Colton Futures," *Economic History* (May, 1927), Vol. 1,259-267; Thomas Odle, "Entrepreneurial Cooperation on the Great Lakes: The Origin of the Methods of American Grain Marketing," *Business History Review* (Winter, 1964), Vol. 38, 439-455; and Harold Irwin, *Evolution of Futures Trading* (Madison, Wis.: Mimir Publishers, 1954).
31. For a discussion of the theory of forward markets see Einzig, *Dynamic Theory*; Egon Sohmen, *The Theory of Forward Exchange*. Studies in International Finance No. 11 (Princeton: International Finance Section, 1966); Fred R. Glahe, *An Empirical Study of the Foreign-Exchange Market: Test of a Theory*. Studies in International Finance, No. 20 (Princeton International Finance Section, 1967).
32. Einzig, *Dynamic Theory*, p. 97.
33. *Ibid.*, p. 6.

Table 1

U.S. EXPORTS (IN MILLIONS OF DOLLARS)

	Worldwide	Europe	Crude Foodstuffs to Europe
1871	464.3	344.8	33.4
1877	622.3	480.4	80.1
1878	712.3	562.9	142.6
1879	728.5	587.6	182.2

Sources: Robert Lipsey, *Price and Quantity Trends in the Foreign Trade of the United States* (Princeton, 1963), p. 154; Matthew Simon and David Novak, "Some Dimensions of the American Commercial Invasion of Europe, 1871-1914," *Journal of Economic History* (1964), p. 594.

Table 2

WHEAT EXPORTS OF THE UNITED STATES (IN MILLIONS OF DOLLARS)

	Worldwide	France	Belgium	Great Britain
1877	47.1	.9	1.7	36.5
1878	96.9	3.8	4.8	73.6
1879	103.7	46.7	9.7	60.3

Source: Annual Statements of the Commerce and Navigation of the United States for the fiscal year ending June 30, 1877-1879. U.S. Treasury Department, Bureau of Statistics (Washington, 1877-1879)

Chapter Ten

The Anglo-American Merchant Banking Houses in the Nineteenth Century

This paper focuses on the activities of the major Anglo-American merchant banking houses during the nineteenth century. My goals here are twofold. First, I plan to review briefly the most important institutional trends in the Anglo-American trade and capital markets over the course of several centuries to provide the proper background. Second, I will discuss the main accomplishments and shortcomings of the leading firms in this dynamic market, with comparisons and contrasts included where appropriate. (1) Let me warn readers in advance that I will devote a disproportionate amount of time and space to the House of Brown, an important firm in the Anglo-American market with Baltimore origins. I wrote a detailed book on the Brown family partnership over two decades ago. (2) I know the Browns best, and I will draw on my prior strengths in this context. I also intend to focus my attention primarily on events on the American side because, again, I am much more familiar with that scholarly literature. Having cited these prejudices and limitations, we may now proceed with the discussion.

The Anglo-American financial sector passed through four distinct phases from British colonization in the early seventeenth century through the end of the nineteenth century. These four stages were: 1) an absence of institutional specialization, 1600 to 1790; 2) an institutional emphasis on trade and trade financing, 1790 to 1820; 3) a mixture of trade-related activities and portfolio investments, 1820 to 1860; and 4) an emphasis on large capital transfers through portfolio investments, 1860 to 1900. The overall trend was to downplay the trade sector and to move toward the capital markets. Irrespective of the purpose of the funding, during this entire era the flow of trade credit and long-term capital was invariably from Europe across the ocean to North America.

Throughout most of the colonial era in British North America, a period of over 150 years, the transatlantic institutional linkages between the providers of

*Unpublished manuscript presented as a paper at a conference organized to celebrate the 200th anniversary of the Rothschilds' operations--London, England in May 1998.

various financial services were never very strong, and few, if any, linkages were enduring. Indeed, the word atomistic immediately springs to mind in describing the institutional structure of this immature market. The financial services provided to American colonial traders involved in international shipments were offered by hundreds of independent British merchants on an ad hoc basis. In the aggregate, the amount of the British capital tied up in American trade debt grew increasing large in the third quarter of the eighteenth century. If the partners in any Anglo-American mercantile firm thought seriously about making an effort to develop a stronger commitment to this rapidly growing market before the middle of the eighteenth century, the effort was not sustained--or, at least, the documentation has not survived. As the volume of trade expanded, the underlying conditions for specialization became more favorable. Beginning in the second half of the eighteenth century, the Barings were the first entrepreneurs on either side of the Atlantic Ocean to act on the idea of creating a transatlantic organizational permanence. We will return to a discussion of the Barings' achievements later in the narrative. Meanwhile, under the prevailing conditions in the capital markets, no firm in London sought to entice investors to purchase the debt obligations of the colonial legislatures for a very sensible reason: almost none existed. (3) Parliament had severely restricted the ability of the thirteen colonies to issue public debt instruments. (4) In the second phase of the evolution of the Anglo-American market, institutional specialization emerged, and the focus was primarily on the overseas trade sector. Two of most the most well known merchant-banking houses--the Barings and the Browns--made commitments to participate fully in the Anglo-American market. These firms not only bought and sold goods on their own account for transatlantic shipment, but, in addition, they offered a range of financial services to other mercantile firms that were likewise engaged in similar trading patterns. The performance of specialized financial services was what differentiated this small group of houses from other less ambitious firms. The leading houses made advances to American shippers against the consignments of goods, mainly cotton and tobacco, to British ports; they created active sterling markets in U.S. ports to serve the needs of local and regional importers and exporters; and, for a modest fee, they began the issuance of letters of credit to American importers, who were thereby able to purchase goods in foreign markets around the globe on more favorable terms than previously.

This last function, the issuance of letters of credit, was the one financial service in the first half of the nineteenth century that qualified an enterprise as a full-fledged merchant-banking house. Only the elite houses with impeccable international reputations for financial strength had sufficient prestige to attract customers for their letter of credit operations. An enhanced reputation in international financial circles often took years, if not decades, to develop. As a consequence, the leading merchant-banking houses typically had very few serious competitors as issuers of letters of credit. This specialized market had oligopolistic characteristics from the outset, and it remained a very concentrated field throughout the nineteenth century. (5)

In the period from 1790 to 1820, the Anglo-American merchant banking houses were only sporadically involved in promoting British portfolio investments in American securities. The opportunities to do so were few and far between. In the 1790s the new U.S. federal government funded its outstanding, non-performing debt, plus the debts of the several states, without the aid of private bankers. Once President Thomas Jefferson took office in 1801, the federal debt was steadily retired. American banks and insurance companies, which in some cases were capitalized at several million dollars, drew largely on the savings of local investors. A number of American securities subsequently traded on secondary markets in London, but the original placements were overwhelmingly transactions negotiated in the U.S. market.

The third phase in the evolution of the Anglo-American financial market was characterized by a mixture of the existing trade-related services and the emergence of new underwriting services linked to the expanding capital markets. The instantaneous success of the Erie Canal, an ambitious venture launched in 1817, triggered a host of expensive transportation projects The funds to finance the construction came from diverse sources, some governmental and some private. Anglo-American merchant banking became involved in these transactions in varying degrees. In many instances, the promoters of American canal and railroad projects engaged private bankers with overseas connections to solicit investors in London and other parts of Europe. But the participation of the private bankers was erratic and irregular. Many firms that had agreed to help promoters raise funds in London for American projects on an ad hoc basis later withdrew their services in the aftermath of the economic dislocations associated with the Panic of 1837. In light of the vicissitudes of the U.S. economy in this period, none of the leading Anglo-American merchant banking houses made the strategic decision to provide investment services on anything approaching a permanent basis during the first half of the nineteenth century. These merchant bankers were already engaged in handling thousands of transactions of all varieties linked to the trade sector, and they considered securities transactions a sideline business rather than a mainstream activity. Nonetheless, given the wide scope of their business activities, which included a mixture of trade financing and occasional investment banking ventures, this era represented the height of the power and influence of those Anglo-American houses engaged in multi-functional merchant banking.

The fourth and final stage in the evolution of the Anglo-American financial markets coincided with the outbreak of the American Civil War. Suddenly, the size of the U.S. federal debt grew enormously, and new opportunities for private bankers immediately arose. Almost simultaneously American railroads sought to raise millions of dollars to finance the expansion of track into the far western states plus improvements in existing lines, mainly the purchase of steel rails. The tremendous volume of American securities generated in the second half of the nineteenth century produced favorable conditions for greater specialization by the Anglo-American houses. Some banking partnerships which had previously provided a mix of routine trading and capital market services decided to forego the trade sector and to concentrate their energies on investment banking functions. The Peabody/Morgan organization was the most prominent private banking firm to readjust its strategies in response to these changing conditions. Originally a merchant-banking house that offered a full range of diverse financial services in the Anglo-American market, the Peabody firm was later carried forward by the father/son team of Junius and John Pierpont Morgan. Under their leadership it had evolved into primarily an investment banking firm by the early 1870s.

****

The second section of this paper addresses, in sequence, the activities of the leading Anglo-American banking houses in the nineteenth century. Chronology orders this discussion. I start with the earliest entries into the market and then move forward to the late arrivals. The six firms discussed are the Barings, Browns, Rothschilds, Peabody/Morgan, Seligmans, and Kuhn Loeb.

The Barings

The Barings were the first important Anglo-American merchant banking house, and based on their overall performance, the Barings were the most accomplished within this class of nineteenth-century business enterprises. The partners were involved in more diverse commodity and financial markets over a longer period time than any of their competitors. The Barings were also more geographically diversified than their Anglo-American competitors, since the partners also conducted an extensive business in Canada, Latin America, and the Far East. The partners were different from other Anglo-American houses too because of their involvement in loan contracting in the London market for European clients, which included the massive bond issues of several governments, including England and France. In these activities, the Barings competed directly with the Rothschilds.

Three Baring brothers established the firm with outlets in both Exeter and London in 1763. The partners began as merchants and only later diversified into the provision of supplementary financial services. This same pattern of internal development prevailed in all six of the firms discussed in this paper. Clear evidence of the Barings' early successes in diversifying the scope of their operations was their inclusion on the list of contractors authorized to market the British government's L20.5 million loan of 1800. By the end of the eighteenth century, the partners had also turned their attention to the international trade sector in North America. (6) Alexander Baring visited the United States in late 1795. He established agency agreements with independent merchants in Boston,

Philadelphia, Baltimore, and New York. More importantly, he signed an agreement with First Bank of the United States, the federally chartered institution with a huge capital of $10 million, to cooperate on the transfer of various funds between the two countries. On the basis of that mutually advantageous association, the Barings became involved in helping to facilitate the transfer of monies linked to the American purchase of the Louisiana Territory from the French government for $15 million in 1803. In cooperation with Hope & Co. in Amsterdam, the Barings helped in placing $15 million in new U.S. bonds with European investors. Given the outstanding credit reputation of the United States after the implementation of the refunding program, these investors had become eager buyers of the federal debt in the early 1790s. Indeed, the transaction in 1803 was one of the rare instances before the American Civil War in which the Anglo-American houses had the opportunity to aid the U.S. government in the sale of bonds to prospective investors at home or abroad.

Following the War of 1812, which ended in a stalemate, the Barings were consistently active in the American foreign trade sector. The partners were frequently outright purchasers of cotton in the United States for shipment to Britain based on the usually reliable advice of their American agents and correspondents. In addition, they periodically made advances to American exporters to attract consignments on which they earned commissions for arranging sales in London or Liverpool. During the 1820s and early 1830s, the Barings operated a lucrative foreign exchange business in cooperation with the Second Bank of the United States. The Barings' sterling bills always passed a premium prices because the risk of non-payment was judged to be exceedingly low. The partners also authorized their agents in the major U.S. ports to issue letters of credit to American importers with adequate capital resources and reliable reputations. In the capital markets, the partners became loan contractors for several of the new canal and railroad projects in the United States. In sum, the Barings acted as all-purpose merchant bankers in the Anglo-American economy, and they were widely recognized as the unchallenged leaders in this broad field through the 1830s.

Sensing possible danger ahead, the Baring partners were well prepared for the Panic of 1837, having curtailed their commitments in the American market during the previous year. Most of their main competitors were severely damaged by the panic and the subsequent economic downturn. Immediately after the panic, the Barings reached what was probably their zenith of power and influence in the U.S. market. Rather than taking full advantage of the temporary weaknesses of their competitors, however, the Barings became exceedingly cautious with regard to the entire U.S. market. Interestingly, an American, Joshua Bates, became the de facto head of the partnership at about this time. Bates, who was born in Massachusetts in 1788, had moved to London in 1816 or 1817, and had steadily progressed in his business career. However, Joshua Bates showed little partiality to his native land.

Under his leadership, the partnership exhibited a vacillating attitude toward the American economy in the 1840s and 1850s. Bates recruited Thomas Wren Ward, a Boston merchant, to serve as a general supervisor for all the Barings' operations in the United States, and Ward was even made a junior partner in the firm. (7) But Ward had only limited influence over the independent houses that acted as Baring agents in other U.S. port cities. Always fearful of a repeat of the 1837 disaster, the Baring partners could never bring themselves to make an unshakable commitment to either the U.S. trade market or to the nation's rapidly developing capital market. Periodically optimistic and aggressive in their involvement in the American economy during this period, the partners invariably pulled in their horns at the first sign of potential disturbances.

Rather than taking the initiative and establishing a network of branch offices in the main U.S. ports, the Barings continued to work through a chain of independent American agents. In several instances the partners had working arrangements with two or three agents in the same port city who competed with one another for new business. In other words, to interject modern Chandlerian terminology into this discussion, the Barings failed to take the steps necessary to build an organizational structure with the potential to take optimum advantage of their enviable competitive position at the end of the 1830s. The appointment of Ward as their primary American agent was only a half-measure. As a consequence of their failure to build a strong organizational network, other firms began to carve out larger market shares in various sectors, leaving the Barings in their wake.

Perhaps one of the main stumbling blocks to any greater expansion in the U.S. market was the fact that the Barings were simultaneously deeply involved in business affairs in other regions of the world, including continental Europe. The partners were unable to perceive at mid-century that one of their best opportunities for maximizing future profits was in the U.S. market. Other regions seemed equally appealing. In trying to become and remain a global enterprise long before that modern-day terminology had entered our vocabulary, the Barings spread themselves too thinly. To compound the problem, the partners regularly withdrew a large proportion of their yearly profits, which kept the capital base stagnant. The maintenance of a luxurious standard of living was more important to many partners than the growth of the enterprise. Several members of the Baring family also served in Parliament and thus became distracted by politics. Reservations about adding new partners, especially permanent non-British residents, may have also inhibited the Baring partners from pursuing expansion plans abroad.

In light of these factors, the Barings' failure to commit greater resources, both capital and personnel, to the United States gave other firms the opportunity to make inroads. By the 1850s the Browns had inherited the leadership position in the foreign exchange and letter of credit markets. (8) Meanwhile, upstart firms like Winslow & Lanier that focused narrowly on investment banking had seized the initiative in the rapidly emerging New York capital market. Once acknowledged as the leaders within the broad Anglo-American merchant banking community, the Barings steadily lost market share in the last half of the nineteenth century. The partners' multi-functional strategy and their broad global involvement became, in time, a liability rather than an asset. By the 1870s, the partners were no longer capable of seizing new business from other houses based in New York that had become more functionally specialized and were more strongly committed to serving the American market.

The Browns

The Brown firm was established in 1800 by Alexander Brown, a modestly successful linen merchant who emigrated from northern Ireland to Baltimore, a port where close relatives had only recently preceded him. Ten years after his arrival in Baltimore, Alexander sent his eldest son William to Liverpool to open what eventually became a branch office of the parent firm. Later, two younger sons opened two additional wholly-owned branch offices in Philadelphia and New York. Like the Rothschilds, the Browns had a unified ownership that functioned smoothly over long geographical distances for many decades. By the 1820s the Browns were involved in a wide range of trade-related financial markets--including the purchase and sale of sterling bills, the making of advances to attract cotton consignments to the Liverpool branch, and the issuance of letters of credit to American importers. In this period the Browns stood just behind the Barings with respect to their overall involvement in the foreign trade sector of the American economy.

The Browns differed from the Barings and most contemporary merchant bankers primarily because of their reluctance to participate extensively in complementary investment banking activities. The location of their overseas branch office in Liverpool, rather than in London, precluded their involvement in all but a few isolated securities transactions. The absence of a presence in what was then the world's key money center did not hurt the partnership's profits, however. From 1816 to 1836, the Browns' capital rose from L150,000 to L1.3 million, increasing at an annual rate of 11.5 percent.

The Browns were hit hard by the Panic of 1837 and only loans from the Bank of England saved them from the embarrassment of repudiating, at least temporarily, their maturing debt obligations. As a result of this crisis, the partners decided to pursue a policy of greater specialization. They gave up entirely trading in merchandise on their own account, which means, strictly speaking, they were no longer acting as merchants--only as bankers. Henceforth the firm concentrated exclusively on providing financial services for the American foreign trade sector. By the mid-1840s the Browns had supplanted the Barings as the leading Anglo-American house with respect to providing services to American importers and exporters, and it was a strong leadership position that the partners never surrendered throughout the remainder of the nineteenth century.

The Browns were enormously successful in serving the U.S. foreign trade market because of heir truly unique organizational structure. The firm had critically important branch offices, manned by partners or salaried employees, on both sides of the Atlantic Ocean. The offices in New York and Liverpool, with the latter superseded by London in 1863, served as dual headquarters. The entire operations of the firm were carefully coordinated and closely monitored. The Browns adopted uniform policies and procedures at all their offices, which included--in addition to New York, Liverpool, and London--branches in Boston, Baltimore, Philadelphia, New Orleans, and Mobile, Alabama. Many nonfamily members joined the house as lowly clerks and advanced through the ranks. Except for William Brown, all of the directing partners in the British branches were British nationals, among them Joseph Shipley--thus the famous branch office title of Brown, Shipley & Co. At a much later date Mark Collet and Francis Hamilton assumed the managerial duties. Mark Collet, incidentally, became governor of the Bank of England in 1887.

Unlike the hesitant Barings, the Browns proved willing to make a strong commitment to the U.S. trade sector. For more than half a century, they assiduously built the organizational capacities to succeed over the long run, and their carefully laid plans eventually translated into a profitable reality. The partners focused on the activities that they knew best, which was serving the requirements of the American foreign trade sector. In the years 1840 to 1857 the firm's capital account grew at a rate of 5.5 percent annually--not as fast in the previous twenty years but still a respectable performance. The Browns constantly reinvested a high proportion of their earnings in their thriving enterprise. In only one exceptionally bad year during this period, 1842, did the partners' withdrawals exceed their profits.

In contrast to most of their competitors, including George Peabody, the Browns breezed though the worst moments of the Panic of 1857 without seeking aid from the Bank of England and without suffering any serious losses. On the eve of the American Civil War, the partnership was flying high. Reminiscent of the status of the Barings at the end of the 1830s, the Browns were thoroughly ensconced as the undisputed leaders of the Anglo-American merchant-banking community at the end of the 1850s, and the partners were exceedingly proud of their achievements.

But developments subsequently turned sour for the Browns as well, and they eventually fell off the Anglo-American pedestal. Million dollar underwritings of government bonds and railroad securities became routine in the U.S. capital markets in the 1860s and 1870s, and these portfolio transactions soon overshadowed the volume of activity in the more mundane foreign trade sector. While the Browns ranked among the leaders in financing the trade sector through the 1890s, that sector's relative importance within the Anglo-American economy continued to fade. In the first decade of the twentieth century, a num ber of American commercial banks with huge financial resources became competitors in the foreign trade sector, and the Browns' position correspondingly fell. In the early twentieth century, the firm merged with the Harriman family enterprise to create Brown Brothers Harriman, a small private bank with an elite clientele.

Rothschilds

The partners' involvement began sometime in the 1820s, or possibly in the early 1830s. The firm invested in transportation projects, either for the partners' own joint account or for the portfolios of valued clients. The partners may have also served as loan contracts for certain canal and railroad companies, plus a few state governments, but the exact details are unknown. The Rothschilds worked through independent American agents, although the names and locations of their representatives are incomplete before 1840. Presumably one or more agents were located in Boston, New York, and Philadelphia--the main U.S. money centers.

Our key source of information about the Rothschilds' Anglo-American activities is linked to the career of their long-term U.S. agent, August Belmont, who served the firm in various capacities for over six decades. Born in Alzey, Germany, in 1813, Belmont joined the Frankfurt office as a clerk at age fifteen. In the early months of 1837 the firm sent him on a mission to Havana, Cuba, via the United States. When he arrived in New York City in March of that year, Belmont found the city in turmoil because of the raging financial panic. The Rothschilds' local agent, the firm of J. L. and S. I. Joseph & Co., had recently suspended payment with outstanding liabilities of reportedly $7 million. Rather than continuing to Havana, Belmont stayed in New York to protect as much as possible his employer's financial interests. He created an independent firm, titled August Belmont & Co., and became, in turn, the Rothschilds' sole American representative. For the next several years, he tried to reduce as much as possible the Rothschilds' exposure to losses on their American securities and to recover what could be salvaged. The partners were extremely satisfied with his performance, and they rewarded him liberally for his efforts.

But that one disastrous experience was apparently enough to stifle the Rothschilds' interest in the American capital market. Although Belmont frequently tried to induce the firm to participate in a series of promising underwriting deals, the partners remained cool to most of his proposals. (9) They joined some syndicates but headed very few. The Rothschilds certainly had the financial resources to dominate the U.S. market had the partners chosen to exert their influence after the investment climate improved in the early 1840s In 1844 the Rothschilds' capital stood at L7,800,000 versus just L750,000 for the Browns and a mere L500,000 for the Barings. (10) Frustrated by the Roths-childs' persistent disinterest, Belmont turned to politics, and he later served for several years as the organizational leader of the Democratic National Party. (11)

Why the Rothschilds failed to respond to the dramatic changes in the federal government's accelerating debt requirements during and then after the American

Civil War deserves consideration. Sponsoring large governmental debt issues had long been the firm's specialty in Europe, and many inviting opportunities in the Anglo-American market arose after 1865. But the Rothschilds held back. To conduct business properly on a grand scale, the partners would have needed to create a genuine branch office in New York City under the direction of a family member. No Rothschilds stepped forward to volunteer for that assignment. Perhaps the family was so closely associated with the monarchical tradition in Europe that none of its senior members ever gave serious consideration to the prospect of dealing regularly with American presidents and cabinet officials who had, in most cases, risen to power from humble and non-aristocratic backgrounds. I am just guessing here, of course, about the snobbery factor; I will leave it to my European colleagues to enlighten me on this issue. Nonetheless, for whatever the reason, the Rothschilds were not major players in what was rapidly becoming one of the most active markets for securities in the entire world.

Peabody/Morgan

Today, the name of J. P. Morgan is universally recognized in financial circles around the globe, but the original enterprise--the firm that made the Morgan family both rich and famous--was actually founded by George Peabody. A native New Englander, Peabody became a successful Baltimore merchant in the 1820s before migrating to London in the mid-1830s. (12) He rose rapidly in the Anglo-American merchant-banking community. Like the Barings, Peabody adroitly performed several functions simultaneously: trading in commodities on his own account: offering trade-related financial services to American importers and exporters, and acting as a securities promoter and contractor. He differed though because his geographical focus was narrowly on the U.S. market. Persistently optimistic about the future prospects of the American economy and the fundamental soundness, in terms of the risks and associated rewards, of investments in the securities of American railroads, he was the most consistent advocate of capital transfers from England to the United States in the 1840s and 1850s.

But Peabody's string of good fortune ran out in the late 1850s. He was caught short in the Panic of 1857, and his firm had to appeal to the Bank of England for a timely rescue package. That crisis dampened his enthusiasm and led to his withdrawal from the partnership in the mid-1860s. Although outside the scope of our primary interests at this conference, it should, nonetheless, be noted in passing that, during his lifetime, Peabody was renown in both England and the United States as an extremely generous philanthropist. He established a standard for charitable giving that other wealthy Americans like Andrew Carnegie and John D. Rockefeller emulated half a century later.

In 1854, Junius Morgan, another native of Massachusetts who had prospered as a merchant in New York City and in Hartford, Connecticut, moved to London and joined Peabody as a junior partner. Morgan soon assumed responsibility for the day-to-day management of the busy office. When Peabody retired in 1864, Morgan became the principal owner. Meanwhile, in 1857, the elder Morgan had sent his son John Pierpont, then aged 20, back to the United States to serve as a clerk in Duncan, Sherman & Co., a firm located in New York City that had a long-standing agency agreement with Peabody. (13) A few years later, the younger Morgan started his own firm. Father and son were not, as it happens, members of a jointly-owned enterprise, but they continued to cooperate on a long series of business transactions over many years. In 1871, J.P. Morgan joined forces with the Drexel family of Philadelphia to create Drexel, Morgan & Co. The Drexels had surplus capital; Morgan provided the managerial skills and the vital link to foreign investors through his father and other cooperative European agents.

The Morgans were well positioned to take advantage of the enormous expansion in the U.S. securities market in the post-Civil War era. They helped raise millions for the federal government and the booming railroads. Their deep involvement in this second market--the private corporate market--is one characteristic that distinguishes the Morgans from the Rothschilds. The American railroads and eventually many industrial enterprises grew to become extremely big businesses, and their capital requirements were nearly insatiable. The Morgans had the transatlantic ties to seek out European investors eager to supplement the limited financial resources of American savers.

Within the borders of the United States alone, the Morgans probably exercised more raw financial power than the Rothschilds ever exercised in any single nation state in Europe. Because of the peculiarities of American political and financial history in the first half of the nineteenth century, the United States was left with no functioning central bank. When major financial breakdowns occurred, J.P. Morgan was essentially drafted by his peers in the private sector, with the acquiescence of government officials, to take the unpopular steps necessary to restore equilibrium. Finally, after years of acrimonious debate, Congress created the Federal Reserve System to deal with these recurring problems in 1913. But from 1890 to 1910 or thereabouts, J.P. Morgan reluctantly played the pivotal role of the nation's de facto central banker since the federal government had long ago abrogated its responsibilities. His decisive role in the Panic of 1907 was especially notable. In sum, Morgan performed both private and public functions, and he amassed a fortune in the process. He left an estate of $68 million plus artwork valued at $50 million in 1913. Whether Morgan's wealth exceeded that of the Rothschilds in the early twentieth century is unknown to me.

Seligmans

Within the Anglo-American merchant banking community, the Seligman family enterprise came the closest in most respects to emulating the Rothschilds' organizational strategies. (14) At the very height of its power and influence, the Seligman firm had partners managing key branch offices in New York, London, Paris, and Frankfurt. The Seligman family's success in the United States is a classic "rags-to-riches" story. Joseph Seligman emigrated from Germany to the United States in 1837. From a base camp in eastern Pennsylvania, he became a country peddler; and he used his modest savings to help bring three brothers across the ocean. By the early 1840s the Seligmans had broadened their lucra-tive peddling routes to include the southern slave states.

In the early 1850s two Seligman brothers, Jesse and Henry, made the acquaintance of a young military officer who would later become one of the firm's important benefactors. This friend was Lieutenant Ulysses S. Grant, a future U.S. president. Even before Grant's war-ending victories on the battlefield in 1865, the Seligmans had expanded their business from merchandising to include complementary financial services. They were loan contractors for the early war bond issues of the federal government. By 1864, the brothers had opened branch offices in London and Frankfurt. They explicitly used the Rothschilds' organizational strategies as an instructive model.

In the late 1860s and 1870s, the Seligmans emerged as major competitors in a wide range of typical merchant-banking fields. They contested the Browns in the foreign exchange markets. Like the Rothschilds, the Seligmans also had influential friends in high places. After his election in 1868, President Grant offered Joseph Seligman, the family patriarch, the cabinet position of Secretary of the Treasury. Joseph declined, and his Jewish heritage and formerly immi-grant status were allegedly crucial factors in reaching that decision. The Seligmans became the financial agents of the U.S. government for the trans-mission of funds overseas. Where the Seligmans differed markedly from the Rothschilds was in their involvement in sponsoring securities issues of many of the largest American railroads. With branch offices throughout western Europe, they were in a favorable position to identify potential investors for millions of dollars worth of new securities. Like the Morgans, the Seligmans were very active participants in underwriting public debt issues and a wide range of corporate securities.

Kuhn, Loeb & Co.

The origins of Kuhn, Loeb & Co. echo the backgrounds of the Rothschilds and Seligmans. Abraham Kuhn and Solomon Loeb were born to German-Jewish parents. They began their business careers as small-town merchants in rural Indiana, then moved to Cincinnati, and finally settled in New York City in 1867. (15) Their firm remained a minor player in the U.S. investment-banking field until Jacob Schiff, who married Loeb's daughter Theresa, became directing partner in the 1880s. In time, Schiff rose to become widely recognized as the nation's second leading investment banker, ranking only behind the influential J.P. Morgan. (16) Schiff was born in Frankfurt in 1847 into a fairly prosperous

German-Jewish household. Well-educated in European schools, he migrated to New York City in 1865 and subsequently joined Kuhn Loeb in 1873. Under Schiff's management, the partnership relied on its close connections with a network of correspondents in London and on the continent to identify investors for American railroads searching for new capital. Kuhn Loeb's outstanding performance demonstrates that a transatlantic ownership pattern was not essential for long-term profitability; but its success does suggest quite strongly that at least one important office supervised by a partner with tremendous authority had to be located in the financial center of the nation from which the demand for investment capital arose--in this case New York City. The Barings and Rothschilds failed to take heed of this organizational imperative; they concentrated on the supply side of the capital equation, not the demand side, and lost their position of leadership in the Anglo-American market.

Kuhn Loeb differed from its competitors in other ways as well. Unlike the Barings, Rothschilds, Morgans, and Seligmans, this firm never focused, in its formative years, on business originating in the public sector. Instead, Kuhn Loeb tied its fate to the private market--the booming U.S. railroads. Again, an expanding financial market had encouraged further specialization. Kuhn Loeb is the only investment house in this survey that rose to prominence almost exclusively by serving the financial requirements of corporate enterprises.

Schiff also disagreed with Morgan about the importance of placing representatives of the major investment banking houses on the boards of directors of the railroads that the bankers routinely financed. Morgan thought the presence of his partners on boards of directors was prudent and necessary since they served as watchdogs for investors in cases of gross railroad mismanagement. Schiff believed that regular monitoring was unnecessarily time-consuming--except, of course, in dire circumstances. The exceptions to his general rule applied after a thorough reorganization of a given railroad's capital structure by court-appointed trustees, persons who were frequently none other than the investment bankers themselves. Schiff's reluctance to become closely associated with the management of the railroads that Kuhn Loeb had financed prevented him from becoming a lighting-rod for public criticism to the same extent as J.P. Morgan.

This is an instance whereby anti-Semitism may have rebounded in Kuhn Loeb's favor. Many American railroad leaders were unwilling, except during a crisis, to add anyone with a Jewish background to their corporate board of directors. That prejudicial attitude helped keep Kuhn Loeb out of the glaring gaze of the public spotlight. Schiff was never subpoenaed to appear before a congressional committee investigating the so-called "money trust." Under the circumstances prevailing in the early twentieth century, Schiff and his partners were quite happy to play second fiddle to the House of Morgan.

Conclusion

Over the three centuries spanning the period from 1600 to 1900, the Anglo-American financial services sector became increasingly large and more sophisticated. The general trend was away from an early emphasis on the foreign trade sector and more toward the burgeoning U.S. capital market, which literally exploded in the second half of the nineteenth century. The flow of money was always westward; Europeans with surplus capital aided U.S. economic development in almost every imaginable way. As the financial markets ripened, greater specialization emerged. The multi-functional merchant-banking houses lost market share as the nineteenth century progressed, and they were superseded by banking enterprises that had a narrower scope.

Initially, the Anglo-American market was institutionally fragmented, but the maturation process advanced steadily after 1750. The leading firms created transatlantic networks of agents or branch offices to expedite transactions of all varieties involving both merchandise and financial services. Trade-related activities predominated through the War of 1812. In the 1820s Anglo-American merchant bankers became simultaneously involved in the U.S. capital markets, helping to locate European investors for a series of capital-intensive transportation projects. These portfolio investments stalled momentarily after the Panic of 1837, but resumed in the 1840s and 1850s. After 1860, the cost of fighting the American Civil War created a huge federal government debt and soon thereafter the U.S. railroads embarked on a massive expansion program in the Far Western states. By the end of the century, the most prestigious and powerful firms in the Anglo-American financial community had largely abandoned their trade orientation to concentrate on investment banking.

The second half of the nineteenth century also witnessed the rise of New York City as the main U.S. money center. Before the Civil War, Boston had a securities market that rivaled Wall Street. New York investment banking firms eased ahead of their rivals in the 1850s, when railroad lines were extended into the Midwestern states. In the 1860s New York bankers became the dominant force in the investment market, with Boston houses like Kidder Peabody & Co. and Lee Higginson & Co. falling into the second tier. By the turn of the century, New York was challenging London on the world stage. London was still far ahead in terms of the number of listed bond issues, but the New York securities market had a growing number of choice equity issues. (17)

Investigating the similarities and contrasts among the six leading firms provides enlightenment on several fronts. Two partnerships were essentially family firms--Rothschilds and Seligmans. The Barings had admitted non-family members by the 1820s, and an American actually headed the London office after 1837. The Browns began as a transatlantic family enterprise. Within a quarter century, non-family partners managed the firm's English branch office. The Morgans had a close family connection in the second half of the nineteenth century, but the mutual-ownership pattern was notably absent. Kuhn Loeb, the

the last major U.S. entrant into this oligopolistic market, never relied on family connections in Europe for its success. On the other hand, it can be stated that Kuhn Loeb, like Rothschilds and Seligmans, had close ties to the larger community of European Jews. Indeed the principals in all three of the Jewish firms could trace their roots to a single German locale, the city of Frankfurt and its hinterlands

Three houses placed a great deal of emphasis on creating strong transnational organizations with branch offices in key cities managed by partners or salaried employees. The Browns, Rothschilds, and Seligmans were atypical of contemporary firms because of their close internal coordination of operations, and they took advantage of their administrative structure to provide customers with superior services. The directing partners in all three firms insisted on the adoption of uniform policies and procedures throughout the organization. The Browns and Seligmans had branches in the United States, but not the Rothschilds. On the other hand, Barings, Morgan, and Kuhn Loeb demonstrated that it was possible to function as a successful enterprise by relying on a network of agents and correspondents.

When financial services were primarily linked to the trade sector, the location of a branch office in the country where the demand for services arose was not critical for success. The Barings were fully capable of serving their American trade customers through a chain of independent merchants in U.S. ports before the middle of the nineteenth century. When the emphasis shifted to the provision of investment banking services for the federal government and the American railroads, then the maintenance of an influential branch office in New York City was a necessity if a house hoped to play a lead role in the transatlantic capital market. Morgan and Kuhn Loeb had singular offices on Wall Street, while the Seligmans made their New York branch their headquarters. The Browns had a New York office but preferred to restrict their business to the trade sector. Without branch offices in New York, the partners of Barings and Rothschilds could not regularly meet with the executives of American railroads to arrange lucrative underwriting transactions. The Browns, Barings, and Rothschilds remained participants in the U.S. capital markets, but they acted primarily as distributors of securities rather than as syndicate organizers.

Over the course of the nineteenth century, the great Anglo-American merchant banking houses underwent a major transformation. The strategy of mixing international trading on their own account with complementary financial services to third parties--foreign exchange transactions, advances against consignments, letters of credit--gave way to greater financial specialization. The Rothschilds abandoned their mercantile activities in the first quarter of the century and immediately stressed investment banking. The Browns ceased merchandising in the late 1830s and concentrated thereafter primarily on the provision of financial services. The Barings, Peabody/Morgan, Seligmans, and Kuhn Loeb shed their mercantile functions at a subsequent date. Except for the Browns, the leading houses in the Anglo-American financial markets at the end of the nineteenth century concentrated on providing investment banking services for governments and large corporate accounts.

Notes

1. The best book on merchant banking in Britain is Stanley Chapman, *The Rise of Merchant Banking* (London: George Allen & Unwin, 1984).
2. Edwin J. Perkins, *Financing Anglo-American Trade: The House of Brown, 1800-1880* (Cambridge: Harvard University Press, 1975).
3. After 1750 the New England colonial legislatures created a small floating debt of three-year treasury bills. It is possible that a few British nationals acquired a fraction of this debt on the recommendation of an American agent, but there was no attempt to place any portion of the colonial government debt overseas.
4. The issue of colonial public debt is closely linked to contentious debates with Parliamentary committees over the issuance of paper money by the thirteen legislatures. See Edwin J. Perkins, "Conflicting Views on Fiat Currency: Britain and Its North American Colonies in the Eighteenth Century," *Business History*, XXXIII (1991), 8-30.
5. Some issuers later added travelers' letters of credit and travelers' cheques to their range of financial services.
6. The definitive book on the Barings is Ralph Hidy, *The House of Baring in American Trade and Finance: English Merchant Bankers at Work, 1763-1861* (Cambridge: Harvard University Press, 1949).
7. Chapman, *Rise of Merchant Banking*, 27.
8. Baron Alphonse Rothschild acknowledged the Browns' status in a letter from New York in 1849: "There is only one banking house here, and that sole concern is that of the Browns." Quoted in Chapman, *Rise of Merchant Banking*, 42.
9. Chapman, *Rise of Merchant Banking*, 21.
10. The data on the Rothschilds and Barings is found in Niall Ferguson, "The Rise of the Rothschilds: the Family Firm as Multinational," a draft paper presented at a conference on financial history in Berkeley, California, in April 1997. The data on the Browns is from Perkins, *Financing Anglo-American Trade*, Appendix A.
11. The one major biography focuses on Belmont's political career; see Irving Katz, *August Belmont: A Political Biography* (New York: Columbia University Press, 1968).
12. The definitive biography is Muriel E. Hidy, *George Peabody: Merchant and Financier* (New York: Arno Press, 1978).
13. The literature on John Pierpont Morgan is vast. The best sources are Vincent Carosso, *The Morgans: Private International Bankers, 1854-1913* (Cambridge: Harvard University Press, 1987) and Ron Chernow, *The House of Morgan: An American Banking Dynasty and the Rise of Modern Finance* (New York: Atlantic Monthly Press, 1990).
14. Ross Muir and Carl White, *Over the Long Haul: The Story of J. & W. Seligman & Company* (New York: privately printed, 1964). The firm's surviving nineteenth-century records are located in a special Bass collection at the main library of the University of Oklahoma.
15. Carosso, *Investment Banking in America*, 19-20.

16. Cyrus Adler, *Jacob Schiff: His Life and Letters* (Garden City, NY: Doubleday, 1928), and Fritz Redlich, *The Molding of American Banking: Men and Ideas* (New York: Johnson Reprint, 1968).
17. Ranald C. Michie, *The London and New York Stock Exchanges, 1850-1914* (London: Allen & Unwin, 1987).

Chapter Eleven

Market Research at Merrill Lynch & Co., 1940-1945: New Directions for Stockbrokers

Let me explain at the outset that this paper is drawn in large part from information gathered in the course of researching and writing a career biography of stockbroker Charles E. Merrill. With several lengthy interruptions, which were necessary to complete other scholarly projects that focused on earlier historical periods, this project has been ongoing for the last six years.

Born in Florida in 1885 and educated at Amherst College and the University of Michigan, Merrill was the most dynamic entrepreneur in the American financial services sector during the middle decades of the twentieth century. He founded Merrill Lynch & Co. in 1915 and served as the directing partner for the next four decades [16, 18]. When he died in 1956, the firm, with over 100 branch offices nationwide, was the acknowledged market leader in the brokerage field--the retail end of the securities business. On Wall Street, Merrill Lynch ranked among the top five houses in underwriting and investment banking--the wholesale end of the securities business. In researching the man and his career, I have benefited from the full cooperation of Merrill Lynch & Co. and the Merrill family; and just in case anyone is wondering, I have received to date no direct financial assistance of any sort from the firm, except free access to the high-speed copy machine. Thus I have retained the liberty to interpret events and personalities without fear of interference or censorship.

My presentation is pertinent to the general theme of this panel because Merrill Lynch was one of the first firms in the securities business to make effective use of opinion polls and customer surveys both in formulating marketing strategies and in reorganizing the administrative system of its numerous branch offices. Before proceeding with the presentation of information drawn from archival sources, I want to comment briefly on the fact that my search for a useful historiographical context proved surprisingly elusive. Quite honestly, I had no idea that so little had been published on the history of market research. I was fairly sure that there was not much in print on the origins of market research in

*Reprinted from *Economic and Business History* (1996), 232-241.

the financial services sector, but the paucity of similar material on basic consumer products prior to World War II came as somewhat as a shock. I want to thank Sally Clarke, Jonathan Silva, and Mansel Blackford, in particular, for drawing me into this panel, since I no realize that I was on to something much bigger than I had ever imagined in terms of the broader significance of this material to the emerging history of marketing, advertising, and distribution.

Most of the books and articles that comprise my abbreviated bibliography focus primarily on the history of advertising and public relations [13, 14, 15,20,24, 25]. Ad agencies and their clients were among the first enterprises to conduct surveys and opinion polls in an effort to determine consumer preferences in the early twentieth century [28]. Several scholars pointed toward Susan Strasser's *Satisfaction Guaranteed: The Making of the American Mass Market* (1989) as the authoritative secondary source on the birth of market research, but I found her ten-page discussion of the topic frustratingly thin [22, pp. 153-62]. Considered in a wider context, much of the recent literature on advertising focuses on the negative impact of these ubiquitous messages on American culture and values--namely the undue emphasis on instant gratification and the promotion of excessive materialism. On that score, I have in mind two recent books--*Fables of Abundance* by Jackson Lears and *Land of Desire* by William Leach [10,11].

For my purposes, however, the existing literature sheds little light on the evolution of strategies designed to convince upper-middle class American households to divert a healthy portion of their current income into investment securities. In this niche of the marketplace, delayed gratification through savings, not instant gratification from acquiring goods and services, was the message of advertisers and marketing departments. Over the course of this century, the superior success rate of advertisers in promoting instant gratification explains, perhaps, why Americans today are reportedly spending too much of their incomes on consumption and, as a consequence, are allegedly salting away insufficient savings to build a nest egg that would maintain their current living standards in their retirement years. Prior to World War II, the only enterprises that as a group were consistently successful in convincing Americans to defer consumption were life insurance companies, and they put the emphasis on prudence and safety [21, 29]. Most of the policies sold were the so-called "whole" life policies, with a portion of the premium covering the actual risk of death plus additional monies that created a pool of savings over time. During the first three decades of the century, many insurance companies were phenomenally successful in selling whole life policies to American households.

Given the fact that brokerage firms were driven from their origins in the early nineteenth century to encourage trading volume and thereby generate commissions on transactions in stocks, bonds, or commodities, it's again surprising to discover how few partners in the leading firms within this broad financial sector had thought systematically about effective sales and marketing techniques prior to World War II. Brokerage was, by its very nature, a sales driven occupation, yet attempts to implement proven selling techniques and organize comprehensive marketing campaigns were slow to develop. Perhaps the main impediment was the prevailing attitude of the New York Stock Exchange itself.

In an effort to achieve a status comparable to recognized professionals such as lawyers, doctors, and accountants, the leadership of the NYSE discouraged member firms from virtually all forms of promotional advertising. "Tombstone" announcements, which listed the participants in a recent underwriting, were about all the rules would allow. Some firms on the periphery made use of direct mail advertising to solicit prospective investors, including Merrill Lynch in the early years, but the largest and most prestigious brokerage and investment houses avoided anything that seemed even mildly aggressive. I wish there was more space to discuss Merrill Lynch's initial experiences with advertising agents, but we have to move on. Suffice it to say that Charlie Merrill produced some highly positive results with direct mail solicitations. He was among those financiers who occasionally questioned other members of the Wall Street community about why they took such a dim view of activities that he thought were perfectly legitimate with regard to informing the public about the services of brokerage firms and investment banks.

In order to provide more context for the later discussion, I want to take a couple of paragraphs to survey Merrill's career up to the eve of World War II [7, 18]. From 1915 to 1930, he was directing partner and CEO of Merrill Lynch & Co. He made a small fortune through what today we call "merchant banking." He invested heavily in the common stocks of the companies for which he had performed various investment banking functions, and capital gains made him wealthy. His specialty was chain stores of all varieties--shoes, clothing, auto parts, and particularly, groceries. For several years, he and his partner Edmund Lynch owned and managed Pathe Studios--the movie producer and film distributor with French origins. After the crash in 1929, Merrill put his financial services career on the back burner and largely abandoned, Wall Street. Using the money from the sale of Pathe to Joseph Kennedy, a founder 'of the RKO movie studio and the father of a future president, Merrill acquired a controlling interest in Safeway Stores, a grocery chain based in Oakland, California, in the mid-1920s. He was very active in overseeing the operations of Safeway throughout the 1930s. By the way, his grandson, Peter Magowan is the current CEO of Safeway Stores--and also one of the key owners of the San Francisco Giants baseball team.

In fighting a proposal by the California legislature to place a prohibitive tax on the outlets of chain stores in 1935. Merrill met Ted Braun, who headed a Los Angeles management consulting firm that routinely used consumer surveys and public opinion polls in advising corporate clients [26]. Braun provided valuable assistance to Safeway in the fight against the chain store tax. The tax proposal finally turned up as a proposition on a state-wide ballot and was defeated handily by voters; citizens decided that they valued the low prices of the chain stores more highly than protecting locally-owned, independent retailers from the rigors of price competition [12].

In late 1939 and early 1940, Winthrop Smith, a former business associate, persuaded Merrill to return to the financial services sector as the directing partner of a new firm created through the merger of Merrill Lynch & Co., which had been essentially dormant during the depression, with E. A. Pierce & Co., which ranked as one of the nation's leading brokerage houses, with approximately 40 branch offices and 300 brokers. Pierce & Co. had been losing money for several years, and Merrill acted as the white knight who rescued it from probable dissolution. In 1941, Fenner & Beane, another brokerage house with a chain of branch offices, and also on the brink of dissolution, came on board to create Merrill Lynch, Pierce, Fenner & Beane. The firm of Fenner & Beane had experimented with customer surveys in the mid-1930s, and I had originally intended to use some of that data in this paper, but, unfortunately, time and space proved a roadblock. [4].

After the stockmarket crash in 1929, brokerage houses remained profitable for the next half decade or so because trading volume on the exchanges held up reasonably well. When stock prices started to recover from their extreme lows in 1934, most brokers thought they were out of the woods, but their optimism was dashed two years later. For reasons inexplicable at the time and still a mystery today, trading volume on the exchanges started to fall precipitously in 1937, and it failed to rebound for six long years. Hundreds of stockbrokers were forced out of the business, and those that remained saw their commission earnings steadily decline; it was especially frustrating because so many other Americans were enjoying the benefits of the economic recovery.

One of Merrill's first acts as CEO in early 1940 was to commission Ted Braun's management consulting firm to conduct a thorough analysis of the operations of the Los Angeles branch of E. A. Pierce & Co. Braun studied the branch office from two perspectives. First, he engaged accountants to conduct an internal review of the revenues and costs associated with servicing different types of brokerage accounts. Second, Braun hired a group of interviewers who, discreetly, without revealing the name of the client, surveyed the attitudes of opinions of a broad sample drawn from the 3,000 customers who maintained accounts at the Los Angeles office. The questions ranged from broad sweeping inquires to other questions narrow and concise; interviewers sought customer views about the capital markets in general and about the performance of the Pierce branch and its personnel in particular. What Braun discovered mirrored the conclusions of the Elmo Roper poll that had been conducted earlier on behalf of the NYSE [27]. Most customers expressed doubts about the fairness of the system to outsiders like themselves, and, not surprisingly, they were suspicious of the veracity and ethics of stockbrokers as an occupational class. On the other hand, most customers gave generally high marks to Pierce brokers in the Los Angeles office, which indicated that criticisms of the capital market were generic in origin and did not reflect negatively on the quality and reputation of the firm's current employees.

Based on his review of the operations of the Los Angeles branch, his discussions with top management at the expanded Merrill Lynch, and his experiences with other firms in the goods and services sectors, Braun proposed one of the most unconventional ideas in the history of the American financial services sector. To long-time participants in the brokerage field, his proposal was thoroughly revolutionary in its implications. Braun recommended that individual brokers no longer be compensated by paying them a percentage of the commission rates linked to specific transactions--at Pierce the split to brokers was 28 percent of the gross commission. Instead, brokers would receive fixed annual salaries that reflected their overall contributions to the profitability of the firm.

If Merrill Lynch genuinely wanted to differentiate itself from other brokerage houses, Braun argued strenuously, the firm needed to inaugurate a dramatic new policy that addressed the lingering concerns not only of existing customers, but more importantly in the long run, the fears of millions of potential future customers. Merely proclaiming that its brokers were more honest than rivals and were more dedicated to meeting the financial goals of investors was unlikely to translate into anything much more than a marginal competitive advantage. Braun's polling data suggested that almost everyone who had ever dealt with a brokerage house had wondered at times about whose interest was paramount whenever the broker recommended either the purchase or sale of securities. Was the broker merely seeking to earn the commission linked to a proposed trade or did the broker genuinely believe the transaction was in the customer's financial welfare? These suspicions about a broker's motivation were inherent and unavoidable, Braun stressed, so long as sales personnel received compensation based on commissions linked to specific trades. The only effective means of altering the fundamental relationship between brokers and their customers was to eliminate completely any incentive to churn individual accounts.

Merrill, whose experience was primarily in the investment banking field rather than in the secondary markets, was initially dubious about the new compensation proposal, but Braun wore him down. In correspondence years later with Lou Engel, who headed Merrill Lynch's advertising department, Merrill recalled the circumstances: "Of all the policies suggested by Ted Braun, this was the toughest one of all for me to adopt...I remember distinctly telling Ted Braun that I would not work for a firm that did not pay a commission." After a pause, "Ted leaned back in his chair, relaxed and said: 'This point is the keystone of all my suggestions. If you do not adopt it, it's no use talking about any of the rest.'" After Merrill had accepted the idea, he "too had a difficult time in selling this policy to my partners." Looking back on his long career in 1954, just two years prior to his death, Merrill confessed: "I think that of all our policies, this is the most important one" [17, Dec. 8, 1954].

To inform the branch managers of the upcoming changes, the partners planned a three-day conference in New York City in April 1940 [2]. Pierce opened the proceedings and quickly introduced the new directing partner--Charles E. Merrill. He began by discussing the rationale for the meeting and the strategic planning that had preceded it. After his introductory remarks, Merrill, in turn, introduced Braun as the man who had produced the facts that had become the cornerstone for a series of innovative managerial decisions. Braun reported in detail on his consulting firm's review of the operations of the Pierce branch in Los Angeles. The office employed nine brokers who handled a total of 2,828 customer accounts, an average of over 300 customers per broker.

Approximately 90 percent of all customers traded primarily stocks and bonds; six percent dealt strictly in commodities; and four percent were involved in both commodities and securities. Women maintained 25 percent of the branch's accounts. The volume of trading activity varied greatly: over 15 percent of all customers had initiated no trades at all over the last year; 55 percent had recorded from one to five transactions; and 30 percent had generated six or more transactions. The slowest 70 percent of accounts produced a mere 15 percent of commissions, while the more active accounts were responsible for 85 percent of commission revenues.

Braun's analysis highlighted the importance of customers who maintained accounts either with debit balances or with credit balances to the firm's profitability, and, in turn, to the commission income of its individual brokers. The most active trading accounts were margin accounts. Customers who bought securities in part with borrowed funds generated average annual commissions of $165 versus only $50 for customers who paid for securities fully in cash. Moreover, the average margin customer produced over $70 annually in interest revenue. The largest revenue sources were a handful of margin accounts with debit balances of over $5,000; these customers had generated more than $500 in commissions and $440 in interest revenue in 1939. On the other side of the ledger, customers who regularly left large cash balances with the firm to finance future transactions were also among the most profitable accounts; they averaged $175 annually in commissions--more than three times greater than cash customers without credit balances.

The second day of the branch managers' meeting was devoted to discussions of organizational, structural, and procedural matters. To members of the audience, the most crucial presentations addressed the new policies related to broker compensation, customer service, and public relations. The big news was that annual fixed salaries would replace fluctuating commissions in compensating brokers. No longer would there be any incentive, or, equally important, the public suspicion of an incentive, for brokers to churn customer accounts. The minimum salary for brokers was set at $2,400 (about $30,000 in 1995 prices), and for about 15 percent of the sales force that figure represented a boost over their earnings in 1939. All brokers who had earned higher than the minimum were automatically granted a $25 monthly increase over their current earnings for the remainder of 1940. No broker was asked to take a cut in take-home pay. The salary program placed limits on how much a given broker could earn during the upcoming year, but that negative feature was offset by the security of a steady income plus the prospect of salary increases in future years—if and when trading volume on the exchanges improved.

Along with changes in the compensation package, the firm instituted a significant reorganization of work assignments and responsibilities at the branch level. Based on Braun's in-depth analysis of the Los Angeles office, Merrill and his key advisors decided to make dramatic changes in the traditional system of servicing accounts. These changes had dual purposes that were viewed as complementary--to provide better service for a varied clientele, while simultaneously boosting volume and improving the firm's overall profitability. The standard method of assigning accounts at every brokerage house in the nation had always been based on individualistic and competitive principles. Managers usually granted the originating broker--the employee who had initially recruited or opened a new account--the option of retaining that customer's future business on a more or less exclusive basis. The net result of this traditional mechanism was that almost every broker at Merrill Lynch (and elsewhere) laid claim to a mixed bag of customers. In most instances the majority of names on a broker's client list were small, relatively inactive, and unprofitable accounts. From one-fourth to one-third of the typical broker's accounts were moderately active, but only marginally profitable. Just a few names on the client list, typically persons with large portfolios financed in part by margin loans, regularly placed orders for securities on a monthly or weekly basis.

In addition to differences in trading volume, almost every broker also handled a wide range of customers with varying objectives: bond investors were primarily interested in capital preservation; common stock investors bought and held securities for long-term growth; and speculators trading puts and calls (options to buy and sell securities at a fixed price) sought to maximize capital gains in the short to intermediate run. Every broker, in short, was expected to be a jack-of-all trader with respect to their knowledge about providing a range of services. In an effort to improve efficiency, Merrill Lynch reassessed the effectiveness of the all-purpose, all-knowing broker and the haphazard system of account allocation.

The new rationale for improved customer service was based on specialization and employee expertise. The task of reassigning accounts fell to the branch manager, who, except in the smaller offices, was no longer expected to act as a part-time broker. To assist in the realignment of customers and brokers--an evolutionary process that was expected to take several years before full implementation--the branch manager was given a new tool for decision making. At Braun's urging, Merrill Lynch executives decided to circulate a customer questionnaire designed to pinpoint the aims and goals of every client. The partners introduced to the brokerage field the personalized financial profile sheet --a universal form that, when completed, identified every client's financial objectives and the jointly agreed-upon strategy for achieving his or her stated goals. The customer filled out the questionnaire, preferably during a face-to-face meeting with a Merrill Lynch broker, and then signed on the dotted line. The central idea was to give each customer the opportunity to tell the firm precisely what level of service he or she wanted from Merrill Lynch; and the firm, in turn, pledged to provide nothing more and nothing less than the customer desired. For example, customers were asked whether they routinely wanted brokers to offer opinion and advice about the purchase and sale of specific securities? Some customers indicated on the survey sheet that all they desired was reliable information on business trends and the finances of certain corporations--and that unsolicited trading advice was unwelcome.

Drawing on the information in the completed questionnaires, the branch manager divided customers into several categories. All the small and inactive accounts in a given branch office were, over time, scheduled for transfer to just a few brokers, usually the most inexperienced men in the office, who now specialized in maintaining and nurturing the accounts of low-activity customers. These brokers handled mostly odd lot orders and performed what was viewed, at least from one standpoint, as essentially a public service to the local community. At the same time these brokers were instructed to remain alert to the fact that some previously inactive clients were on the verge of increasing their trading volume and were therefore eligible to graduate into the ranks of profitable accounts. After the transfer of small accounts took effect, the client list of brokers with the responsibility for handling the genuinely profitable accounts was expected to drop significantly--in the Los Angeles branch most client lists declined from around 300 names to only 150 names or thereabouts. The mainstream brokers now had more time to concentrate on providing superior services to accounts that were already generating a profitable volume of trades.

In a further effort to match clients with the one broker most qualified to meet their specific needs, branch managers used the information on the individual survey sheets to divide customers into three broad groups: investors, speculators, and persons who periodically alternated between prudent investing and speculation depending on current market trends. In the Los Angeles office about one-third of active accounts seemed to fall roughly into each category. Based on this data, those brokers who were more oriented toward capital preservation and long-term growth in their selection of securities were matched with clients who emphasized safety and income. Brokers who were comfortable with high risks and volatile price movements served customers who indicated a speculative bent; these same brokers usually handled the 5 percent or so of active accounts that traded commodities on a regular basis. Customers who fit most logically in the alternating investor/speculator group were assigned to brokers who were reasonably at home in both camps. There was, in other words, still a place in the organization for all-purpose brokers, but they now became a minority within the office rather than the overwhelming majority.

Under the new compensation and account allocation plans, the personnel in each branch office were encouraged to act as a team in meeting the needs of local customers and in developing new business. Brokers in the same office no longer had a strong incentive to compete internally with each other for new accounts--at least, not for small or modest accounts; now they could concentrate on explaining to business prospects why Merrill Lynch's broad services were superior to those of their competitors. Executives in New York planned to judge the performance of each branch as a comprehensive unit. Local branch managers were granted the power to adjust salaries to reflect each employee's contribution to the overall success of the branch.

To support their brokers in the field, Merrill and his new partners planned to break with the old taboos on Wall Street and launch an aggressive advertising and public relations campaign. In one light-hearted comment to the assembled managers, he remarked as follows: "If R. H. Macy had the same approach toward business getting expenses that all members of the New York Stock Exchange have, I assure you R. H. Macy & Co. would be out of business by next April--and it wouldn't be April Fool's Day either" [2]. The new emphasis was on educating the public about the functioning of the exchanges and the benefits arising from long-term investments in selected securities of profitable and growing corporations. The NYSE itself had parted with tradition and started running a series of generic advertisements in the late 1930s but the impact on trading volume had been minimal. At Merrill's insistence, his partners allocated $100,000 to the advertising budget over the next year. An analysis of income and wealth patterns indicated that there were approximately 5 million households nationwide--mostly upper middle class households in mid-sized cities--which owned few, if any, securities, and they were considered likely prospects for solicitation. Braun announced that the firm had contracted to place advertisements covering up to two-thirds of a page in Time Magazine, with a circulation of over 750,000, for 28 weeks. According to Braun, Time was "the best single medium in the United States to reach the maximum number of potential customers for this business" [2]. The firm also scheduled ads to run in newspapers with a combined circulation of 14 million in cities with branch offices.

The new organizational and marketing strategies adopted at Merrill Lynch in 1940 proved remarkably successful, and amazingly they required little modification over the next quarter century. From the start, Merrill had assured everyone in the organization that the partners' radical departure from long-standing precedents on Wall Street was experimental and that major adjustments were possible if serious problems unexpectedly arose. As it happened, few actually emerged. Indeed, the firm maintained the salary compensation program until deregulation and the elimination of fixed commission schedules led Merrill Lynch to abandon the practice and revert to industry norms in the 1970s.

Meanwhile, implementing the new policies and holding the organization together in the early 1940s proved difficult because trading volume on the exchanges continued to fall in 1941 and 1942 (Table I). The 126 million shares traded on the NYSE in 1942 was so low it actually dropped below the level reached four decades earlier in 1900. (Today, the same number of shares is frequently traded in a mere two or three hours.) Despite the unfavorable investment climate, the campaign to attract new customers was enormously successful. From April through December 1940, the number of new accounts exceeded 50,000--an increase of about one-third in the customer base. In an 162 appearance before members of the Financial Advertisers Association in September 1941, senior partner Edward Pierce told the audience that the firm's advertising had produced some very positive results. "Even those who have ridiculed our efforts," Pierce added, might one day realize the benefits accruing from "the right kind of public relations campaign" [NY Herald Tribune, Sept. 11, 1941). That year the firm added 30,000 new customers; in 1942 another 27,000 signed on; in 1943 another 49,000; and in 1944 another 46,000. By the end of WW II, Merrill Lynch served approximately 250,000 customers. During this period, the brokerage firm generated 8 to 12 percent of all trading on the NYSE.

Despite sharp cost reductions in rents and communications services, the firm lost over $300,000 in 1940. The next year was marginally profitable, with earnings of $459,000. In 1943 pre-tax earnings jumped to $4.8 million, which translated into a 70 percent return on the partner's invested capital; the imposition of extremely high wartime taxes reduced the after-tax figure to $1.1 million and a 16 percent return on capital [17]. In the postwar era, the partners continued to earn handsome returns on their capital. From a big-picture perspective, Merrill Lynch truly brought Wall Street to Main Street; the firm's brokers helped hundreds of thousands of upper middle class households accumulate substantial portfolios of blue chip stocks through sustained programs of regular life-cycle investing. Many professors will likely obtain the same results by investing regularly in the stock funds offered by TIAA-CREF over a 25- to 30-year period.

The partners' decision in 1940 to shift the firm's broker compensation system from commission splitting to fixed salaries was a bold move, with many potential dangers. Previously the firm's annual expenses were roughly fifty percent variable (the brokers' split of the gross commissions), and fifty percent fixed (for office leases, equipment depreciation, phone lines, bookkeeping, and the like). Under the new compensation system fixed costs rose to about 85 percent of total expenses. Merrill and his partners were assuming tremendous risk in very uncertain times.

To summarize and conclude, when Charles Merrill decided to return to the financial services sector in 1940, he relied heavily on the data and the recommendations generated by Ted Braun's management consulting and public relations firm. Based on the information in other published public opinion polls and from a confidential survey of the customers of a single branch office, Braun presented a sweeping reorganization plan that was to be coordinated with an aggressive marketing and advertising program. Initially skeptical, Merrill soon accepted the logic of Braun's grand design to reinvigorate the firm; the new focus was on the solicitation of millions of upper middle class households that typically owned life insurance policies but few, if any, common stocks.

The decision to move forward with such a truly revolutionary program would not have been possible without the data gathered from a group of outside consultants who analyzed the financial environment from several angles. The fruits of market research made a huge impact on Merrill Lynch; and the brokerage firm, in turn, made a tremendous impact on the development and maturation of the American financial services sector in the post-WW II era. The

SEC's reforms in the public realm and Merrill Lynch's new strategies in the private realm were highly complementary; together they revived the securities markets in the mid-1940s, and, in time, led directly to the expanded Wall Street that we know today.

Notes

1. T. A. B. Corley, "Competition and the Growth of Advertising in the U.S. and Britain, 1800-1914," *Business and Economic History*, 17 (1988), 155-167.
2. Conference of Branch Managers, April 1940. Merrill Lynch & Co. Corporate Files. World Trade Center, New York City.
3. N. H. Engle, "Gaps in Marketing Research," *The Journal of Marketing*, (April 1940), 345-353.
4. Fenner & Beane, Proceedings of First Managers Conference, July 1935, New York City, ML Files.
5. 0iarles Goodrum and Helen Dalrymple, *Advertising in America: The First 200 Years* (New York, 1990).
6. Hugh Hardy, ed., *The Politz Papers: Science and Truth in Marketing Research* (Chicago, 1990).
7. Henry Hecht, *A Legacy of Leadership: Merrill Lynch, 1885-1985* (New York, 1985).
8. Donald Holland, "Volney Palmer: The Nation's First Advertising Agency," *Pennsylvania Magazine of History and Biography* (1974), 353-3081.
9. Pamela W. Laird, "From Success to Progress: The Professionalization and Legitimization of Advertising Practitioners, 1820-1920," *Business and Economic History, 21* (1992), 307-316.
10. William Leach, *Land of Desire: Merchants, Power, and the Rise of a New American Culture* (New York, 1993).
II. Jackson Lears, *Fables of Abundance: A Cultural History of American Advertising* (New York, 1994).
12. Godfrey Lebhar, *Chain Stores in America, 1859-1962*, 3rd ed. (New York, 1963).
13. Roland Marchand, *Advertising the American Dream: Making Way for Modernity, 1920-1940* (Berkeley, 1985).
14. ____________, "The Corporation Nobody Knew: Bruce Barton, Alfred Sloan, and the Founding of the General Motors 'Family,"' *Business History Review* (1991), 825-875.
15. ____________., The Inward Thrust of Institutional Advertising :General Electric and General Motors in the 1920s," *Business and Economic History*, 18 (1989), 188-196.
16. Martin Mayer, "The Fabulous Firm of Merrill Lynch," *The Reporter* (March 1955).
17. Merrill Lynch & Co., Archives and Annual Reports, ML Files.
18. Edwin J. Perkins, "Charles E. Merrill," in Larry Schweikart, ed., *Encyclopedia of American Business History and Biography: Banking and Finance, 1913-1989* (New York, 1990) 283-90.
19. David A. Revzan, *A Comprehensive Classified Marketing Bibliography*, Pt. 2 (Berkeley, 1951).
20. John Staudemaier and Pamela W. Laird, "Advertising History," *Technology and Culture*, (1989), 1031-1036.
21. J. Owen Stalson, *Marketing Life lnsurance: lts History in America* (Cambridge, MA, 1942).

22. Susan Strasser, *Satisfaction Guaranteed: The Making of the American Mass Market* (New York, 1989).
23. Richard Tedlow, *New And Improved: The Story of Mass Marketing in America* (New York, 1990).
24. Ibid., "The National Association of Manufacturers and Public Relations during the New Deal," *Business History Review*, (1976), 25-45.
25. _________, "From Competitor to Consumer: The Changing Focus of Federal Regulation of Advertising, 1914-1938," *Business History Review* (1981), pp. 35-58.
26. "Theodore Braun: A Biographical Sketch," Public Relations Office, Braun & Company, Los Angeles, California.
27. "What Does the Public Know about the Stock Exchange? Roper Survey Reveals Extent of Misconceptions and Misinformation about the Services of the Exchange," *Exchange Magazine* (January 1940).
28. Mary Ellen Waller-Zuckerman, "'Preconceived Notions' and the Historian's Dilemma: Market Research by Women's Magazine Publishers in the Interwar Years," in Terence Nevett el. al., eds., *Marketing History: The Emerging Discipline* (East Lansing, 1989).
29. Viviana Rotman Zelizer, *Morals and Markets: The Development of Life Insurance in the United States* (New York, 1979), 331-353.

Chapter Twelve

Presidential Address
Business History Conference

Banks and Brokers

One nice feature of these presidential addresses is that they follow no set pattern. Some speakers talk about past accomplishments in the field or where they think the profession may be headed. Others discard the serious stuff altogether, and just show old photographs of their Hungarian grandparents. Listeners never know exactly what is going to happen in these after-dinner adventures. For once in a long career, the speaker has a captive audience of peers and, within reasonable limits, you can talk about any damned thing that pops into your mind. And there are no great audience expectations to worry about either; few dessert eaters really anticipate that the speaker is going to say anything genuinely profound or memorable--or at least I hope not. My approach tonight will be to present a smorgasbord of remarks on a series of topics; and if you have no interest in one subject, perhaps the next one will catch your ear.

What I actually remember most clearly from previous presidential addresses--including, of course, those sensational photos of Lou Galambos's ancestors--are the life stories that illuminate how our friends and colleagues first got interested in business history as an academic discipline. Like many of us, I entered the business history field through a serendipitous route. After earning a bachelors degree in political science at William & Mary in the early 1960s, I moved on to the MBA program at the University of Virginia. The Darden School at Virginia unapologetically copied its curriculum and methodology from the Harvard Business School--meaning that it relied almost exclusively on the case method of instruction. That learning system, which emphasizes the identification of an underlying problem, or two or three overlapping problems, from a morass of seemingly unconnected and often purposely irrelevant facts, proved remarkably sound training for my later shift into a history curriculum. I often tell students, undergraduates and graduates alike, that all history--social, political, economic, or whatever--is just one immense and unending case study, and that our task is to sift through the mountains of evidence and figure out what is really important within a given context or in response to certain questions.

*Reprinted from *Economic and Business History* (1995), 1-8.

From Charlottesville, I went to work in the Big Apple for the Chase Manhattan Bank--a disastrous work experience, by the way. I was totally unprepared because never in the MBA program had we discussed how to react when, in your mid-twenties, you find yourself working for a large corporate enterprise where everyone immediately above you in the managerial hierarchy was mediocre at best and incompetent at worst. The only rational response was to run for the exits, and to make a long story somewhat shorter. I left New York a year and one half later and, after a few more years in Norfolk, Virginia, at a much smaller bank. I ended up in Blacksburg, Virginia, as an instructor in the accounting department at Virginia Tech. I decided almost immediately that academic life was well-suited to my talents and personality; but I still had to make a choice about which discipline to choose in pursing a doctoral degree. Accounting and business administration just seemed way too boring for a lifetime of scholarly work, and I doubted that I had the math skills to succeed in an economics curriculum.

One very positive aspect of life at Virginia Tech was that, in casually walking around the campus and town (population 15,000), I met various faculty from a wide array of academic departments, including history. When I expressed some interest in the history field during my first year on campus, most faculty were mildly discouraging, citing my general lack of a respectable background in the discipline--just two upper-division courses at the college level. There was, however, one major exception to this chorus of negativity. Gus Williamson, a former Johns Hopkins graduate, explained one day during a visit to his office that there was a small niche in the history discipline called business history and, given my previous training, I might have sufficient credentials to pursue a doctoral degree. To test my level of interest, he suggested that I stroll over to the university library and check out a single book; let me see if I can recall its title; oh yes, I think it was something like *Strategy and Structure*, and the author was someone named Alfred D. Chandler, who, to me, was totally unfamiliar. Let me assure you that I knew within an hour of checking out that singular book that I would likely be able to do this kind of history--and maybe even do it fairly well one day. From that day in 1966, I set out to become a business historian.

The next step was to gain admittance to a strong doctoral program. Since Al Chandler was then at Johns Hopkins, that university seemed the logical starting point. It just so happened that I was driving through Baltimore on the way to New York City during spring break, and I wrote Chandler in advance to request what I thought would be brief introductory interview. After a half hour or so of cheerful conversation in his office, interrupted by telephone calls from department chairs elsewhere trying to hire a new faculty member (this was in the mid-1960s) Al announced in a rather matter-of-fact manner that he was prepared to admit me to the Hopkins graduate program. Puzzled and surprised, I protested: "but Professor Chandler, I haven't even filled out an application form, or sent along my college transcripts, or taken the GREs." Those technicalities didn't matter, AI assured me; I was unofficially admitted and could come to work with him the next year. When I walked back to the waiting car to announce to my traveling companions that I had unexpectantly been granted admittance to the Hopkins doctoral program, everyone was equally incredulous that a casual interview could have produced such a magical outcome; but, as I later learned, that's how they conducted academic affairs at Johns Hopkins in the mid-1960s--strictly off-the-cuff and spontaneously. Maybe they still do. At any rate, from that date forward--a period covering about 3 decades--it has been clear sailing for me in the economic and business history field. Al Chandler, as well as Lou Galambos, who came along later, were both just wonderful mentors.

Now comes one of the very best parts in any presidential address. I get to tell you what you ought to be emphasizing henceforth in teaching about the expansion of the American economy over the last three or four centuries, and you just have to just sit there and take it all in. First, historians ought to pay more attention to the colonial and early national eras. Over the last quarter century, that is, since I have been a member of the profession, scholars have made enormous strides in terms of getting a handle on this formerly "terra incognito." What they have found is that there was substantial economic growth long before industrialization. High population growth alone kept the North American GDP rising at about 3 percent per annum, and accumulating evidence suggests that per capita increases were on the order of 5 percent per decade. Only Holland and England were enjoying sustained per capita growth in this same period--and at lower rates. English North America was already well along the road to becoming a rich nation in comparison with its contemporaries in the mid-eighteenth century--a phenomenon prominently mentioned by Adam Smith in the *Wealth of Nations*, published in 1776.

Most American farm households produced substantial surpluses and disposed of them in active markets at home and abroad. Indeed, one of the key reasons why this nation reached such heights in the nineteenth century was not only the impact of canals, railroads, and industrial technologies, but because U.S. citizens started from a very high material base. Indeed, in certain respects, British North America was never an undeveloped country in the modern sense of the term; rather it was always a developing economy with high savings rates and a strong entrepreneurial spirit--an argument that I advanced in an article published several years ago in *Business History Review*--so I won't bore you with a rehash of it now.

I mentioned earlier that I had worked at the Chase Manhattan Bank immediately after graduation from the MBA program, and that experience explains in large part why financial history became my special niche within the field. I can tell you with a great deal more certainty now than I could have done a decade ago that economic and business historians also ought to pay more attention to the financial services sector in explaining the growth of the American economy. The U.S.--and U.K. as well by the way--have been blessed by such an array of efficient financial services over the last three centuries that it is just too easy for historians to take these blessings for granted--to pass over casually the routine facts on banks and capital markets without realizing their vital importance in providing the environment for economic success. When Paul Uselding, a former president of this organization and a former assistant professor of economics at

Johns Hopkins, asked me at my dissertation defense in 1972 how important this financial stuff was to the growth of the American economy, I must confess that I had no idea where it ranked on a scale of 1 to 10.

What I learned in the course of researching and writing a recently published book on the evolution of financial services from the colonial period through the War of 1812 was, I must confess, a gratifying revelation. I did not set out to argue the importance of financial services when I started that project, but what I delightfully discovered was the following: that even prior to the rise of superior transportation systems and industrial technologies in the 1820s, the United States already had a rapidly maturing financial sector. Commercial banks and insurance companies had outstanding issues of common stock that totaled in the millions of dollars. They were the big businesses of the early national era. (I better include the post office too, just in case Richard John is out there in the audience taking notes.) Active too in the early nineteenth century, but on a lesser scale, were brokers of all varieties who dealt in stocks and bonds, foreign exchange, and lottery tickets. Although American capital markets in the first decade of the nineteenth century were small compared to Great Britain, many of the securities traded, government bonds and common stocks, were so well regarded that investors, residing here and abroad, bid the prices up to such heights that the yields were surprisingly low--often only 4 to 6 percent. Overall, the institutional infrastructure associated with the U.S. financial services sector was largely in place and functioning exceptionally well by 1815. In short, the financial revolution preceded and moved forward in advance of the new technologies applied to manufacturing and transportation.

Banks were important later in economic development as well, of course, and I want to recommend Naomi Lamoreaux's new book on the changing role of financial institutions in the New England region over the course of the nineteenth century. My review is forthcoming in the American Historical Review and it's a very positive assessment too, just in case anyone was wondering. Let's give a tip of the hat to Larry Neal, as well, for his outstanding book on the rise of capital markets in London and Amsterdam in the seventeenth and eighteenth century, and to Geoff Jones for his brilliant work on the international reach of British banking over the last two centuries. We can also look forward to new books by Dick Sylla and George Smith and by Paul Miranti on American financial markets.

Having done most of my previous work on the eighteenth and nineteenth centuries, I have now moved forward into the twentieth. My current project, just about complete by the way, is the career biography of stockbroker Charles Merrill, the founder of Merrill Lynch & Co. My biography will be the first in print on this important figure in twentieth century finance. Merrill was, I will argue, as critical to the development of the capital markets in the twentieth century as J. P. Morgan was in the nineteenth. Merrill had a broader vision than Morgan, and the firm that bears his name eventually rose to become the market leader, first, in secondary markets--trading shares on the exchanges--and, next in investment banking--the issuance of new securities to finance new plant and equipment.

Much of how modern brokerage firms operate now can be traced back to the innovations that Charles Merrill had introduced in the early 1940s. New Deal reforms paved the way, of course, but Merrill went much further to open up the whole process to public scrutiny. He launched an aggressive advertising campaign; he hired researchers to produce a steady flow of reliable information on hundreds of firms that had outstanding securities; and in an unprecedented departure from Wall Street tradition, he issued voluntarily, in 1940, the first annual report by any Wall Street firm that revealed the income statement and balance sheet of his new partnership. All in all, Merrill rightfully deserves most of the credit for bringing Wall Street to Main Street and for drawing the upper middle classes, people like most of us, into the capital markets--and especially into the common stocks of growing companies. With over 100 offices nationwide, Merrill, in conjunction with his partners and employees, showed millions of often reluctant investors how, over a lifetime of moderate saving, they could build a sizable nest egg for retirement.

Many of us living in academia are major beneficiaries of Merrill's initiatives. Through investments in the common stock portfolios of TIAA/CREF and at my university in any of Fidelity's mutual funds, people with incomes that may never rise above $75,000 can over a 25 to 30 year period accumulate a pool of money that might approach $1 million. When I tell my skeptical middle-aged colleagues at USC that great riches are in store for them one day, they often look at me with jaundiced eye, because after all, they exclaim, it has taken 15 years just to creep up to $150,000. But I keep assuring them that, over the next 15 years, their accumulation, if it compounds at the 12 percent rate historically true for stocks on the New York Exchange, will generate an additional $700,000 and carry them near the one million dollar mark by retirement.

While we are on the topic of money and retirement funds, let me grab the attention of everyone in the room over 55, an age I just reached last May. In updating your final wills and testaments, I want you to remember this splendid organization. Whatever monies we decide to leave to our alma mater will likely be only a drop in a very large bucket. So consider channeling your charitable instincts in the direction where it is most likely to do the most good, where it will provide more bang for the buck. Will Hausman didn't prod me to insert this plug, but the Williamson fund, which provides the income for our biannual award, is always in need of strengthening. Over the past four or five years, Bill Lazonick has also been able to come up with funds from outside sources to finance the travel of promising graduate students to our annual meetings. In the future we need to raise more internal funding for this purpose. So think about BHC the next time you sit down with your lawyer to divide up your estate. I promise you that Harvard and Stanford, with endowments already of over $1 billion, don't really need your money all that much. But we do. In this organization, a few thousand dollars will make a huge impact.

To get back to Charles Merrill; he was alive from 1885 to 1956. He was born, no one would ever guess, right here in Florida. The town was Green Cove Springs, up north near Jacksonville, where his father was a physician who served the local community and, more importantly in terms of income, the wealthy visitors who flocked to the tourist hotels in the winter months. When I began this project, I was almost totally ignorant of the development of the Florida economy. Before the turn of the century the population of the whole state was not much over 100,000, and settlement did not extend much beyond 100 miles south of the Georgia border. Even more, perhaps, than California, Florida was a frontier region in the twentieth century. Starting even before the Civil War, when steamboats carried passengers from New York and Philadelphia to Jacksonville, this state's economy has always relied heavily on tourism. Hollywood is only one part of the California economy; in Florida entertainment and leisure are the life blood of the economy and always have been. Younger scholars who are seeking subjects different from the old standbys --like basic industries and transportation might take a closer look at what's been happening here in Florida over the last century. Florida is, I suspect, the premier service sector economy in the United States.

I also want to spend some of my time this evening talking about where business history fits into the broader history curriculum. Bill Lazonick focused on the role of history in the economics curriculum several years ago in his presidential address in Toronto, and I will attempt to do some of the same for historians. My guess is that I have been involved in the broader field of American history over the last 15 years about as much anyone in this room because, as a result of my reputation as a keen editor of my colleagues' first drafts, I was called upon in the late 1970s to serve as managing editor and later as an associate co-editor of the respected historical journal, *Pacific Historical Review.* I escaped those duties temporarily in 1991, but Norris Hundley's decision to retire this past summer brought me back again as de facto managing editor in an essentially caretaker role. The *PHR* has been around since the 1930s and receives a small annual subsidy from the American Historical Association. It publishes scholarship in two categories: first, articles that focus on U.S. interaction with the Pacific Ocean region, and, second, articles that focus on events in the states located west of the Mississippi River in the 20th century. Over the years, I have read at least 500 article manuscripts for this journal. What they reveal, and I am sure it will come as no surprise to anyone here, is that business history has become increasingly marginalized in the broader scheme of things. Gender, class, and ethnicity are all the rage. With few exceptions, most historians' attitudes toward our capitalist system and the majority of its business leaders are hostile and suspicious. Perhaps equally disturbing, economic factors are often simply ignored or dismissed as unimportant by historians in other fields. The collapse of the Berlin Wall may have opened up eastern European economies to the capitalist onslaught but a similar event has not occurred within the history profession. Some claim that leftist historians, cornered and on the defensive, have become even more negative about capitalism and even more strongly attached to pure Marxism--that is, Marxism without the Leninist dictatorial element.

Given these trends within the historical profession over the last quarter century, I know that some of you are quite disturbed about where business history might be headed in the first half of the next century. That future I cannot predict, although I do not worry about it so very much, because I suspect that the current generation of undergraduates are not likely to find the socialist agenda very pertinent in discussing the evolution of global society. So rather than musing about the outcome of future trends, I propose instead to look at the brighter side of what has occurred within our field over the last two decades. Rather than wringing our hands about being shut out of the panels at the annual meeting of the American Historical Association or the Organization of American Historians, like many political historians--who, incidentally, have a legitimate beef--we economic and business historians have been busy creating and strengthening our own alternative professional environment. We are fortunate to have three organizations to serve scholars in our field, and all three hold annual meetings and publish regularly most of the papers presented. I suspect that I have been simultaneously involved in the parallel activities of Business History Conference, the Economic and Business Historical Society, and the Economic History Association more frequently than anyone in the profession. I'm also a member of the organization of British business historians, which was formed within the last decade, and I recently joined another new group of business historians serving both UK and the European continent. BHC has been meeting for about four decades now, and its membership has mushroomed from not more than about 150 as recently as 20 years ago to a figure somewhere in the vicinity of 500. The number of foreign scholars on the membership rolls continues to grow, and in response to the more international character of our membership, we are planning an annual meeting somewhere across the Atlantic in 1997.

Thus by rejecting us and forcing us to stick to our knitting, the broader historical profession has prompted economic and business historians to make enormous strides over the last quarter century in virtually every topic area. And frankly, I like it better this way. Meetings of 100 to 200 specialists are far more rewarding both intellectually and socially than mass meetings of thousands of historians milling aimlessly around the lobbies of giant hotels in the nation's largest cities. I'd rather travel to Williamsburg, Virginia, Ft. Lauderdale, Florida, or Columbus, Ohio, than to New York City or Chicago, Illinois, hands down. In short, our isolation within the broader history profession has had a number of very positive benefits--and in my view, at least, many more positives than negatives. It goes without saying--but I will say it anyway--that the quantity and quality of scholarship produced by economic and business historians--by many of you out there in the audience--has been absolutely outstanding during this period. If the social historians believe our type of history is out of fashion, that's their problem not ours; we can get along very well on our own, thank you very much.

In the same breath, I want to add that I believe there is something that most of you can do, however, to reach out to at least one other group in the historical profession. I have in mind more interaction with the practitioners of labor history. I know from personal experience that it is possible to obtain some very positive results from this sort of interaction, because my colleague Steve Ross and I have been cooperating successfully for nearly 15 years at the University of Southern California. For example, we alternate in teaching a lower division course entitled American Business and Labor History that qualifies for our university's general education program. If you want more information on how we go about it, pull out the 1986 proceedings volume for this organization when you get back home and read "Integrating Business and Labor History," a paper that Steve and I jointly delivered at the Columbus meeting in 1985. We have also had success in training graduate students at USC; we routinely recommend each other's fields to the graduate students studying under us.

To date there have been no major problems or conflicts arising from this system of dual training in business and labor history. We believe our program is truly unique within the borders of the United States. Among the recent USC graduates who have benefited from this comprehensive program are Jim Kraft and Clark Davis, both of whom have participated in recent BHC conferences; and we have more graduate students in the pipeline with similar training. Steve and I have been proselytizing colleagues in other departments around the country for a long time about the benefits to students and faculty alike from integrating more closely the fields of labor and business history. I wanted, therefore, to take advantage of this opportunity to let everyone know that we have continued to practice what we earlier preached, and that I continue to recommend that business historians make the effort to provide their students, especially graduate students, with greater exposure to the labor historians in their respective departments.

In closing, I want to wrap things up on a more personal note. I want to state forthrightly and sincerely how much the intellectual and social atmosphere of this organization has added to the enjoyment and satisfaction of my career choice over the last quarter century. For me, the annual conventions are like a happy family reunion. I always relish seeing again those of you who have been good friends for many years, and equally as much, I enjoy meeting the newcomers to our discipline. Whenever I talk with prospective graduate students who might be considering a career in business history, I always tell them that one of the most positive aspects is that there are many marvelously friendly and supportive people in the field. I have published numerous books and articles over the last quarter century, but serving as your president has been, without question, the highlight of my professional career. Thanks so much to you, my treasured colleagues in economic and business history, for honoring me with this office and giving me the opportunity to share these thoughts and sentiments with you tonight.

Edwin J. Perkins

Emeritus Professor
Department of History
University of Southern California

Home Address:
3029-N Calle Sonora
Laguna Woods, CA 92637
e-mail: perkinsej@aol.com
Phone: (949) 472-2213

Born: Charlottesville, Virginia, 1939

Education:

Ph.D.	The Johns Hopkins University	1972
M.B.A.	University of Virginia	1963
B.A.	College of William and Mary	1961

Employment:

2002-2004	University of Southern California, Department of History, Visiting Professor
2003	Mesa State College, Grand Junction, Colorado, Aspinall Distinguished Professor, Spring Semester
1998	Fulbright Distinguished Lecturer, Moscow State University, February to May 1998.
1973-1997	University of Southern California, Department of History, Assistant Professor, 1973-77; Associate Professor, 1978-86; Professor, 1987-97
1995	Visiting Professor, Ohio State University, Spring Quarter
1966-1968	Virginia Polytechnic Institute & State University, Blacksburg, Virginia -- Instructor in College of Business.

Editorships:

Pacific Historical Review, Managing Editor: 1978-1979, 1994 - 1995; Associate Editor, 1979-1991, 1995-1996. Published by the Pacific Coast Branch of the American Historical Association, University of California Press.

Journal of Economic History, Editorial board, 1993-1997.

Journal of the Early Republic, Editorial board, 1995-1998.

Essays in Economic and Business History, Managing Editor, 1983-1994. Selected papers from the annual meetings of the Economic and Business Historical Society. A joint publication of the society and the History Department, University of Southern California, Vols. III to XII.

General series editor, "The Evolution of American Business: Institutions, Industries, and Entrepreneurs." Twayne/G.K. Hall/Macmillan, New York, 1987-1992.

Publications:

Books:

Wall Street to Main Street: Charles Merrill and Middle Class Investors, Cambridge University Press, 1999.

American Public Finance and Financial Services, 1700-1815, Columbus, Ohio State University Press, 1994.

The Economy of Colonial America, second, revised edition, hardback and paper. New York: Columbia University Press, 1988.

A Prosperous People: The Growth of the American Economy, co-authored with Gary Walton, Economics Department, University of California, Davis. Prentice-Hall, 1985.

The World Economy in the Twentieth Century. Cambridge, Mass.: Schenkman Publishing Co., 1983.

Men and Organizations: The American Economy in the Twentieth Century. Editor, New York: G. .P. Putnam's Sons, 1977.

Financing Anglo-American Trade: The House of Brown, 1800-1880, Cambridge Mass.: Harvard University Press, 1975.

My book edition of Bailey Diffie's posthumously published manuscript. *A History of Colonial Brazil, 1500-1792.* Melbourne, Florida: Krieger Publishing Co., 1987.

Articles

"Market Research at Merrill Lynch & Co.: New Directions for Stockbrokers," *Economic and Business History*, XXV (1996), 232-41.

"Bankers and Brokers," *Economic and Business History*, XXIV (1995), 1-8, Presidential address -- Business History Conference, Fort Lauderdale, Florida, March 1995.

"William Graham: Branch Manager and Foreign Exchange Dealer in Baltimore in the 1850s," *Maryland Historical Magazine*, LXXXVII (1992), 11-23.

"Conflicting Views on Fiat Currency: Britain and Its North American Colonies in the Eighteenth Century," *Business History*, XXXIII (1991), no. 3, pp. 8-30. Special issue on international banking and finance also published in hardback.

"The Entrepreneurial Spirit in Colonial America: The Foundations of Modern Business History, " *Business History Review*, LXIII (1989), 160-86.

"Lost Opportunities for Compromise in the Bank War: A Reassessment of Jackson's Veto Message," *Business History Review*, LXI (1987), 531-550.

"Integrating Business History and Labor History," co-authored with Steven J. Ross, *Business and Economic History*, XV (1986), 43-52.

"Langdon Cheves and the Panic of 1819: A Reassessment," *Journal of Economic History*, XLIV (1984), 455-461.

"Tort Law and Business Enterprise in Nineteenth-Century America," co-authored with Professor Gary T. Schwartz, UCLA School of Law, *Essays in Economic and Business History*, III (1984), 218-230.

"Lenin and the Shift from Workers' Control to One-Man Management, 1917-1920," *Essays in Economic and Business History*, III (1984), 131-151.

"Partnership Accounting in a Nineteenth-Century Merchant Banking House," *Accounting Historians Journal*, VII (1980), 59-68, co-authored with Sherry Levinson, M.B.A., University of Southern California.

"Tourists and Bankers: Travelers' Credits and the Rise of American Tourism, 1840-1900," *Business and Economic History*, VIII (1979), 16-28.

"Business-Government Relations in Historical Perspective," *USC Engineer* (December 1978), 20-24.

"Foreign Interest Rates in American Financial Markets: A Revised Series of Dollar-Sterling Exchange Rates, 1835-1900," *Journal of Economic History* (June 1978), 392-417.

"The Emergence of a Futures Market for Foreign Exchange in the United States," *Explorations in Economic History* (Spring 1978), 193-211.

"Managing a Dollar-Sterling Exchange Account: Brown, Shipley & Co. in the 1850s," *Business History* (January 1974), 48-64. Reprinted in Geoffrey Jones, ed., *Multinational and International Banking* (London, Edward Elgar Publishing, 1991), 529-45.

"Financing Antebellum Importers: The Role of Brown Brothers in Baltimore," *Business History Review* (Winter 1971), 421-451.

"The Divorce of Commercial and Investment Banking: A History," *Banking Law Journal* (June 1971), 483-528.

Contributor

"Growth Stocks for Middle Class Investors: Merrill Lynch & Co., 1914-1941," in Makoto Kasuya, ed., *Coping with Crisis: International Financial Institutions in the Interwar Period* (Oxford and New York: Oxford University Press, 2003).

"Currency and Finance: British," 551-59, in *Encyclopedia of the North American Colonies* (New York: Charles Scribner's Sons, 1993).

"The Socio-economic Development of the Colonies," 53-63, in Jack P. Greene and J. R. Pole, ed., *Blackwell Encyclopedia of the American Revolution*, (Oxford, England: Basil Blackwell, 1991.)

Four essays in Larry Schweikart, ed., *Encyclopedia of American Business History and Biography*. New York: Facts on File, Bruccoli Clark Layman, Vol. I., Banking and Finance to 1913 (1990) – "Biddle," 51-63; "Brown," 73-80; and "Cheves," 108-111, Vol. II, Banking and Finance, 1913-1989 (1991) – "Merrill," 283-290.

"Monetary Policies" in *Encyclopedia of American Political History*, Jack P. Greene, editor (New York, Charles Scribner's Sons, 1985), II, 831-40.

Essay on Charles Merrill (1,500 words), founder of the brokerage firm, Merrill Lynch & Co., for *Dictionary of American Biography*, John A. Garraty, editor (New York, Charles Scribner's Sons, 1980), Supplement VI, 448-449.